Nationality Between Poststructuralism and Postcolonial Theory

Nationality Between Poststructuralism and Postcolonial Theory

A New Cosmopolitanism

Philip Leonard

palgrave
macmillan

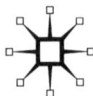

First published 2005 by
PALGRAVE MACMILLAN
Houndmills, Basingstoke, Hampshire RG21 6XS and
175 Fifth Avenue, New York, N.Y. 10010
Companies and representatives throughout the world

PALGRAVE MACMILLAN is the global academic imprint of the Palgrave Macmillan division of St. Martin's Press, LLC and of Palgrave Macmillan Ltd. Macmillan® is a registered trademark in the United States, United Kingdom and other countries. Palgrave is a registered trademark in the European Union and other countries.

ISBN-13: 978–1–4039–1912–0   hardback
ISBN-10: 1–4039–1912–7   hardback

This book is printed on paper suitable for recycling and made from fully managed and sustained forest sources.

A catalogue record for this book is available from the British Library.

Library of Congress Cataloging-in-Publication Data

Leonard, Philip, 1967–
    Nationality between poststructuralism and postcolonial theory : a new cosmopolitanism / Philip Leonard
        p. cm.
    Includes bibliographical references and index.
    Contents: Cosmopolitan locations – Before, across and beyond : Derrida, without national community – New concepts for unknown lands : Deleuze & Guattari's non-nationalitarianisms – Atopic and utopic : Kristeva's strange cosmopolitanism – In the shadow of shadows : Spivak, misreading, the native informant – To move through, and beyond, theory : Bhabha, hybridity, and agency.
    ISBN 1–4039–1912–7
    1. Criticism–History–20th century. 2. Nationalism in literature. I. Title.

PN94.L46 2005
801'.95'0904–dc22   2005049750

10   9   8   7   6   5   4   3   2   1
14   13   12   11   10   09   08   07   06   05

Printed and bound in Great Britain by
Antony Rowe Ltd, Chippenham and Eastbourne

PN
94
L46
2005

Contents

Acknowledgements

This book has benefitted enormously from the assistance, support, and guidance that friends and colleagues have generously given. For their help I should like to thank Steven Connor, Dan Cordle, Dick Ellis, Lynne Hapgood, Bernard McGuirk, and Greg Woods. John Marks, Douglas Smith, Patrick Williams, and Dave Woods carefully read versions of some of the chapters here, and their suggestions were extremely welcome. I am especially grateful to Leslie Hill, whose generosity made the impossible possible. Students who opted for my final year modules 'History and Culture' and 'Poststructuralist Debates' allowed me to work through some of the ideas explored here, and the Department of English and Media Studies at The Nottingham Trent University granted me the study leave that allowed this book to be completed. I wish to thank both Emily Rosser Helen Craine, and Paula Kennedy at Palgrave for their editorial support and advice. This book could not have been written without Sam Haigh's untiring support.

An earlier version of Chapter 3 appeared in *National Identities*, 5: 2 (2003).

Earth, yield me roots
Shakespeare, *Timon of Athens*

1
Cosmopolitan Locations

When Terry Eagleton, in a review of Gayatri Chakravorty Spivak's *A Critique of Postcolonial Reason,* declares that Spivak's 'flamboyant theoretical avant-gardism conceals a rather modest political agenda'[1] he rehearses the allegation, made repeatedly since the late 1970s, that poststructuralism indulges in a ludicism that prevents it from offering a compelling critique of the social, the political, and the cultural. Poststructuralist theory, Eagleton tells us, is caught up in a 'self-theatricalizing'[2] introspection; its notion of resistance permits little more than a vigilant complicity with dominant institutions, and its theory of cultural power fails to provide a convincing analysis of social systems and the injustices embedded within them. These claims tellingly reiterate other work – by other critics, as well as Eagleton – that excoriates poststructuralist theory for being unsystematic, ahistorical, rarified, abstruse, or banal; for being, in other words, a diversion from properly effective forms of radical critique.

Eagleton's 'In the Gaudy Supermarket' does, however, have more to offer than earlier hostile responses to poststructuralism, since this essay sees poststructuralism's political significance as something that is now tied to debates in postcolonial theory. According to Eagleton, critics like Spivak and Homi Bhabha may well be 'devotees'[3] of earlier poststructuralist thinking, but for him their work is distinctive because it illuminates the path out of dark and cabbalistic writing by poststructuralism's high priests. Again, Eagleton's claims here are not without precedent. Benita Parry, Aijaz Ahmad, Arif Dirlik, and Bart Moore-Gilbert have each identified what they see as poststructuralism's social, cultural, and political failings, and conclude that it displays little concern for cultural emancipation, is inattentive to class-struggle, and disregards revolutionary nationalism.[4] These criticisms often turn on

1

the belief that poststructuralism construes all social experience and cultural phenomena as a form of textuality: colonialism and postcoloniality, according to these responses, are treated by poststructuralism simply as a discursive simulation, with the materiality of imperial oppression – and the responses it engenders – becoming, in effect, less important than fictions of empire.

Like Eagleton, critics such as these also believe that certain theorists – most notably Spivak and Bhabha – take poststructuralism in different directions when they question the cultural violences that are associated with imperialism, colonialism, and postcoloniality. According to these readings, poststructuralism becomes politicized only when postcolonial theory reconfigures it as an instrument for theorizing the uneven distribution of power across national and international systems. Some of the most influential developments in postcolonial theory are seen to surface either as a prudent departure from, or as a selective amplification of, poststructuralism's narrowly textual concerns; common to both readings is the idea that postcolonial theory possesses a critical trajectory that is conspicuously absent from poststructuralism. Poststructuralist theory, as a result, is viewed as a static, schematic, and systematic tradition – one hardening 'into theoretical dogma'[5] – that neither concerns itself with intercultural violence nor reflects on its own status as metropolitan theory. Poststructuralism 'itself' and 'before' postcolonial theory, it would seem, has nothing to say about colonial power, postcoloniality, globalization, transnationality, anticolonial resistance, or minority discourses.

I The ends of Europe

Nationality Between Poststructuralism and Postcolonial Theory begins from the premise that such a genealogy relies on an unsustainable distinction between poststructuralist and postcolonial theory. One concern here is to show that Spivak and Bhabha are not the only 'poststructuralists' who rethink culture by challenging the uneven distribution of global power, since Derrida, Deleuze and Guattari, and Kristeva each draw attention to the fissures that open up in the articulation of national identity. The contention that is most commonly associated with work that shuttles between poststructuralist and postcolonial theory – that grave uncertainties disarticulate the West's assertions of its historic and international authority – also needs to be seen in the thinking of those, like these theorists, who are often construed as narrowly 'poststructuralist' and somehow pre-postcolonial. They too insist that, since the West's prominence is still built around the attempt both to determine its own distinctively civilized character and to establish the barbaric alterity of the foreigner, theory must continue to expose the anxious and impossible nature of this global hierarchy.

The theorists considered here offer a series of both intersecting and disjunctive critical interventions that disconcert the West's investment in ideas of cultural legitimacy, national authenticity, and racial particularity, and they show that poststructuralism 'itself' and 'before' postcolonial theory is always and already informed by issues that are usually associated with postcolonial theory. Indeed, many of those who are credited with being poststructrualism's major precursors themselves prioritize questions of community, regionality, ethnicity, and nationality: Nietzsche, Husserl, and Heidegger, for example, each redefines the origins of European nationality in ways that vigorously contest the equation of modernity with progress. While it may be obvious to point out that these attempts to radicalize European identity replace one form of Eurocentrism with another, poststructuralist and postcolonial theory provocatively argue that such accounts also – and perhaps more importantly – undermine the sense of national and cultural particularity that they promote.

'They are not a philosophical race...'

Nietzsche certainly fails to provide the decisive account of European identity that is suggested by his cavalier and aphoristic treatment of different national types. Evidence of this treatment is readily available: of the English, for example, *Beyond Good and Evil* scornfully declares 'They are not a philosophical race, these Englishmen... European *noblesse*... is *France's* invention and accomplishment, while European commonness, the plebeianism of modern ideas is – *England's*'.[6] Vignettes such as this suggest that each nation possesses an internal and self-evident character – a character that can be captured by a few broad strokes of the polemicist's pen – though these seemingly casual remarks about different national traits are buttressed by Nietzsche's profoundly melancholic critique of modernity's decadence. The Greeks, he claims in *Twilight of the Idols*, 'remain the *supreme cultural event* of history – they knew, they *did* what had to be done'.[7] Implicit in this assertion is a challenge to the Hegelian historiography that views history as a turbulent refinement of consciousness, a process that will eventually lead to the attainment of human perfection. Against such an understanding of history, Nietzsche sees degeneration and decay as the defining traits of Europe's development, and in *Beyond Good and Evil* he describes how, for him, this decline is deleteriously affecting the distribution of racial and national groups.

> Europeans are coming to resemble one another more and more, and are more and more free of the conditions that would give rise to races connected by climate and class. They are increasingly independent of any *particular* environment that might inscribe its identical demands into their bodies and souls over the course of centuries.[8]

European history becomes, then, the history of a progressive departure from progress; rather than representing the maturation of an ancient culture or the evolution of human civilization, European nations have corrupted the principles of their founding culture, have turned away from their regional bonds, and have turned local differences into an insipid uniformity.

On the other hand, while appearing to offer such a nostalgic reading of the conceptual ground in which European nations are rooted, Nietzsche also states that this founding moment cannot be conceived as a pure origin. Rather, he describes Europe's appearance as a transitional event that is intrinsically derived from, and therefore tainted by, other cultural traditions. 'Nothing is more foolish', he writes in *Early Greek Philosophy*, 'than to swear by the fact that the Greeks had an aboriginal culture; no, they rather absorbed all the culture flourishing among other nations, and they advanced so far, just because they understood how to hurl the spear further from the very spot where another nation had let it rest'.[9] If remarks like this counter Nietzsche's claim that European nations possess a unique and definable character, then his pronouncements on nationalism develop the antifoundationalist tendencies of his writing by dramatically rejecting the idea that authentic ethnicities can or should be preserved. This rejection is most evident in *Human, All Too Human*, where Nietzsche proclaims that national and racial uncertainty is on the rise in Europe:

> Commerce and industry, traffic in books and letters, the commonality of all higher culture, quick changes of locality and landscape, the present-day nomadic life of all landowners – these conditions necessarily bring about a weakening and ultimately a destruction of nations, or at least of European nations; so that a mixed race, that of the European man, has to originate out of all of them, as the result of continual crossbreeding.[10]

Here, however, cultural association is not cast in a negative light, but is seen by Nietzsche as both an inexorable and a productive process. Seeking to inhibit this transnational process is, Nietzsche claims, an 'artificial nationalism' that promotes ruling interests to the detriment of European cultural development:

> The isolation of nations due to engendered *national* hostilities now works against this goal, consciously or unconsciously, but the mixing process goes on slowly, nevertheless, despite those intermittent countercurrents; this artificial nationalism, by the way, is as dangerous as artificial Catholicism was, for it is in essence a forcible state of emergency and martial law, imposed by the few on the many, and requiring cunning, lies, and force to remain respectable.[11]

European nations are not, it seems, able to return to a state of unadulterated insularity by closing their borders or by restricting political, economic, and cultural associations. Instead, Nietzsche argues that European nationalism not only produces unstable social systems (since its truths are propped up by lies and cunning), but that this nationalism also departs from the cosmopolitanism that, strangely, created Greek distinctiveness. For Alan D. Schrift, this dimension of Nietzsche's work is decisive, since 'Nietzsche's critiques of nationalism and the metaphysical assumptions underlying rigid identity politics should show us... that a politics of difference is not only just; it is also good'.[12] Nietzsche calls for a kind of thinking that refuses to accede to modernity's distortions and embraces the transfiguration of values that is necessary if Europe's complacency and hypocrisy are to be overcome. What this transfiguration also demands, however, is a departure from the sense of national character and ethnic belonging that have become embedded in the idea of Europe.

'If we understand ourselves properly...'

Nietzsche's provocative rethinking of Europe's territorial and cultural foundations finds some support in Husserl's claim that Europe was, in the early decades of the twentieth century, experiencing an intellectual catastrophe. Like Nietzsche, however, Husserl also seems unable to arrive at a resolute account of Europe's distinctiveness. Writing during the twilight years of the decadence that Nietzsche appears so eagerly to anticipate, Husserl takes Europe to task for missing an opportunity to reinvigorate its philosophical heritage, and he laments the decline of a tradition that, he thinks, could have saved humanity. Such is the contention of his 1935 lecture 'Philosophy and the Crisis of European Man', in which he describes the failure of the human sciences to embrace modernity's revolutionary anti-positivism. These sciences, he believes, continue to view their task as the study of independently meaningful regions of human activity: the fact that diversity exists within and between families, communities, and nations is taken as self-evident, and the human sciences begin from the assumption that they can and should identify social and cultural differences. It is because they look only to the differences between groups of people that the human sciences fail to consider the structure (or 'spirit') that is common to all people. 'The practitioners of humanistic science have', he submits, 'completely neglected even to pose the problem of a universal and pure science of the spirit and to seek a theory of the essence of spirit as spirit'.[13]

'Philosophy and the Crisis of European Man' mourns the demise of an intellectual tradition that once reflected on humanity's common character, and thus did not fall foul of the methodological and ontological confusion that afflicts the contemporary human sciences. This tradition, Husserl points out, was born in Greece in the sixth and seventh centuries B.C. and constitutes a 'completely new type of spiritual structure'[14]; it possessed a universal attitude (because it sought to understand reason as a human faculty), but it also reflexively interrogated its own judgments of truth and value. Crucially, for Husserl, this mode of thinking not only started in Greece, but is exclusively and essentially a feature of European culture. This shared heritage accounts for the way in which 'the European nations have a special inner affinity of spirit that permeates all of them and transcends their national differences'.[15] This regional particularity also leads Husserl to assert that 'to Europe belong the English dominions, the United States, etc., but not, however, the Eskimos or Indians of country fairs, or the Gypsies who are constantly wandering about Europe'.[16]

Husserl's universalism harks back to a form of philosophy that is for him, in the early decades of the twentieth century, becoming eclipsed by a flawed rationalism and a dubious positivism, and the ensuing darkness that is beginning to envelop reason constitutes 'the crisis of European man'. But Husserl is not content to see this crisis as one afflicting Europe alone. Instead, this calamity will, if unchecked, prove to be disastrous for humanity as a whole: the West, he believes, has a 'mission' to save humanity from the ruinous effects of the crisis in philosophy. Indeed, so convinced of this mission is Husserl that his arguments often expose themselves as firmly Eurocentric: he announces, for example, that 'Philosophy has constantly to exercize through European man its role of leadership for the whole of mankind'.[17] At times, this lament also lends itself to a colonial sensibility. Thus, when 'Philosophy and the Crisis of European Man' declares that other cultures envy Europe's innate superiority, it echoes the assimilationalist sentiment that permeates certain colonial traditions. In Europe, he states,

> lies something unique, which all other human groups, too, feel with regard to us, something that, apart from all considerations of expediency, becomes a motivation for them – despite their determination to retain their spiritual autonomy – constantly to Europeanize themselves, whereas we, if we understand ourselves properly, will never, for example, Indianize ourselves.[18]

Had Husserl's argument ended here, then we might fairly claim that his work exhibits the kind of Eurocentrism that poststructuralist and postcolonial theory have vigorously contested. But as much as these theories might object to Husserl's Eurocentrism, they might also point to how his account of European identity constantly slides into uncertainty. When Husserl assigns different forms of thinking to particular geopolitical settings, he effectively construes philosophy as a restricted conceptual system: European thought might well strive for the universal, but its understanding of humanity's general character nonetheless remains informed and constrained by its particular cultural location. However, certain comments in 'Philosophy and the Crisis of European Man' work against this attempt to fix philosophy's provenance. Although he finds a 'special inner affinity' between European nations, Husserl is also reluctant to assign this bond to an origin that is exclusively European:

> If, then, we follow historical connections, beginning as we must with ourselves and our own nation, historical continuity leads us ever further away from our own to neighbouring nations, and so from nation to nation, from age to age. Ultimately we come to ancient times and go from the Romans to the Greeks, to the Egyptians, the Persians, etc.; in this there is clearly no end.... To an investigation of this type mankind manifests itself as a single life of men and of peoples, bound together by spiritual relationships alone, filled with all types of human beings and of cultures, but constantly flowing each into the other. It is like the sea in which human

beings, peoples, are the waves constantly forming, changing, and disappearing, some more richly, more complexly involved, others more simply.[19]

Greek distinctiveness does not, Husserl claims here, lie in the fact that it springs forth anew, but is to be found in its channelling of other intellectual currents towards yet another form of understanding. Already shaped by external forces, then, Europe's origin becomes a particularity that begins as a cosmopolitan hybridity.

'... for the first time in Greece'

Heidegger too constructs Greece as philosophy's bedrock, and yet he again finds the frontiers that unite Greece to be precariously contingent. Such a vacillation can certainly be found in 'The Origin of the Work of Art' – an essay published in 1950, but based on lectures delivered in 1936. Commentators on Heidegger's political convictions point out how many of this essay's claims disconcert his supposed faith in Germany's unique mission, as well as more general notions of national belonging. This essay primarily undertakes a critique of aesthetics by disputing the specious notions of artistic production and reception that have prevailed in debates on the status and function of art. Rejecting the notions of creativity, beauty, expression, mimesis, intention, or context that have been central to aesthetic theory, Heidegger instead argues that the importance of art lies in its capacity to force us from the thought to the unthought: art, Heidegger declares, is not truth, but 'truth setting itself to work'.[20] Importantly, when Heidegger argues that art disturbs technical understanding, he finds it necessary to show how its different, non-propositional, thinking is rooted in a Greek foundation. For Heidegger, as for Husserl, the originality of Greek thought lies in its dogged efforts to understand the limits of thought, in its struggle to determine Being as presence: 'Art as poetry is founding' he writes, and 'This foundation happened in the West for the first time in Greece'.[21] What follows in Western history is not a succession of subsequent attempts to think the unthought; rather, later thinking hardens the poetic act of naming into a system of received ideas: '*Roman thought takes over the Greek words without a corresponding, equally authentic experience of what they say, without the Greek word*. The rootlessness of Western thought begins with this translation'.[22]

Heidegger's unhappiness with the deracination of Western thought results from its mechanistic and uniform appropriation of Greek conceptuality, and were his argument to end here it would amount to little more than an elegy for a time when thought was poetic. However, 'The Origin of the Work of Art' also declares that truth can set itself to work not only in poetry, but also in 'the act that founds a political state'.[23] Suddenly, truth becomes attached to state structures, and this politicization of thought takes a further turn when Heidegger argues later in this essay that 'Genuinely poetic projection is the opening up or disclosure of that into which human being as historical is already cast. This is the earth and, for an historical people, its earth, the self-closing ground on which it rests together with everything that already is, though still hidden from itself'.[24] Echoing the discourse of the 1933 Rectorship Address (in which he credits the German people with a supreme destiny), Heidegger here suggests that only 'an historical people' – rather than all people – are capable of 'poetic projection'. Since the Rectorship Address invests Germany with such a unique historical mission, then readers might conclude that in 'The Origin of the Work of Art' Heidegger continues to assert that Germany alone has a mission to restore Europe's inaugurating grandeur.

As many commentators on Heidegger observe, only the most elementary reading can allow his work to be described as nationalist in this way. 'Although Heidegger's readings sometimes contain a rhetoric of "homecoming"', Timothy Clark argues, 'to identify Heideggerian poetics merely with the mythical-political programme of German renewal is too reductive, and amounts to a refusal to bear the insecurity of the open space to which Heidegger leads us'.[25] In 'The Origin of the Work of Art' this 'open space' is difficult to reconcile either with a National Socialist vision of the German state, or with a more general vision of Europe's intrinsic community. While this essay appears at times to regard Greek thought with a melancholic gaze, and seems to call for Germany to reinvigorate this inaugurating moment, at other times it insists that the originality of Greek thought remains irrecuperable. Philosophy must, for Heidegger, return to interrogating the nature of truth, but after posing the question 'Does this require a revival of Greek philosophy?' he answers: 'Not at all. A revival, even if such an impossibility were possible, would be of no help to us', since 'Unconcealedness is... the most concealed thing in Greek existence'.[26]

To this less nostalgic direction in Heidegger's work it is necessary to add his more complex account of what 'a people' is. Towards the end of 'The Origin of the Work of Art', he enigmatically claims that:

> Poetry is the saying of the unconcealedness of what is. Actual language at any given moment is the happening of this saying, in

which a people's world historically arises for it and the earth is preserved as that which remains closed. Projective saying is saying
which, in preparing the sayable, simultaneously brings the unsay-
able as such into a world. In such saying, the concepts of an historical people's nature, i.e., of its belonging to world history, are
formed for that folk, before it.[27]

Here, Heidegger's distinction between poetry's 'projective saying' and
'actual language's' predicative ambitions dramatically interrupts his
apparent belief in a realizable German mission. Declarations of national
essence are, he suggests, part of 'actual language', and if Germany's
mission is to restore a Greek poetics, then the Germany that Heidegger
allegedly promotes is one that can be neither represented nor concep-
tualized. In other words, the idea of Germany is, for Heidegger, an
inoperative one, and if this is the case it certainly would not provide
succour for the nationalism that surrounded him in the 1930s. Unable
to function as a structured and institutionalized aggregation of 'a
people', the projective enunciation of community or nation instead
becomes an act of discursive invention in which the fiction of the
nation precedes and shapes the nation's emergence. When a culture
reinvents itself as a modern nation-state, its mission is therefore to
attain this predetermined immanence by entering world history as the
nation it already sees itself as being. For Leslie Paul Thiele, 'The nation
attempts to produce itself out of itself, to actualize its essence as a work
of art, to achieve its historical potential in the present. With the Nazis,
this entailed a violent sculpting of the German nation'.[28] Germany's
destiny might well be a world historical one for Heidegger, but this
destiny also seems to be one that cultures acquire when they adopt
narratives of national identity. No longer possessing the incomparable
spirit that Heidegger appears to attribute to it, Germany becomes yet
another self-legitimating fiction that, for him, betrays poetic thought
when it becomes territorialized by a technical understanding of
culture.

Complicities

Questions of national authenticity and cultural originality certainly
shape the thinking of those who are seen as the precursors to poststructuralist theory. However, Nietzsche, Husserl, and Heidegger each
reveal that notions of bordered nationality, of territorial rootedness, of
ethnic singularity inevitably lead to conceptual aporia. Against the
grain of their declared investments in the idea of Europe's exceptional

origin, they each show how concepts of national unity, of racial particularity, of ethnic exceptionality cannot convincingly account for cultural belonging. Instead, their work reveals – often clandestinely – that notions of authentic and cohesive territoriality are always out of joint with themselves and impossible to sustain. Poststructuralism's contribution to postcolonial theory has most often been found in the disclosure of caesurae like these: not only challenging the racial, ethnic, and national hierarchies that continue to inform European thought, poststructuralism also provides theory with a range of critical strategies for exposing the uncertainties that persistently return, even in work – such as that of Nietzsche, Husserl, and Heidegger – that interrogates and challenges European principles.

The theorists considered in this book do not offer strategies for conclusively overcoming or eliminating the inconsistencies and contradictions that permeate European conceptual structures, and neither do they set out to devise theoretical procedures that are uncontaminated by European or Eurocentric principles. In addition to showing how nationality becomes ambiguous in the moment that it is inscribed as a finite totality, Derrida, Deleuze and Guattari, Kristeva, Spivak, and Bhabha also draw attention to how even anti-ethnocentric, anti-racist, and counter-colonial thinking is not always vigilant towards its own collusion with the structures of power and conceptual systems that it confronts. Again, those seen as poststructuralism's prercursors provide examples of this collusion, and Derrida finds one such complicity in Lévi-Strauss's ethnography. Rejecting divisions between developed and primitive cultures, and documenting the mythemes that for him remain constant across human societies, Lévi-Strauss questions the presumption that the West alone is civilized. For Derrida, however, Lévi-Strauss falls short of providing a plausible or far-reaching critique of the West's discriminating logic. Lévi-Strauss's study of the Namikwara in *Tristes Tropiques* is inherently phonocentric, Derrida argues, since it is committed to 'the exclusion or abasement of writing':[29] Lévi-Strauss does not simply (if contentiously) assert that the introduction of written language to the Nambikwara violently transforms a people without writing, he also attributes to this culture an essential goodness or innocence that is communicated through the sincerity and spontaneity of speech. As much as Lévi-Strauss professes that this distinction between cultures with and without writing is non-evaluative (and as much as he avoids attributing notions of progress or civilization to the art of writing) he nevertheless, Derrida insists, relies upon a Western distinction between verbal language (as *logos*, the truth of the spoken word, where utterance and intention correspond) and writing (as the debasement of nature and the contamination of self-presence). For Derrida, 'The traditional and fundamental ethnocentrism which, inspired by the model of phonetic writing, separates writing from speech... is thus handled and thought of as anti-ethnocentrism'.[30]

Robert Young identifies a similar complicity in his essay on 'the two Saussures'. Although a conceptual gulf separates Ferdinand de Saussure's anti-positivist account of language from Léopold de Saussure's belief in biologically innate and culturally insurmountable racial divisions, Young argues that Ferdinand's ideas are compromised by their investment in the notion that linguistic communities are shaped by ethnic unity: 'Saussure's arguments about language and ethnicity' are, he claims, 'based on an assumption of ethnic and cultural uniformity that leads them back to the "positive fact" of the communal bonds of the social – on which Saussure's logic ultimately depends even though his fundamental argument consists of the attempt to exclude it'.[31] Even Emmanuel Levinas, who is widely credited with provoking the 'ethical turn' in recent critical and cultural theory, offers strangely conflictual ideas about national identity. For Bhabha, Levinas's notion of ethical proximity – a 'relation with the non-encompassable... the welcoming of alterity'[32] – troubles assumptions about territorial belonging. 'The difference of proximity', Bhabha writes, 'refuses to posit the relations of persons or cultures as different on the normalizing grounds of an abstract universality of meaning, or on a shared, synchronized temporality of present being'.[33] In what he describes as his confessional and non-philosophical writings, however, Levinas appeals to notions of territorial rootedness when he considers Israel's territorial legitimacy. *Difficult Freedom*, for example, describes the state of Israel as 'the place where man is uprooted from his recent past for the sake of an ancient and prophetic past, where he seeks his authenticity'.[34] In passages like these Levinas subjects the different cultures that inhabit Israel/Palestine to the same temporality, and this is precisely the sort of manoeuvre that Bhabha contests in *The Location of Culture*.[35]

II The postnational nation

Narratives of cultural particularity not only fail in their own terms to make sense of social collectivity and territorial belonging, they also return to haunt resistance thinking, and poststructuralism's contribution to postcolonial theory is often linked to the critique of essentialism's persistence in both dominant and resistant accounts of national identity. What has become increasingly evident in the last decade, however, is that poststructuralism offers postcolonial theory more than just a series of interventions that displace the concepts of nationality that are embedded in both the assertion and critique of the West's authority. Certainly, those associated with poststructuralism collectively argue that originary hybridities are central to the West's identifications, and that these hybridities work against some of the most entrenched and violent attempts to separate one racial, cultural, or national character from another. But poststructuralist theory has also, in various ways, sought to trigger a shift in the understanding of regional, national, international, and global identity by developing concepts that facilitate a different understanding of identity – concepts that avoid the unwitting rearticulation of a colonial or neocolonial sensibility.

For its critics, this rethinking of national identity amounts to little more than an anarchic celebration of the demise of the nation-state. Poststructuralism is often viewed by its detractors as part of a voguish and asinine avant-gardism that finds in contemporary transnational movements, in new communications technologies, and in virtual spaces an absolute dispersal of national boundaries, of regionality, of local communities: we no longer know who we are, its advocates apparently declare, so we should abandon all forms of identification and should instead embrace our fluid and polymorphous postnationality. As well as disputing the attempt by critics like Eagleton to detach poststructuralist theory from the critique of colonial and postcolonial systems, this book will also contest such accusations that poststructuralism pursues an emptily utopian and postnational agenda. Derrida, Deleuze and Guattari, Kristeva, Spivak, and Bhabha certainly find the idea of a securely bordered territoriality unconvincing, but the concepts of transnational, cosmopolitan, resistant, and postcolonial difference that they develop are, more subtly, concerned with how theory might think beyond the nation-state; in other words, these theorists are not interested in declaring the nation-state's burgeoning obsolescence, but instead interrogate the conditions for thinking the future of national and international identities. Indeed, these theorists not only refuse to promote the postnational dispersionism that is frequently associated with them, they also provide a more compelling sense of conceptual and cultural transformation than is offered by their critics.

An exceptional community

One reaction against the supposedly anarcho-globalist tendencies in recent theory can be found in Roger Scruton's *England: An Elegy*. This book pays tribute to a nation that, for Scruton, has embodied the virtues of civilization; in part a valediction to England's waning character – genteel, loyal, chivalrous, heroic, reserved, urbane, eccentric, and adventurous – this book is also a rejoinder to what he sees as the vituperative proclamation that nationality, as a mode of social affiliation, is in terminal decline. Against the slanderous broadside that has been launched against England's historic status, Scruton undertakes a revaluation of the English national character that would see it recover its fading glory in an increasingly postnational world. For him:

> The empire was acquired by roving adventurers and merchants who, trading with natives whom they could not or would not trust, summoned the law of Old England to conclude the deal and, in the wake of the law, the sovereign power that would enforce it. But it was not only the empire that was acquired in this way. Almost the entire social order of the country arose from private initiatives. Schools, colleges and universities; municipalities, hospitals, theatres; festivals and even the army regiments, all tell the same story: some public-spirited amateur, raising funds, setting out principles, acquiring premises…. That is the English way. It is the way of people who are at home, and who refuse to be bossed about by those whom they regard as outsiders. Their attitude to officialdom reflected their conviction that, if something needs doing, then the person to do it is you.[36]

That this passage indulges in a quite stupendous bathos is obvious, and its simple homilies provide comfort only to those who locate social responsibility in naked self-interest. Scruton's account of English culture and its imperial appetites does little more than reiterate the parochial ethnocentrism that construes colonial intervention as an act of cultural benevolence, and what motivates this revisionism is a desperate caricature of the challenge to England and empire in recent thought.

Less visible, however, is the problematic theory of community that is central to the notion of Englishness that Scruton offers as a foil to postnational culture. When developing his idea of the English character, Scruton tries to avoid the essentialist traps that have, in the recent past, ensnared reflection on ethnicity and nationality: rather than argue that the English character is rooted in the landscape, or that its spirit flows through the blood of true-born Englishmen, he maintains that Englishness is attained culturally, and is built on layers of sedimented tradition:

As with the landscape... the human form is shaped by culture: what is identified as raw material – the 'racial' inheritance – may turn out on closer inspection to be a cultural acquisition. Not the blue eyes, but the cool glance; not the pale lips, but the shy smile; not the tall figure, but the erect carriage – these are the features that spoke to our ancestors of 'race' and 'breeding', and of course they belong to our cultural rather than our genetic endowment.[37]

This endowment, he goes on to claim, is what allows communal bonds to be forged between people with a shared heritage: 'The raw material of a country', he argues, 'is shaped by consciousness and culture. The fundamental force... is the common language. People form communities by talking'.[38]

Scruton here sounds a little like Nietzsche: for him, as for Nietzsche, the contours of the landscape become etched on the bodies of the people who live from it. However, whereas Nietzsche ultimately disconcerts the topological determinism that he also promotes, Scruton locates nature as the *ne plus ultra* when claiming that communities and nations offer a valuable form of social organization.

Nations are useful, because they enable people to rationalize their common fate, to *define* themselves as a 'we', and to prepare themselves for the competition – which may, at the limit, become a life-and-death struggle – between 'us' and 'the others'. But not all ways of forming a first-person plural are so conscious. There are other, more instinctive and more immediate, forms of membership which serve the purpose just as well or better, and which have the desired result of making it possible for people to live together in a state of mutual support.[39]

By claiming that communities and nations represent an expression of a universal human nature – that they are a 'first-person plural' – Scruton begins to sound more like Rousseau and Kant than Nietzsche. The individual is seen to possess natural instincts that both predate the social and need to be managed by a shared rationality; existing only to enable the individual's welfare, communities and nations would not, ideally, interfere with its interests. As the theorists considered in this book insist, however, these notions of community and nation are always ambivalent, and Scruton's claims do indeed work against themselves. He acknowledges that hybridizing processes produced the English, but he also argues that their distinctiveness has been shaped by both a particular history and a unique landscape which owe nothing to other cultures. The consequence of this reasoning is that the English 'we' denotes only those who possess a legitimate claim to their heritage: that is, Englishness once again becomes an exclusive – racial – property. And Scruton argues that the bonds between people are forged through language, but he also claims that individual identity precedes – and can be known outside of – social structures such as language; despite being external to the formation of the individual, these structures are nonetheless essential to the functioning of the individual. According to this mutable reasoning, then, Englishness creates the people who come together to form the English community.

The politics of recognition

England is so full of conservative prejudice that criticizing it is a little like reprimanding a frail relative who, in all likelihood, will not see another summer. A more engaging account of the nation-state's transitions is developed in Jürgen Habermas' *The Postnational Constellation*. For Habermas, recent technologies of communication, transportation, and commodity production are resulting in the emergence of new 'Networks' that control the movement of goods and capital. What these globalizing Networks also produce is a departure from the idea of the republican state on which Western modernity is modelled. But Habermas does not simply conclude with this simple, and now familiar, diagnosis of the nation-state's declining fortunes. He is more concerned with how the erosion of territorial frontiers is generating a series of political paradoxes, such as the fact that Western democracies drive globalization, even though globalization's transnational thrust threatens the very borders that secure the democratic state's autonomy.

In contrast with Scruton, Habermas views the emerging postnational condition, and the contradictions it engenders, not as the rampant degeneration of valuable organizational frameworks that allow us to tame our wilder passions and express our intrinsic capacity for sociable coexistence. Instead, Habermas argues that the idea of the nation has hardened people's sense of affinity by providing them with a symbolism that confirms their shared heritage: 'Constructed through the medium of modern law', he writes, 'the modern territorial state thus depends on the development of a national consciousness to provide it with the cultural substrate for a civil solidarity. With this solidarity, the bonds that had formed between members of a concrete community now change into a new, more abstract form'.[40] Habermas does not go as far as Scruton in this account of the origins of the social – unlike Scruton, his analysis is not based on the idea that individuals precede social systems

– but he does suggest that authentic ('concrete') forms of collectivity predate the arrival of the nation. Certainly, he does not dwell nostalgic-ally on what the pre-modern past might have looked like; instead he considers how the arrival of the postnational world means that new narratives, new symbolic forms, and new cultural values are starting to emerge, and are reshaping people's consent so that it fits the new world order. This process of constant political management is what interests Habermas: faced with the disempowering consequences of globaliza-tion, he argues, Western democratic states develop regulatory proced-ures that allow them to preserve their integrity. Departing from notions of national cohesion, democratic cultures can restructure themselves around notions of participatory and inclusive citizenship: democracies 'guarantee a sort of emergency backup system for maintaining the integrity of a functionally differentiated society'.[41]

In order to arrive at this explanation of the capacity for state-based democracies to moderate the centrifugal effects of a burgeoning post-nationality, Habermas dismisses other theories that explore the rela-tionship between cultural difference and cultural totality. Included in these other models is a 'postmodern neoliberalism' that, for him, celeb-rates globalization as the shattering of old certainties and the disper-sion of the state's sovereignty:

> postmodern neoliberalism cannot explain how the deficits in steer-ing competencies and legitimation that emerge at the national level can be compensated at the supranational level without new forms of political regulation.... The relative hardness or permeability of boundaries itself doesn't reveal much about the openness or closed-ness of a given community.[42]

Postmodern neoliberalism, in other words, fails to comprehend exactly how European societies operate because it refuses to see that these soci-eties successfully reintegrate themselves in response to external dangers. Admittedly, Habermas does not name those who promote this mis-guided neoliberalism, but his characterization of it does point to those who disagree with his claim that cultural totality constantly reasserts itself over the forces of differentiation and dissemination. By implica-tion, then, Derrida, Deleuze and Guattari, Kristeva, Spivak, and Bhabha would find themselves falling into the company of postmodern neolib-erals: since they argue that differences persistently trouble the cohesion of cultural systems, they can only, from Habermas' point of view, mis-construe the ways in which global systems are being reshaped.

A sense of how recent developments in poststructuralist theory might begin to dispute Habermas' claims can be derived from his support for multiculturalism. For Habermas, 'Multicultural societies require a "politics of recognition" because the identity of each individual citizen is woven together with collective identities, and must be stabilized in a network of mutual recognition'.[43] In order for a multicultural society to function and survive, then, it has to develop a inclusive political system that is based upon mutuality and deliberative consensus. That Habermas here places rationality outside of any geopolitical affiliation is problematic enough, but he compounds this problem by then suggesting that a functional multiculturalism is produced not by consent, but by a dominant group that is willing to accommodate other ethnicities, languages, and religions:

> For nation-states with their own national histories, a politics that seeks the coexistence of different ethnic communities, language groups, religious faiths, etc. under equal rights naturally entails a process as precarious as it is painful. The majority culture, supposing itself to be identical with the national culture as such, has to free itself from its historical identification with a *general* political culture, if all citizens are to be able to identify on equal terms with the political culture of their own country.[44]

Multiculturalism is thus possible when the state knowingly welcomes different ethnicities into its fold and permits other cultures to influence its development. But this process of accommodation would not entail a dramatic departure from the political structures that buttress the democratic state; the state's existing political configuration would instead remain essentially unaltered by this process of reconfiguration, and multiculturalism would consist simply in the expansion of the democratic state. Further, it also appears that, in this account, subaltern groups or resistance movements have almost no bearing on the emergence of multicultural states. Their role is, instead, simply to add qualities that are palatable to the state's prevailing appetites. Augmenting a social system that is already open to outsiders, other ethnicities merely provoke a separation of national culture from the state: once this separation has been achieved, all that remains for minorities is to sit on the margins of political life.

For those associated with poststructuralist and postcolonial theory, this kind of thinking ultimately reinforces the melancholic idea of national identity that is also at work in Scruton's *England*, maintaining

Manichean distinctions between domesticity and difference by continuing to see the majority culture as one that, despite its capacity for pluralism, remains secure in its sense of cultural belonging. What such accounts problematically assume is that the displacing effects of modernity's counter-narratives can be overcome by political reason and social consensus: if the state has to rearticulate itself in response to internal and external differences, then its authoritative narratives remain permanently fissured. From this alternative perspective, then, what other communities bring to democratic multiculturalism is the realization that cultural difference cannot be smoothly incorporated into the state's evolving constitution; the multiculturalism that emerges and becomes established can only be a profoundly uncertain one, and this anxiety demands a different understanding of both national identity and national difference.

The following chapters consider how Derrida, Deleuze and Guattari, Kristeva, Spivak, and Bhabha interrogate modes of national identification and differentiation by challenging the politics of inclusive recognition that continue to inform social, cultural, and political theory, by disputing the still widespread belief that Europe can or should recentre itself as a stable collectivity that possesses an inherent character, and by refusing to endorse the vague utopianism that often accompanies the critique of frontiered territoriality. This book also contests the repeated assertions that poststructuralism becomes politicized by postcolonial theory or offers merely a negative critique of claims to the nation's ontological substance. Against such assertions, it argues that theorists associated with poststructuralism provide a range of concepts that provoke a dramatic rethinking of nationality and globalization. These concepts certainly name the various movements that trouble entrenched assumptions about local, national, and international identity, though they also work alongside and against each other in a mode of relentless critique and auto-critique that departs from the drive for systematicity and closure that remains in social, cultural, and political theory; it is this mode of conceptual invention and intervention that can allow theory not only to subject the foundations of the nation-state to a compelling critique, but also to trigger new narratives of national and international identity. Whereas some responses to the nation-state's shifting status offer little sense that it is always out of joint with itself, and while others declare the present to be a moment of transnational pluralism, the concepts that emerge between poststructuralism and postcolonial theory begin to think the cosmopolitan locations that have always shaped Europe, but are yet to come.

2
'Before, Across, and Beyond': Derrida, Without National Community

Community is where communication masquerades as communion, where artifice is disguised as essence, where the subject experiences ecstasy and death, and where theory fails. These are just some of the conclusions that Jean-Luc Nancy arrives at in *The Inoperative Community*. Principally concerned with how the roots of social and political systems have been conceived, Nancy argues that theories of culture's origin gravitate towards the idea that the individual is an agent who creates social and cultural structures in its own image. Community, according to such an immanentist understanding of cultural foundations, represents the extension of a subject for whom association is a basic necessity. Nancy locates one such model of the community in Rousseau's work: here community is seen as an authentic form of regional collectivity, one that binds together groups of people who possess shared characteristics and who live in close proximity with each other. For Rousseau, however, this local affiliation is increasingly threatened by modernity's anonymous institutions: modern political systems interrupt neighbourly bonds between individuals, and the objective of political theory should therefore be to re-assert the intimacy of local association. This idea of community has been so influential, Nancy claims, that it is now a central feature of political thought:

> The lost, or broken, community can be exemplified in all kinds of ways, by all kinds of paradigms: the natural family, the Athenian city, the Roman Republic, the first Christian community, corporations, communes, or brotherhoods – always it is a matter of a lost age in which community was woven of tight, harmonious, and infrangible bonds and in which above all it played back to itself,

through its institutions, its rituals, and its symbols, the representation, indeed the living offering, of its own immanent unity, intimacy, and autonomy.[1]

Disputing such nostalgic interpretations of the individual's essential
sociability, *The Inoperative Community* reiterates the now commonplace
sentiment that subjects are produced by, not the producers of, social
systems. Hence, for Nancy, immanentist notions of community do
not, as their proponents assume, extend political thought by revealing
the source of collective organization, but instead circumscribe and constrain reflection on the political by attributing to it a restricted and
essential foundation. Nancy's insight, however, is to take this argument further by considering how the subject is not shaped as a
uniform and distinctive entity, but is broken apart by community's differentiating logic: community can only set the subject in motion as a
separate being by distinguishing it from other inhabitants of the social
and not, as is often thought, by asserting the intrinsic autonomy of the
individual. No longer an extension of the subject's absolute sovereignty, community becomes for Nancy yet another fiction, one providing a refuge for those who recoil from modernity's vertiginous
anti-foundationalism. 'Community, far from being what society has
crushed or lost', he argues, 'is *what happens to us… in the wake of*
society'.[2]

Despite contesting nostalgic notions of community, *The Inoperative*
Community does not simply engage in a critical assessment of flawed
reasoning. Nancy's text is also concerned with how a transformed
understanding of community can offer new ways of conceiving the
political. Although the notion of community has been rooted in
essences and foundations, it also reveals itself to be both impossible
and ineluctable: narratives of common belonging certainly indulge in
melancholia and invoke nebulous phantasms, but versions of these
narratives are needed if social structures are to be transfigured. It is for
this reason that, although problematic, the idea of community can act
as the starting point for different approaches to culture. Once the
subject ceases to act as the source and guarantor of regional affiliation,
social, cultural, and political theory can relinquish their attempts to
restore a past populated by self-reliant and harmonious communities,
and can instead begin to conceive community as an ecstatic form of
association, as a 'bond that forms ties without attachments', a 'bond
that unbinds by binding'.[3] Such a transformed notion of community,
he cautions, must ultimately escape theory's grasp: 'Perhaps we should

not seek a word or a concept for it, but rather recognize in the thought of community a theoretical excess... that would oblige us to adopt another *praxis* of discourse and community'.[4]

One compelling example of how community might be reconceived as a bond without attachments can be found in Derrida's work: from *Of Grammatology* to *Of Spirit*, from *Margins of Philosophy* to *Politics of Friendship*, Derrida contests the ways in which the term 'community' has been used to signify an immanent interiority. Nancy's insistence that the idea of community masks melancholic assumptions about subjectivity certainly finds itself endorsed throughout Derrida's work, and the first section of this chapter reflects on his challenge to immanentist attempts to root identity in a fixed and regional character. The second section considers how, for Derrida, an unsustainable notion of community operates not just as a principle for local organization, but also extends to shape the borders of the nation-state. Focusing in particular on *Specters of Marx,* this section explores Derrida's challenge to the primacy that is given to Europe and the US in liberal definitions of the international community.

Some commentators claim that such a critique concerns itself solely with Western authority, and that Derrida, by implication, regards all modes of national identification (including those that resist colonial and neocolonial processes) as a uniformly hegemonic reproduction of the Western nation-state. To read Derrida's work in this way, the final section argues, is to disregard its attempts to develop a conceptual vocabulary that would render and give place to collective identity in different ways. Derrida's work is not, as it might appear to be, concerned simply with combating frontiered notions of belonging, or with exposing the violences that are fundamental to European thought, and this section explores how some of Derrida's more recent writings (such as *The Monolingualism of the Other* and the dialogue 'Autoimmunity: Real and Symbolic Suicides') bear witness to deconstruction's affirmative dimensions. This work not only sees Derrida turning more directly towards conventional discourses of international politics in order to question the West's authority. What also needs to be discerned in this recent material is the series of quasi-propositional concepts that allow Derrida to promote a different sense of international justice.

I   'What is initiated is already corrupted'

Introductions to Derrida's thinking frequently overlook his attempt to address local, national, and global forms of identity. Synopses of deconstruction often lead us to believe that it is exclusively concerned

with philosophical abstractions and conceptual lacunae: deconstruction, commentators often insist, is interested only in exposing Western
culture's unsustainable efforts to determine identity as essence. These
synopses credit Derrida's work with, at best, a limited interventionist
value: foregrounding the constitutive contradictions that reside within
the West's founding concepts, Derrida offers critical and cultural theory the seemingly underwhelming pronouncement that meaning and
identity, as they are imagined by metaphysical thought, should no
longer be treated as adequate or convincing first principles.

Although such a concise overview of Derrida's ideas might suit those
interested in intellectual economy, it fails to acknowledge that deconstruction – even in its embryonic stages – provokes a dramatic recon-
sideration of political concepts. Vital to Derrida's account of originary
différance, for example, is his claim that the concepts of nature and
culture both define and erase each other:

> one could reconsider all the pairs of opposites on which philosophy
> is constructed and on which our discourse lives, not in order to see
> the opposition erase itself but to see what indicates that each of the
> terms must appear as the *différance* of the other, as the other differ-
> ent and deferred in the economy of the same... culture as nature dif-
> ferent and deferred, differing-deferring; all the others of *physis* –
> *tekhnē, nomos, thesis*, society, freedom, history, mind, etc. – as *physis*
> different and deferred, or as *physis* differing and deferring.[5]

'Différance' here does not simply name a philosophical process that is
dissociated from the principles of political organization, it also points to
the slippages that occur when such concepts as society, freedom, and
history are articulated. These concepts cannot be located purely within
a self-sufficient realm of rational culture (a realm that would be construed as a skilfully crafted (*tekhnē*) territorial interiority (*nomos*) that
has reasoned propositions (*thesis*) as its foundation), since they only
acquire their meaning in relation to non-rational, aconceptual, and
unruly exteriorities. For 'Différance', in other words, some of the most
basic principles of culture and civilization need to be scrutinized for
their immanent instabilities, rather than be treated as axiomatic truths.

Both 'The Ends of Man' and *Of Grammatology* are more direct in their
confrontation of social and political issues. The opening pages of 'The
Ends of Man' situate Derrida's discussion of metaphysics and anthropology in the context of its articulation. Forming the backdrop to
Derrida's essay are the assassination of Martin Luther King, the beginning of the Vietnam Peace talks, the invasion of universities in Paris by

'the forces of order',[6] and students' subsequent reoccupation of those universities. Derrida also points out that when invited to deliver 'The Ends of Man' at an international colloquium in New York, he agreed to do so if he were allowed to express solidarity with those 'who were fighting against what was then their country's official policy in certain parts of the world, notably in Vietnam'.[7] That he was given permission suggests for Derrida only that 'the *form of democracy*' is 'the political milieu'[8] for philosophical colloquia: although diverse positions may be expressed at these colloquia (even positions which defy official policy), the fact that permission can be denied as well as given reveals that one of the cornerstones of democracy – free speech – exists only as a myth. For Derrida,

> It would be illusory to believe that political innocence has been restored, and evil complicities undone, when opposition to them can be expressed in the country itself, not only through the voices of its own citizens but also those of foreign citizens, and that henceforth diversities, i.e. oppositions, may freely and discursively relate to one another. That a declaration of opposition to some official policy is authorized, and authorized by the authorities, also means, precisely to that extent, that the declaration does not upset the given order, is not *bothersome*.[9]

In addition to exposing democracy's distinctly undemocratic protocols, 'The Ends of Man' also questions the assumption that cultural identity is the expression of an immanent character. This essay documents the history of an error in post-war French thought – an error that Derrida associates with Sartre's misreading of phenomenology's response to anthropology, a misreading that can, in turn, be attributed to the inaccurate translation of Heidegger's term '*Dasein*' as 'human-reality'. While this translation may allow a rethinking of man and humanity to take place (as 'a reaction to a certain intellectualist or spiritualist humanism which had dominated French philosophy'[10]), it nevertheless, for Derrida, continues to render 'Being' in terms of an unproblematized unity of man. Sartre's 'phenomenological ontology is a philosophical anthropology', Derrida argues, since, 'the history of the concept of man is never examined. Everything occurs as if the sign "man" had no origin, no historical, cultural, or linguistic limit'.[11]

Derrida's response to this conceptual hiatus is only partly the result of scholarly concern. Certainly, he finds it 'astonishing' that Sartre treats 'Being' and '*anthropos*' as synonyms in work by Hegel, Husserl and Heidegger: it is 'the most serious mistake' and an 'anthropologistic misinterpretation' in which 'the critique of anthropologism remained totally unnoticed'.[12] More important than exposing Sartre's short-comings, for Derrida, is the need to re-establish phenomenology as a challenge to humanism's uninterrogated anthropocentrism. Derrida's concluding ellipsis 'But who, we?' does not simply arise out his atten-tion to the aporias running through Hegel's notion of *Aufhebung* or the ineffable quality that Heidegger finds in *Dasein*. This question suggests, rather, that if man is neither autochthonous nor self-identical then, by extension, culture cannot be understood purely as the outcome of common interests or qualities; community, by this reasoning, can no longer form the basis for defining cultural identity.

The question of community is taken further and Derrida's concerns about it are made more explicit in *Of Grammatology*. Like Nancy, Derrida here questions Rousseau's attempt to distinguish between social groups that possess unique attributes. Reading Rousseau's 'anthropo-geographic'[13] distinction between Northern and Southern cultures ('North/winter/cold/need/articulation; South/summer/warmth/passion/accentuation'[14]) against the grain of strict differentiation that is promoted in the *Essay on the Origin of Languages*, Derrida writes:

This *birth of society* is therefore not a passage, it is a point, a pure, fictive and unstable, ungraspable limit. One crosses it in attaining it. In it society is broached and is deferred from itself. Beginning, it begins to decay. The South passes into its own North. Transcending need, passion engenders new needs which in turn corrupt it. Post-originary degradation is analogous to pre-originary repetition. Articulation, substituting itself for passion, restores the order of need…. If culture is thus broached within its point of origin, then it is not possible to recognize any linear order, whether logical or chronological. In this broaching, what is initiated is already cor-rupted, thus returning to a place before the origin. Speech lets itself be heard and understood in the South only through articulation, through chilling itself in order to express need anew…. The South and the North are not territories but abstract places that appear only to relate to each other in terms of each other.[15]

Cultures of the North and South inform each other, and this means that they do not, as Rousseau supposes, possess distinctive or independ-ent characters. Just as the South ceases to be a domain of pure expres-sion, so the North loses its status as an autonomous realm of structured articulation. *Of Grammatology* arrives at these conclusions after observing that although Rousseau appears to view cultural differences as absolute, he nonetheless believes that these differences ultimately rest on a natural social order which, for him, takes the form of the family. This order maintains itself by a universal and consecrated law of incest prohibition that cannot itself be spoken or signified; writing, according to this reasoning, has the status of an appurtenance that is exterior to a full positivity, but which dangerously aids an extra-linguistic plenitude by bringing it into rational discourse. What interests Derrida is that Rousseau's account of this natural origin inadvertently works against itself because language here does not simply allow the recognition and articulation of this foundation, but is central to its very existence. Although the order of the family exists as an ineffable and inconceivable origin, this natural association can only come into being after its dissociation from structured discourse. And if language and nature mutually inform each other, then, Derrida argues, society's natural foundations must already be contaminated by signifying conventions.

For social and cultural theory the consequences of such claims are far reaching, since Derrida's critique of Rousseau's account of culture's natural foundations can be extended to all essentializing accounts of social formation. Degradation is intrinsic to any supposedly immutable order, just as repetition is inherent in any supposedly founding identity. The frontiers circumscribing territories thus lose their anthropogeographic certainty, and must be treated instead as artifices and abstractions that are essentially unsustainable; rather than being understood as the collocation of self-present neighbours, communities must instead be defined as both structurally interdependent and beyond absolute delimitation.[16]

II   Injunctions

Other work by Derrida develops this critique of immanentist constructions of community, and *Specters of Marx* provides one of his most sustained efforts in recent years to question foundationalist accounts of social collectivity. *Specters* represents Derrida's attempt to uncover the bonds between Marxism and deconstruction, and for him the points of convergence between these supposedly distinct theoretical approaches are complex and varied. At the most evident level, and in terms of intellectual history, deconstruction's emergence and Marxism's influence in the post-war period are indissociable: apocalyptic and eschatological themes – the end of History, the end of Man, the end of Philosophy, and the end of Marx – as well as the 'socio-economic disasters of Soviet bureaucracy' form 'the element in which what is called deconstruction developed'.[17] Further, just as deconstruction's emergence can be seen as challenge to these celebratory teleologies, so 'pre-deconstructive' traits can be found in some of Marx's texts; indeed, Derrida goes so far as to say that in *The German Ideology* Marx addresses 'deconstructive critiques'[18] to Max Stirner.

While it draws attention to some general correspondences between Marxism and deconstruction, *Specters* refuses desperately to fold Marxism and deconstruction into each other so that they become synonyms for the same critical activity. Instead, Derrida ventriloquizes Blanchot's essay 'Marx's Three Voices' by pointing out not only that Marxism is an increasingly heterogeneous critical tradition, but that Marx's legacy is itself disparate and disjointed.[19] In following this path into Marx's work, Derrida challenges what he sees as 'the neutralizing anesthesia of a new theoreticism' that accompanies 'philosophico-philological'[20] attempts to evaluate recent Marxist theory by reading it against an incontestably singular and authoritative body of Marx's writing. Responding to Marx in this way – reducing his texts to proper readings and to the property of institutionalized knowledge – would (perhaps inadvertently) 'muffle the political imperative in the untroubled exegesis of a classified work', eventually 'enervating a *corpus*, by silencing in it the revolt'[21] that characterizes Marx's injunctions.

This absence of doctrine and systematicity for Derrida signals the continuing urgency of Marx and Marxism, and for him it allows theory to challenge recent accounts of regional, national, and transnational identity. Many of the concerns of *Specters of Marx* are triggered by Hamlet's apostrophe 'The time is out of joint!', an exclamation stifled by jubilatory announcements of the triumph of the new world order, by proclamations that the global free market has conquered communism, and by declarations that liberal democracy and neo-capitalism represent the culmination of history (assertions that are most notoriously advanced in Francis Fukuyama's reworking of Hegel and Kojève, *The End of History and the Last Man*). Against the euphoria surrounding the assertion that an 'ideal finality'[22] has been reached, Derrida points out that this 'worldwide hegemony' seeks to install itself 'in paradoxical and suspect conditions',[23] since its rhetoric is 'both jubilant and worried, manic and bereaved'.[24] This ambivalent mourning of the death of Marxism anxiously 'conjures away' troublesome social and cultural phenomena and denies itself the 'force and virtuality' of 'the *spirit* of the Marxist critique'.[25] It is this '*spirit*' of the Marxist critique', rather than the notion that Marxism is a clearly defined system, doctrine or 'ontological totality' with 'fundamental concepts',[26] that *Specters of Marx* seeks to elicit. This spirit is signalled by the substantial yet equivocal presence of ghosts, phantoms, revenants and spectres throughout Marx's writings: from the 'decalogue of specters'[27] in *The German Ideology*,[28] through the opening line of *The Communist Manifesto* ('A specter is haunting Europe – the specter of communism'), to the theory of the alchemical metamorphosis of commodities into the idealized (simulacrous, shadowy, ghostly) form of the monetary sign in *The Critique of the Political Economy of the Sign*, Marx both disavows phantasmatic apparitions and frames his speculations by a 'spectropoetics'.[29] It is this ambivalent disavowal and return of revenants in Marx's work that, for Derrida, allows it to be read as disparate and disjointed *'hauntology'*.[30] Unlike its homophone, *ontologie*, this hauntology would not treat materiality as the primary determinant of identity, but would instead consider the supplementary relationship that exists between the material and the imaginary. Theory, Derrida insists, must not deprive itself 'of the means with which to take into account, or to render an account of, the effects of ghosts, of simulacra, of "synthetic images", or even, to put it in terms of the Marxist code, of ideologems'.[31]

While some might discern in these claims just another version of structuralist Marxism, where material practices and ideology are seen as co-relative and reciprocally constitutive, others argue that *Specters of Marx* attributes cultural forces and the materiality of oppression to undiagnosable, supernatural, and shadowy causes. Daniel McGee, for example, argues that *Specters of Marx* needs to be treated as part of an increasingly voguish 'post-Marxist' cultural critique, one that induces a diversionary narcosis rather producing the analysis of social forces that is needed if advanced capitalism is to be resisted:

> Insofar as post-Marxism convinces us that our most pressing political concern is to ensure the cultural immortality of our ancestors and thus ourselves, it may well distract us from improving the conditions of living people.... post-Marxism provides contemporary intellectuals with a theoretical vision of the technology for misrecognizing politics that Marx called 'the opiate of the masses'.[32]

Mark Lilla similarly concludes that Derrida's recent political writings, such as *Specters of Marx,* display an 'intellectual desperation' since they promote a willed and unspeakable 'idea of justice', rather than offering a more pragmatic programme for intervention.[33] For Lilla, 'the post-modernist section of any American bookshop is such a disconcerting experience', not because these books advance any form of disruptive critique but because they offer only a bathetic sense of the political:

> The most illiberal, anti-enlightenment notions are put forward with a smile and the assurance that, followed out to their logical conclusions, they could only lead us into the democratic promised land, where all God's children will join hands in singing the national anthem. It is an uplifting vision and many Americans believe in uplift. That so many of them seem to have found it in the dark and forbidding works of Jacques Derrida attests to the strength of American's self-confidence and their awesome capacity to think well of anyone and any idea. Not for nothing do the French still call us *les grands enfants*.[34]

Of course, criticisms like Lilla's can be arrived at only through a stupendous and willful misprision. No doubt, there are books that advocate the sort of vague utopianism that Lilla finds in the 'post-modernist' sections of American bookshops; to think that this utopianism – rooted in the notions of determinable topology, redemptive theology, democratic finitude, speculative logic, and characterized as a nation unified by the spoken word – is at work in *Specters of Marx* is truly to believe that texts are absolutely indeterminate.

Community and the political

Against the sort of criticisms that are arrived at by McGee and Lilla, Derrida insists that the non-propositional extrapolation of Marxism's interventionist spirit would galvanize the conditions for conceptual transformation, and would begin to address ideological processes with a greater complexity than can often be found in both Marxist and non-Marxist theory. Indeed, rather than rashly speculating on democratic futures or offering a naïve utopianism in the way that Lilla declares, *Specters* reiterates the recognizably Derridean contention that cultural criticism is always informed by the systems of knowledge that it contests. And, as Fredric Jameson writes in defence of *Specters* , 'there is still a very strong Marxian flavour about the conviction that genuinely new concepts will not be possible until the concrete situation, the system itself, in which they are to be thought, has been radically modified'.[35] Theoretical contributions to the work of political and social transformation lie not, then, in indulgent conjecture on possible futures, but in maintaining the possibility for more equitable and democratic forms of social organization, even if they lie beyond current concepts of culture and identity. This task requires a vigilance towards the continued shaping of cultural critique by dominant forms of understanding, and such a vigilance can be found, Derrida tells us, in Marxism's (often neglected) modification of its theoretical protocols:

> To continue to take inspiration from a certain spirit of Marxism would be to keep faith with what has always made of Marxism in principle and first of all a *radical* critique, namely a procedure ready to undertake its self-critique. This critique *wants itself* to be in principle and explicitly open to its own transformation, re-evaluation, self-reinterpretation.[36]

Specters of Marx emphasizes Marxism's conceptual and methodological reflexivity, but it is also anxious to point out that the radical critique that flows from this re-evaluation would not find itself caught in a self-regarding narcissism. Instead, such a critique would begin to provide the theoretical resources for a different form of affirmative praxis; no longer trapped by the demand to produce a new ontology, this hauntological Marxism would point to the possibility for a different future. Among the various terms that Derrida associates with this affirmation are 'the messianic', 'promise' and 'justice':

> Now, if there is a spirit of Marxism which I will never be ready to renounce, it is not only the critical idea or the questioning stance.... It is even more a certain emancipatory and *messianic* affirmation, a certain experience of the promise that one can try to liberate from any dogmatics and even from any metaphysico-religious determination, from any *messianism*. And a promise must be a promise to be kept, that is, not to remain 'spiritual' or 'abstract', but to produce events, new effective forms of action, practice, organization.... A deconstructive thinking, the one that matters to me here, has always pointed out the irreducibility of affirmation and therefore of the promise, as well as the undeconstructibility of a certain idea of justice.[37]

Affirmation here proceeds through atheses: 'the messianic' signifies 'a structure of experience rather than a religion',[38] designating an undesignatable hospitality and an opening towards a 'future that cannot be anticipated';[39] 'promise' refuses a constative or prophetic naming of the future; 'justice', which Derrida differentiates from the institutional legitimation of legality and illegality by judicial systems, resists taxonomy and legal calculation, and can be found in the ceaseless questioning of norms, concepts and principles.

Non-predicative concepts such as these can, according to Richard Beardsworth, initiate transformations in our understanding of 'the political': 'Our political concepts, and, therefore, the fields in which these concepts are discursively organized, acquire meaning and operate', he states in *Derrida & the Political*, 'need to be reinvented'.[40] For Beardsworth, this reinvention provokes a rethinking of political theory's static preoccupation with Kant and Hegel – a preoccupation that sees political thought caught in an opposition between transcendence and empiricism, between the notion of attainable rights and the idea of immanent community. Resurfacing in the United States as the debate between those who advocate rights-based non-foundationalism (Ronald Dworkin, Robert Nozick, and John Rawls) and those who adopt 'an expressive understanding of community'[41] (Charles Taylor, and Alisdair MacIntyre), this division has persisted: 'For the liberals', Beardsworth points out, 'rights are the very condition of community. For the communitarians, community is the very condition of rights'.[42] What is excised from this debate for Beardsworth is an interrogation of a prioricity, as well as any consideration of 'the relation between rights, community and violence'[43] that is to be found in the work of Kant and Hegel. By reintroducing this relation to the Kantian-Hegelian legacy, Derrida, according to Beardsworth, reminds political theorists that the idea of community should be treated neither as a predetermined fact nor as a salutary goal.

Specters of Marx develops the concepts of the promise, justice, and the messianic, and it does so while continuing to challenge the ways in which political theory has figured community. *Of Grammatology*, 'Différance' and 'The Ends of Man' cast doubt upon ethnographic, philosophical and anthropological notions of community (as a neighbourly self-proximity communicated by the spoken word, as an expression of intrinsic traits, or as the unity of man) by arguing that these notions arise out of inconsistent and unsustainable ideas about subjectivity, nature, signification, and the social. *Specters of Marx* reasserts this critique of immanentist thinking, but it differs from Derrida's earlier work by appearing to take an altogether more censorious tone with regard to the idea of community.

Fukuyama's *The End of History and the Last Man* provides one of the main sources for Derrida's discontentment in *Specters of Marx*. According to Fukuyama, the modern liberal state is vigilant towards all of its citizens, recognizes and protects the rights of all people, eliminates the division between master and slave, and is governed by consensually determined policies. In the modern nation-state, Fukuyama submits,

> the authority of the state does not arise out of age-old tradition or from the murky depths of religious faith, but as the result of a public debate in which the citizens of the state agree amongst one another on the explicit terms under which they will live together. It represents a form of rational self-consciousness because for the first time human beings as a society are aware of their own true natures, and are able to fashion a political community that exists in conformity with those natures.[44]

Transparency, rationality, self-consciousness, truth, and nature here operate as wholly unproblematic axioms, and Fukuyama assumes that the integrity and equanimity of modern liberal communities are beyond reproach. While Derrida is certainly concerned with the series of conceptual inconsistencies and omissions that allow Fukuyama to arrive at his conclusions about humanity, nature, subjectivity, or knowledge, he is more troubled by Fukuyama's idea that European Christian thought should provide the model for liberal communities:

> The model of the liberal State to which he explicitly lays claim is not only that of Hegel, the Hegel of the struggle for recognition, it is that of a Hegel who privileges the 'Christian vision'... it is in the name of a Christian interpretation of the struggle for recognition... and thus of the exemplary European Community that the author of *The End of History and the Last Man* [Christian man] criticizes Marx.[45]

Fukuyama's claim that the European Community constitutes a 'state of universal recognition'[46] is, for Derrida, not only built on a faithfully Hegelian teleology, but is also entirely Christocentric. Fukuyama treats Christianity as a conceptual tradition that dissociates itself from authoritarian governance, even though he attributes to it a universal importance. Neither respecting difference nor seeking equality, the liberal community – exemplified by the EEC for Fukuyama – can establish itself only by placing Christian principles at the centre of legal and ethical systems. Fukuyama, then, is disinclined to consider the undemocratic foundation of democracy or the illiberal status of the liberal state, and is happy to locate the ideality of community politics in the tangible world of existing political institutions and alliances, but for Derrida liberal definitions of the community are neither politically acceptable nor accomplished as a material reality.[47]

Other headings

Specters of Marx answers those critics who seek to draw a line between Marxism and deconstruction, and if some commentators are unhappy with what they see as a dematerialization of Marxism by Derrida, others believe that this book offers a timely intervention into debates about both poststructuralism as cultural theory and about the status of Marxism in the late-twentieth century. '*Specters of Marx* is a major, courageous political statement', Teresa Brennan writes, 'Marx's stakes have never been lower, but the most influential philosopher of recent times has chosen this point to insist that deconstruction is only an extension of a "certain spirit of Marxism"'.[48] Jameson is less convinced, feeling that *Specters of Marx* misses an opportunity to consider class-based forms of differentiation and discrimination, though he nevertheless believes that Derrida's version of the messianic reinvigorates Walter Benjamin's Judaeo-Marxist notion that revolutions are unpredictable – 'unexpected by anyone, even their organizers... It is this temporality which is the messianic kind, and about which the very peculiarity of the messianic idea testifies, which can thus not be "hoped" for in any familiar way'.[49]

Specters of Marx stages the denouement of Derrida's dialogue with Marxism, but it also shows how deconstruction refuses to separate questions of identity (such as those that are provoked by the notion of community) from questions of national and international identity. 'If one had to answer... the question of what deconstruction is a deconstruction of', Young observes in *White Mythologies*, 'the answer would be, of the concept, the authority, and assumed primacy of, the category of "the West"'.[50] And yet, while deconstruction's preoccupation with nationality and cultural difference may be entirely evident to many of Derrida's readers, this preoccupation either continues to be dismissed or is attributed to other critics and theorists whose work is situated at the interface of poststructuralism and postcolonial theory.

Contesting either response is a relatively straightforward task, since Derrida regularly argues that European thought and culture are saturated by forms of epistemic violence. '*Geschlecht* II', for example, resolutely opposes attempts to conjure away the cultural location of Trakl's poem 'Occidental Song': contrary to Heidegger's claim that Trakl's text points to a pre-Western form of being, this primordiality for Derrida has '*no other content and even no other language* than that of Platonism and Christianity' and must therefore be situated within an 'ultra-Occidental horizon'.[51] More directly, 'Choreographies' confronts 'a certain Europeanization of world culture',[52] and *The Other Heading* asserts that 'Europe has always recognized itself as a cape or a headland... the point of departure for discovery, invention, and colonization'.[53]

Blunter still are Derrida's claims in 'Racism's Last Word', where he describes the political and juridical enforcement of apartheid in the South African as a 'quasi-ontological segregation'.[54] What is important to Derrida here is that rule by segregation in South Africa directly stems from and (at the time that this essay was written, at least) continues to embrace European approaches to governance and civilization. Apartheid, Derrida maintains, 'was a European "creation"' and continues to be propagated by 'a certain white community of European descent'.[55] As a result of this cultural heritage, South Africa shapes itself as

> a regime whose formal structures are those of a Western democracy, in the British style, with 'universal suffrage' (except for the 72 percent of blacks 'foreign' to the republic and citizens of 'Bantustans' that are being pushed 'democratically' into the trap of formal independence), a relative freedom of the press, the guarantee of individual rights and of the judicial system.[56]

Apartheid, then, is not just modelled on a European understanding of democratic enlightenment. It also reveals that this version of political refinement can comfortably accommodate extreme forms of subjugation. Segregation in South Africa might well have been buttressed by laws and amendments passed in the 1950s and 1960s, but apartheid is nonetheless, Derrida argues, a testament to Europe's history of conceiving civilization in racial terms.

Even the most apparently innocuous concepts, such as the concept of friendship, are drawn into Derrida's critique of European thought and culture. Friendship, he maintains, has been conceived (in the tradition that runs from Aristotle and Cicero to Montaigne, Kant and Schmitt) in 'autological' terms which privilege the proximate and the same over the distant and the different. Friendship has been grounded in the nameable, the knowable and the finite because the friend is someone configured (according to Cicero) '"in our own ideal image"'.[57] And this configuration provokes political questions, Derrida observes, since the narcissistic interpretation of friendship provides the foundation for more general structures within a culture, such as Western democracy (a 'community of friends'[58]), notions of filiation (exemplified by the family), and fratriarchy (the canonical androcentrism of democracy). Of course, this relationship between community and friendship equally informs the way that Greco-Christian nations have organized themselves in relation to other cultures. Like Derrida's other work, such as the essays on *Geschlecht* and genre, *Politics of Friendship* points out that concepts of filiation conceive 'stock, genus or species, sex, blood, birth, nature, nation'[59] as immutable and natural. Importantly, since friendship and affiliation are constituted as the converse of enmity, they belong on the same structural continuum that includes nationalistic forms of discrimination: 'in every racism, every ethnocentrism – more precisely in every one of the nationalisms throughout history', he argues, 'a *discourse* on birth and nature, a *phúsis* of genealogy... regulates, in the final analysis the movement of each opposition: repulsion and attraction, disagreement and accord, war and peace, hatred and friendship'.[60]

One inference that might be drawn from these remarks is that deconstruction is as hostile to concepts of national identity as it is critical of the idea of community. *Specters of Marx* appears to endorse this challenge to the West's ethnocentric privileging of local affiliation by suggesting that a comprehensive denunciation of both national identity in general, and nationalism in particular, is needed. For example, the preface to *Specters of Marx* anticipate Derrida's later account of justice as a ghostly responsibility, but it also claims that this justice cannot be reconciled with the dogmatic assertion of cultural totality that Derrida finds in nationalism and imperialism. Justice, in other words, bears witness to a responsibility

> beyond all living present, within that which disjoins the living present, before the ghosts of those who are not yet born or who are already dead, be they the victims of wars, political or other kinds of violence, nationalist, racist, colonialist, sexist, or other kinds of exterminations, victims of the oppressions of capitalist imperialism or any of the forms of totalitarianism.[61]

When moving towards its conclusion *Specters of Marx* again describes nationalism only as a form of cultural violence. In contrast with justice as 'event', and unlike the hesitant and tremulous dislocations of the messianic, nationalism remains entranced by the illusion of racial and cultural certainty, an illusion that is conjured up by the phobic disavowal of national difference:

> In the virtual space of all the teletechnosciences, in the general dislocation to which our time is destined – as are from now on the places of lovers, families, nations – the messianic trembles on the edge of this event itself. It is this hesitation, it has no other vibration, it does not 'live' otherwise, but it would no longer be messianic if it stopped hesitating: how to give rise and to give place [*donner lieu*], still, to render it, this place, to render it habitable, but without killing the future in the name of old frontiers? Like those of the blood, nationalisms of native soil not only sow hatred, not only commit crimes, they have no future, they promise nothing even if, like stupidity or the unconscious, they hold fast to life .[62]

How to give place to justice, to the messianic, and to the future without once again rooting new identities in a fixed and deterministic regionality? *Specters* does provide an answer to this question: in the (unthinkable) concept of the 'new International' there is, for Derrida, the possibility for affiliations and associations that are not constrained by forms of national identification. Triggered by the '*international* character'[63] of communism, these alliances would be forged 'without coordination, without party, without country, without national community... without co-citizenship, without common belonging to a class'.[64] What this suggests, of course, is that in its efforts to initiate alternative concepts of place and identity, *Specters* treats all nationalisms – including resistant, counter-colonial, and anti-globalization nationalisms – as uniformly phobic inscriptions of frontiered belonging.

III 'A tragic economy'

Such a suggestion leaves some of Derrida's readers alarmed that his work only exposes rifts in the dominant, and that it pays no heed to the effects of minority and resistance activity: 'the post-structuralist theoretical move of splitting and multiplying a monolithic identity... from within', Rey Chow states, 'is by itself inadequate as a method of reading'.[65] Others question whether concepts of national identity should provide Derrida with the *overriding* sense of Western hegemony, European authoritarianism, or neo-colonial pre-eminence that seems to be at work in much of his writing on cultural differentiation. Pheng

Cheah is one reader who is concerned that Derrida's tendency to equate nationalism with xenophobic exceptionalism simplifies its significance by turning it into just another hegemonic ruse. Echoing other work on nationalism, Cheah argues that nationalism's function is not as straightforward as Derrida suggests:

> The question I wish to pose is whether, in the light of the failed promises of postcolonial nationalism and... also its continuing imperativity as an agent of ethicopolitical transformation in neo-colonial globalization, Derrida's dismissal of nationalism as an ideology may be hasty.[66]

This objection – that Derrida's work resides wholly within Europe and fails to look to counter-hegemonic insurgency – problematically construes deconstruction as a theoretical intervention that is not itself minoritarian, one that does not form part of an empire that writes back to its centre. Derrida's own multiple coding and trans-frontier significance are now well documented: many of the obituaries written after Derrida's death in 2004 find his work to be simultaneously French and Jewish and Algerian and American and global; for both Spivak and Young, the Franco-Maghrebian and Marranic dimensions of Derrida's life and work are often ignored by those who situate him as a Western or European thinker.[67] For Hélène Cixous too, the concurrence of French, Algerian, Jewish, and Berber motifs in Derrida's thinking is decisive. *Portrait of Jacques Derrida as a Young Jewish Saint* connects Derrida's intercultural hybridity with Cixous' own 'passporosity'[68] as a Jewish woman who grew up in French Algeria. And she extends the lines of flight that take Derrida incessantly away from his proper name in his paranomastic autobiography 'Circonfession', finding in it not a departure from national identification, but the sense that national and cultural affiliations are both insufficient and overcoded. In 'Circonfession',

> it was the Marrano he was calling, the Marrano that he already was although he didn't know it. One of those Jews without knowing it and without knowledge, Jew without having it, without being it, a Jew whose ancestors are gone, cut off, as little Jewish as possible, the disinheritor, guardian of the book he doesn't know how to read, half buried and all the more tenacious for that.[69]

It is not necessary, however, just to look to Derrida's proper name, or only turn to biographical accounts of his own interlingual transcontinentality, when disputing the charge that he is unable or unwilling to address counter-colonial activity. In some of his later writing – especially *The Monolingualism of the Other*, 'On Cosmopolitanism' and 'Autoimmunity: Real and Symbolic Suicides' – Derrida considers the legal, political, and ethical dimensions of multiculturalism, international terror, and immigration. Importantly, these texts do not simply document the disfigurations that the forces of globalization (or, more accurately for Derrida, *'mondialisation'*[70]) inflict on national identity, since he here develops concepts of resistance that do seek to effect an 'ethicopolitical transformation'.

The Monolingualism of the Other sees Derrida reflecting on his own childhood in Algeria, on his relationship with the French language, and, in a less personal sense, on how the national particularity of minority groups might be understood. Here Derrida yet again appears to adopt an opprobrious tone in his account of nationalism's function. Echoing Bakhtin, he argues that although languages are radically improper and structure their own dispossession, it would be a mistake to treat all linguistic structures as equally appropriative. Instead, cultural theory can explore the different configurations of language and power that are to be found in different periods, while at the same time avoiding the geopolitical determinations that occur when regions are treated as the source of discursive structures. It is possible, Derrida states, 'to analyse the historical phenomena of appropriation and to treat them *politically* by avoiding, above all, the reconstitution of what these phantasms managed to motivate: "nationalist" aggressions... or monoculturalist homo-hegemony'.[71] Deconstructive challenges to 'monoculturalism' can therefore arise in part from a non-nationalistic understanding of language's status in the formation of national types.

A common perception of Derrida's work is that it is content merely to disclose the supplementation of interiority by exteriority and expose the essentially alienated condition of all cultural belonging. Deconstructive theory, according to this perception, ultimately concludes that all cultural systems operate as a uniform aggregation of untotalizable identities, and one consequence of such a conclusion would be that any defense of linguistic specificity is a futile task. This, however, is an argument that Derrida conspicuously refuses to support in *The Monolingualism of the Other*. Certainly, he objects to the idea that any language forms an interior, finite, and calculable structure, but he does not wholly advocate the dispersal or disarticulation of linguistic specificity. While a reconceptualization of language (as alienation) and nationality (as cultural non-originality) can avoid the traps of nationalism, he maintains that a sense of cultural – and linguistic – singularity can be (and has been) crucial to the critique of colonial and global authority. As Herman Rapaport observes, 'this book is not so much an attack on the narrowness of monolingualism as it is a recognition that monolingualism is more hospitable to otherness than we might at first assume'.[72]

Importantly, although *The Monolingualism of the Other* insists that threatened groups can preserve their singularity by safeguarding their national languages – although linguistic anamnesis is necessary to combat the erosion of regional languages that results from an increasingly uniform world order – this rememoration does not, for Derrida, entail a simple restitution of a national sovereignty. Rather, *The Monolingualism of the Other* asks,

> what if some humans were more worth saving than their language, under circumstances where, alas, one needed to choose between them? For we are living in a period in which the question at times arises. Today... certain people must yield to the homo-hegemony of dominant languages. They must learn the language of the masters, of capital and machines; they must lose their idiom in order to survive or live better. A tragic economy, an impossible counsel.[73]

Offering neither a indiscriminate denunciation of national identity nor an unconditional endorsement of nationalism as an oppositional force, Derrida is instead attentive to the unworkable imperative that provokes minority narratives of national identity. Caught in the '*double inter-dict*'[74] that requires them to frame their identity in the language of dominance, marginalized groups are left with a schizophrenic imperative: '*We only ever speak one language*' and '*We never speak only one language*'.[75] Certain groups, then, face an 'impossible appropriation',[76] since they have to surrender to discourses of national identity in order to face threats from dominant cultures, even though this mimetic act leaves minorities ensnared in an incessant departure from and return to cultural particularity. It is this condition of double alienation ('This structure of alienation without alienation, this inalienable alienation'[77]) that is specific to the monolingualism of the marginalized, and allows it to be differentiated from the monolingualism of the master. As Geoffrey Bennington points out,

> What we need to understand still is how that intrinsic multiplicity or plurality brings in a thought of singularity or the unique – for it is precisely this that will allow us to distinguish in principle (though

perhaps not always easily in fact) between the new promised language of invention and the language of master or coloniser which it
can also resemble.[78]

In sharp contrast with Derrida's other work, which suggests that a
sense of nationality is wholly autological and aggressive, *The Monolingualism of the Other* therefore finds the monolingualism of national
identification to operate differently when voiced by the powerful and
the disempowered.

The attempt to separate politically engaged theories of nationalist
resistance from a deconstruction that is supposedly deaf to minority
voices therefore finds itself countered by Derrida's account of language
and national identity in *The Monolingualism of the Other*. Derrida is not,
of course, alone in thinking that minority groups, such as colonized
populations, are forced into the aporetic adoption of national identification: well before the appearance of *The Monolingualism of the Other*,
much of the critical work on the interventionist potential of counter-
colonial independence movements viewed nationalism simultaneously
as an empowering discourse and an impassable road to cultural emancipation.[79] For example, Derrida's distinction between two types of
monolingualism echoes Frantz Fanon's account of the resistance to
colonial hegemony. The struggle against colonialism cannot, according
to Fanon, take place through the affirmation a pre-colonial national
consciousness, since this affirmation would simply reverse the colonial
dialectic, rather than substantially challenging the dialectical economy
that regulates concepts of culture. Instead, resistance must be conducted as an assertion of identity at the level of the nation-state, by
seizing colonial territorial designations: 'To fight for national culture',
Fanon writes in *The Wretched of the Earth*, 'means in the first place to
fight for the liberation of the nation, that material keystone which
makes the building of a culture possible'.[80] Or, as Neil Lazarus writes,
paraphrasing Fanon, 'Colonialism cannot be overturned except through
anti-colonial struggle; and, in a world of nations, the colonial state
cannot be captured and appropriated except as a nation-state'.[81]

Derrida shares Fanon's conviction that monoculturalism does not
always operate as the simple reassertion of hegemony, but that certain
groups can only ensure their survival through the adoption of dominant languages and concepts. Indeed, when *The Monolingualism of the
Other* claims that resistant groups often have to 'learn the language of
the masters', it suggests that this language might include Western discourses of national identity, perhaps even (albeit provisionally, simu-

lacrously, or spectrally, and under particular circumstances as Fanon would agree) nationalist discourses. But Derrida does not just conclude that the declaration of a frontiered national identity by minority groups is a strategically necessary and politically expedient operation. Derrida goes further than Fanon when he argues that the entry into the dominant by other cultures represents an exorbitant intervention, one dramatically altering the conceptual economy that provides the nation with legitimacy and authority. This process, *The Monolingualism of the Other* claims, needs to be rethought as a form of invention – as a structural event that splits apart the fusion of dominant languages to national particularity and allows a transformative resignification of cultural belonging. Although 'This monolingualism of the other certainly has the threatening face and features of colonial hegemony',[82] and although minority narratives are themselves often commandeered by ruling discourses, Derrida insists that they nevertheless hold open the possibility for a different future:

> Reappropriation always takes place. As it remains inevitable, the aporia involves a language that is impossible, unreadable, and inadmissible. An untranslatable translation. At the same time, this untranslatable translation, this new idiom *makes things happen* [*fait arriver*], this signature brought forth [*fait arrivée*], produces events in the given language, the given language to which things must still be given, sometimes *unverifiable* events: illegible events. Events that are always promised rather than given. Messianic events. But the promise is not nothing; it is not a non-event.[83]

Marginalized groups might well repeat hegemonic discourses but, since this repetition is a necessarily transformative act, it brings heteronomy to where homogeneity has prevailed; minority groups certainly find themselves following a tragic counsel but this counsel carries within it the promise of future that can be negotiated, even if this future cannot be clearly predicted.

Cosmopolitan aporia

Derrida restates his commitment to non-programmatic intervention in 'Autoimmunity: Real and Symbolic Suicides'. In this dialogue, Derrida responds to the demand that he, like other intellectuals, social theorists, and political commentators, provide conclusions about the supposedly inconceivable events of 9/11, and about the war on terror that ensued. Much of this dialogue is given over to three issues that concern

Derrida. First, he questions the terms and concepts that acquired greater currency after the attacks on the World Trade Center and the Pentagon, and he is especially concerned with how political discourse has hastily embraced portentous declarations of a different world order. '9/11' and 'September 11' provide him with examples of the attempt to index what has often – excitably – been seen as an unprecedented event that changed the world in unimaginable ways; this phrasing disturbs Derrida not only because it suggests that the world before this date was a uniform sameness, but also because it renders the incidents of '9/11' exceptional and confined to this day alone. Rather than viewing '9/11' as an unanticipatable and unparalleled event, Derrida argues that it needs to be treated both as a foreseeable act of violence (for which parallels do exist) *and* as moment of profound cultural uncertainty. Precedents for an attack of this magnitude can be seen, he claims, in the bombing of Hiroshima and Nagasaki during the second World War, and a similar targeting of office workers can be found in both the Oklahoma City bombing and the attack on the Twin Towers in 1993; by way of parallels, he cites the scale of civilian killing in Cambodia, Rwanda, Palestine, and Iraq.

Second, in addition to voicing his misgivings about the names '9/11' and 'September 11', Derrida also questions the concept of 'international terrorism' that came to dominate political discourse after the attacks. Derrida expresses reservations about the division between terrorism and legitimate resistance, and he points out that distinctions between national and international terrorism are often difficult to maintain: Algeria, Northern Ireland, Corsica, Israel, and Palestine have each, he observes, witnessed forms of insurgence that take place within the borders of a nation-state, but are directed against occupation by another nation. But Derrida does not only show how complex questions of national identity and resistance are elided in recent debates about international terrorism. He also traces the genealogy of the term 'terrorism' and observes that 'the political history' of this word 'is derived in large part from a reference to the Reign of Terror during the French Revolution, a terror that was carried out in the name of the state and that in fact presupposed a monopoly on violence'.[84] A dramatic semantic shift seems, then, to have taken place at some point in the discourse on terrorism: no longer a name for the state's authoritarian, cruel, and often illegal suppression of insurrectionist activity, this term is now used to suggest that the brutal transgression of national and international law is solely the pursuit of those engaged in action against states deemed to be democratic and civilized. What this means, in other words, is that the language of the US-led war on international terrorism serves to construct 'civilized' states as the victims of violence, and it precludes the possibility that leading states, including the US, may themselves engage in forms of national and international aggression. 'The United States was not always, let it be said by way of a litotes, on the side of victims',[85] Derrida remarks.

Third, while he is concerned that '9/11' grants greater honour to the Americans and Europeans who died on that day than it does to others who have died in analogous circumstances, and while he believes that 'the war on international terrorism' functions as a hegemonic sleight of hand, Derrida argues that this discourse nevertheless points to a trauma that *is* impossible to comprehend:

> Is, then, what was touched, wounded, or traumatized by this double *crash* only some particular thing or other, a 'what' or a 'who', buildings, strategic urban structures, symbols of political, military, or capitalist power, or a considerable number of people of many different origins living on the body of a national territory that had remained untouched for so long? No, it was not *only* that but perhaps especially, through all that, the conceptual, semantic, and one could even say hermeneutic apparatus that might have allowed one to see coming, to comprehend, interpret, describe, speak of, and name 'September 11' – and in so doing to neutralize the traumatism and come to terms with it through a 'work of mourning'.[86]

The reasons for this incomprehension lie partly with the way in which '9/11' defies established notions of national belonging and international conflict. Indeed, Derrida argues, the very notion of secure territoriality now lies more obviously in ruins than it has in the past, since the United States' (and, in a wider sense, Western) division between the protected interiority of the nation and the groundless aggressivity of foreigners has become increasingly difficult to sustain. Despite the efforts of some in the US (as well as some in allied countries) to rewrite the attacks on September 11 as the opening salvo in a new intercivilizational war, what needs to be seen, Derrida insists, is that the United States has to some extent been party to acts of violence against itself. He writes,

> Immigrated, trained, prepared for their act in the United States by the United States, these *hijackers* incorporate, so to speak, two suicides in one: their own... but also the suicide of those who welcomed

them, armed, and trained them. For let us not forget that the United States had in effect paved the way for and consolidated the forces of the 'adversary' by training people like 'bin Laden', who would here be the most striking example, and by first of all creating the politico-military circumstances that would favor their emergence and their shifts in allegiance.[87]

The early sections of the dialogue between Derrida and Borradori seem, then, to question attempts to render '9/11' exceptional, to challenge efforts to consign terrorist acts to those who lack legitimation by the world's governing nations, and to expose the *'autoimmunitary process'* whereby the US 'in quasi-*suicidal* fashion, "itself" works to destroy its own protection, to immunize itself *against* its "own" immunization'.[88]

Were his account of these circumstances to end here, then Derrida might find himself once again attracting the accusation that he fails either to acknowledge minority groups' role in the resistance to the West's dominance or to offer strategies for challenging the interests that drive globalization. But in his reading of September 11 Derrida is not, of course, content merely to identify the internal inconsistencies that disconcert the authority – and the particularity – of dominant nation-states. Rather, the later sections of this dialogue see Derrida putting forward a series of suggestions for intervening in and transforming the forms of global governance that now prevail. Distancing his own notion of counter-hegemonic intervention from the tactics that the name 'bin Laden' metonymizes, Derrida argues that an internationalization of resistance is necessary in the response to *mondialization*. 'Bin Laden' signifies for him a succession of brutal practices and a form of religious dogmatism that *'open onto no future and… have no future'*.[89] Derrida here again recalls the concepts of the promise and of messianic affirmation that, he believes, can initiate a transformation of the ethico-political sphere: what 'bin Laden' proposes, he feels, is an intransigent version of Islamism that seeks theological closure rather than the emancipatory promise of justice. 'If we are to put any faith in the perfectibility of public space and of the world juridico-scene, of the "world" itself, then there is', Derrida asserts, *'nothing good* to be hoped for from that quarter'.[90]

Occasionally forthright pronouncements like these are concerned not simply to malign figures like 'bin Laden'.[91] Rather, 'bin Laden's' actions are for him to be contrasted with forms of intervention that can contest the West's hegemony, but without asserting an alternative totality. Justice, the promise, democracy to come, and messianic affirmation continue to provide Derrida with a vocabulary for articulating this intervention, though 'Autommunity' adds to this lexicon by stressing the cosmopolitanism of deconstruction's challenge to North American and European authority. Arguing that the much-vaunted globalization of the world does not facilitate the democratic reinvention of the globe that is announced by some, Derrida insists instead that it both is and is not occurring to all cultures. Information, commodities, and populations are certainly more mobile now than they have ever been, he points out, and although this mobility means that national borders are increasingly permeable, this does not mean that the opportunities offered by globalization are evenly distributed. 'From this point of view globalization is not taking place', he argues,

> It is a simulacrum, a rhetorical artifice or weapon that dissimulates a growing imbalance, a new opacity, a garrulous and hypermediatized noncommunication, a tremendous accumulation of wealth, means of production, teletechnologies, and sophisticated military weapons, and the appropriation of these powers by a small number of states or international corporations. And control over these is becoming *at once* easier and more difficult.[92]

If the term 'globalization' fails to provide political and cultural theory with resources for rethinking the sovereignty that remains attached to the concept of the nation-state, then for Derrida 'cosmopolitanism' and 'hospitality' point to a future that would allow national and international identity to take on new dimensions. Chapter 4 shows how Derrida's 'On Cosmopolitanism' unsettles notions of original ethnicity by challenging the legislative restrictions that host nations have imposed upon transnational populations. 'Autoimmunity' similarly ties cosmopolitanism to an idea of unconditional hospitality, loosens the distinction between native residents and immigrant, and emphasizes the capacity for a new internationalist thinking to transfigure dominant nations' belief in their status and their sovereignty. For Derrida, this cosmopolitanism would, in the immediate term, be served by an international legal system that would not prioritize the interests of powerful nations – a role that the UN has yet to adopt, he argues – but it would also be served by a conceptual shift that would allow an alternative understanding of cultural belonging to emerge:

> Cosmopolitanism as it is classically conceived presupposes some form of state sovereignty, something like a world state, whose concept can be theologico-political or secular.... For a deconstruction to be as effective as possible, it should not, in my view, oppose

the state head on and in a unilateral fashion. In many contexts, the state might be the best protection against forces and dangers.... But, ultimately, these necessary transactions must not obstruct a deconstruction of the state form, which should, one day, no longer be the last word of the political.[93]

Deconstructive cosmopolitanism entails for Derrida, then, neither a thoroughgoing critique of the nation-state, nor a unreserved celebration of the limited and undemocratic transnationalisms that currently characterize globalization. While it certainly highlights the uneven distribution of power and capital by the forces of globalization, and exposes the violences that are conducted in the name of national security, this cosmopolitanism also discloses the aporia that traverse the state when it is constructed as both a sovereign interiority and a part of *mondialization*. Offering political and cultural theory an alternative to the unsustainable opposition between national particularity and a generalized internationalism, this cosmopolitanism not only allows the nation-state to be rethought as a space that is always in excess of itself. A different understanding of global citizenship would also mean an end to the regionalism that has prevented certain groups from participating in the transformation of national and international culture.

'An impossible-possible'

When in 'Autoimmunity' Derrida states that cosmopolitan justice needs to both to begin from and to exceed the existing institutions of international law – that 'We must thus be dutiful beyond duty, we must go beyond law, tolerance, conditional hospitality, economy, and so on'[94] – he reaffirms his conviction that cosmopolitanism is only possible with a thought that resists thinking. Unlike other, more speculative, accounts of hybridity, this cosmopolitanism acts as non-predicative concept that seeks to hold open the futurity of the future. However, while it might be tempting to equate cosmopolitanism with other asignifying signifiers in deconstruction's ever-expanding lexicon – to treat it, that is, as a synonym for other deconstructive concepts, such as *différance*, denegation, ashes, genre, justice, or messianism – such a temptation needs to be resisted.

A certain contiguity – what Simon Critchley describes as a chain of 'palaeonymic displacements'[95] – *can* be discerned in Derrida's various responses to entrenched notions of identity, and in his efforts to avoid speculative delineations when drawing out concepts of difference.

His challenge to the construction of community as an interior auto-logy, for example, does not merely seek to denounce a problematic understanding of collective association, and neither does it argue that different affiliations and alliances can only begin to emerge with a deprivileging of the proximate. Derrida is equally concerned to find alternatives to the narcissism, chauvinism, and prejudice that have been so central to the idea of community, and some of these alternat-ives can be encountered in 'the language of madness', in the 'incon-ceivable concepts' and in the 'untenable syntagms and arguments' of Nietzsche, Bataille, and Blanchot. Ineffable, inscrutable, and asyntactic, these articulations, Derrida maintains, begin to signify differently, and begin to speak of a 'community of those without community'.[96] The resonances with Nancy are unmistakable here: refiguring the social as an ecstatic form of association demands 'a politics, a friendship, a justice' which '*begin* by breaking with their naturalness or homogene-ity, with their alleged place of origin'.[97] For Nancy, theory can only fail in its attempts to encompass this inoperative community, and for Derrida too, theory is compelled to drift from sense in the very moment that it begins to think community – indeed, the political – differently.

Specters of Marx similarly displaces entrenched notions of identity while also challenging theory's speculative dimensions. The idea of community remains an important one for Derrida here, but *Specters* is more concerned with rethinking the increasingly uncertain relation-ship between national and international identity. Since community is no longer conceivable as an interior association, *Specters* argues, the bordered particularity that has been attached to nation-states must also be seen as conceptually unsustainable. In place of fixing groups accord-ing to their territorial attachments, Derrida calls for an alternative form of association. This new International does not, as it might appear, entail a rejection of national identifications, but is instead

a link of affinity, suffering, and hope, a still discreet, almost secret link, as it was around 1848, but more and more visible, we have more than one sign of it. It is an untimely link, without status, without title, and without name, barely public even if it is not clandestine, without contract, 'out of joint', without coordination, without party, without country, without national community (International before, across, and beyond any national determination), without co-citizen-ship, without common belonging to a class. The name of the new International is given here to what calls to the friendship of an alliance without institution among those who... continue to be inspired by at least one of the spirits of Marx or of Marxism... and in order to ally themselves, in a new, concrete, and real way, even if this alliance no longer takes the form of a party or of a worker's international, but rather of a kind of counter-conjuration, in the (theoretical and practical) critique of the state of international law, the concepts of State and nation, and so forth.[98]

The 'new International' here becomes a critical counter-affirmation, a ghostly, almost invisible alliance; 'Barely deserving the name community', Derrida later writes, 'the new International belongs only to anonymity'.[99] What such passages reveal is that, even when he appears most emphatically to denounce the '*primitive conceptual phantasm* of community, the nation-state, sovereignty, borders, native soil and blood',[100] Derrida nevertheless insists that different alliances can only emerge out of and in response to national identity's structuring hegemony. As much as he draws attention to the mad and unlocalizable, the exnominated and atopic 'without' that traverses ('before, across and beyond') colonial, neo-colonial, globalized Europe, there nevertheless remains in his work the conviction that the iterative rewriting of national identity can make a difference. Shadowy and spectral, unavowable and messianic, the most that can be said about the different singularities of the new International is that they would no longer be informed by the fixed borders and frontiered territoriality that currently shape national and global culture.

Both *The Monolingualism of the Other* and 'Autoimmunity' offer adjacent challenges to the bond that ties cultural dominance to national identification. The monolingualism of the other is not just a different idiom, one which subjects hegemonic discourses to an audacious repetition. It also, for Derrida, allows new – inconceivable and illegible – idioms to emerge, since minority articulations prevent dominant groups and nations from securing the monolingualism that would legitimate their authority. 'Autoimmunity' does not conclude with the simple observation that, after 9/11, notions of national particularity and state security are no longer operative, and Derrida goes further than arguing that international justice needs to be extended to those who are currently prevented from participating in global governance. He is also eager to stress that this cosmopolitan justice cannot be encompassed by a simple thinking of the future, cannot be asserted as just another axiom, and cannot develop within a calculable system of regulations. Deconstructive cosmopolitanism would not, then, seek to determine yet another set of rules for inventing the future, but would work to expose the aporia that arrive in the structural aperture between the constituted and the unconditional, 'between order and its beyond'.[101] Neither railing against a closed hegemony nor declaring the pure difference of a future that is truly universal, this cosmopolitanism instead challenges existing institutions – such as the law and the nation-state – by maintaining the possibility for another, international, justice.

Community without community, the new International, the monolingualism of the other, and cosmopolitanism seem, then, to provide cultural theory with a cogent method for rethinking national identity, since these athetic concepts collectively provoke us into reconceiving regional, national, and global identities. Indeed, Derrida points to the connections between these, and other, deconstructive motifs when, in 'The University Without Condition', he describes his work as a thinking of 'the impossible possible':

> The examples with which I have attempted to accede to this thought (invention, the gift, forgiveness, hospitality, justice, friendship, and so forth) all confirmed this thinking of the impossible possible, of the possible as impossible, of an impossible-possible that can no longer be determined by the metaphysical interpretation of possibility or virtuality.[102]

Tempting though it might be to see these athetic concepts simply as an uneventful reworking of established deconstructive strategies, Derrida's thinking of the impossible-possible does not function as a static or uniform mode of cultural intervention. Such a response would treat deconstruction as a method that serially applies the same reading protocols to a range of ideas and practices, and it suggests that these concepts are now part of deconstruction's vocabulary because Derrida has only recently addressed questions of national and international identity. This response would, most obviously, have to overlook the attention that Derrida devotes to these questions in the early and middle period of his writing, from *Writing and Difference*, *Of Grammatology*, and *Margins of Philosophy*, to 'Racism's Last Word', '*Geschlecht* II', and *Of Spirit*. Less obviously, the notion that deconstruction invariably applies the same method would also have to disregard the subtle and unanticipatable movements that are triggered in Derrida's thinking when he considers different modes of power and resistance. If theory is routinely defeated in its efforts to arrive at overarching explanatory models, then it must, Derrida insists, respond to the shifting cultural landscape by maintaining the possibility for an incessant, unconditional, and impossible rethinking both of 'the political' and of theory itself. Community without community, the new International, the monolingualism of the other, and cosmopolitanism are some concepts that develop when Derrida reflects on the specific cultural transformations that are effected by the breakdown of immanentist notions of community, by the internationalization of workforces, by the singularity of minority discourse, and by the *'mondialization'* of the nation-state's sovereignty. These (inconceivable) concepts testify to the impossible-possible condition of cultural critique, and they draw attention to the conceptual restlessness that is needed if individual and collective identities are to undergo significant transformation.

3
'New Concepts for Unknown Lands': Deleuze & Guattari's Non-Nationalitarianisms

In a radical departure from the idea that European modernity leaves as its legacy an emergent global syncretism, an intensification of world-wide culture, and a collapsing of spatial distance into a uniform prox-imity, Hardt and Negri argue that power has become delocalized and diffuse, to be found not in the ascendance of a newly dominating nation-state, but in the operations of transnational markets that are irreducible to national territoriality. 'Empire' is the newly inflected term for what is, according to Hardt and Negri, a global condition that encompasses all cultural forms, yet leaves world culture disharmonious and acentred. Working to deconstitute systemic totalities at the very moment that it restructures the international community, Empire is illimitable since its rule extends to enclose all social strata, but at the same time it seizes for itself an interiority that transcends history: 'Empire', they write, 'can only be conceived as a universal republic, a network of powers and counterpowers structured in a boundless and inclusive architecture'.[1]

Hardt and Negri insist that this post-imperial stage of capitalism is, despite the extent of its reach, vulnerable to insurrection, since its many contradictions – combined with its overdetermination of national sovereignty – provide a global 'multitude' (workers, the poor, nomads) with the resources to rethink collectivity. What seems equally decisive here, for Hardt and Negri, is that the non-systemic and bound-less flows of people, information and capital that serve both to expand Empire and to provoke insurgence against Empire are the very flows that impede critical scrutiny of the new world order. The concept of Empire dwells beyond the determinable and, as a consequence, polit-ical and cultural theory has to relinquish its positivistic endeavours: new critical tools for reading the terrain of Empire need to be developed, they argue, in order to recognize that challenges to Empire can only come from a 'productive excess' that is 'beyond measure' – a *'new place in the non-place*, the place defined by productive activity that is autonomous from any external regime of measure'.[2]

Empire clearly occupies an important place in the study of global rule and its impact upon national identities, but its theoretical innovations are certainly not without precedent. Hardt and Negri draw attention to the ways in which their arguments are informed by directions in post-colonial and globalization theory, though it is their debt to Deleuze and Guattari's work that they make most explicit: 'Their work', Hardt and Negri claim, 'demystifies structuralism and all the philosophical, sociological, and political conceptions that make the fixity of the epistemological frame an ineluctable point of reference'.[3] However, while Hardt and Negri find in Deleuze and Guattari's writings a vital rethinking of materialism as 'biopower', they also claim that this work ultimately turns the social into an 'ungraspable event':

> Deleuze and Guattari... seem to be able to conceive positively only the tendencies toward continuous movement and absolute flows, and thus in their thought, too, the creative elements and the radical ontology of the production of the social remain insubstantial and impotent. Deleuze and Guattari discover the productivity of social reproduction... but manage to articulate it only superficially and ephemerally, as a chaotic, indeterminate horizon marked by the ungraspable event.[4]

This chapter argues that for Deleuze and Guattari the 'event' is not entirely 'ungraspable' or beyond thought, but can be signified by a non-expressive language that both reveals the diminishing role of the nation-state and points to different conceptions of the social. In particular, this chapter will look at how Deleuze and Guattari not only invent new concepts (nomadism, becoming-minor, global polymorphy, smooth space, and deterritorialization) that can allow us to rethink the foundations of the European nation-state, but also claim that the act of conceptual invention is itself a non-nationalitarian process.[5]

Vanishing-point

The editors of a recent special issue of *Cultural Studies* admit that are trying to fool no-one with their title, 'Deleuze and Guattari in Cultural Studies': 'after all,' they state, 'it's not as if Deleuze and Guattari are not already here'.[6] The same could be said of Deleuze and Guattari and postcolonial studies or of Deleuze and Guattari and globalization theory, since one concept that runs persistently throughout their work – the concept of 'deterritorialization-reterritorialization' – names both the movement by which nation-states incessantly unground their own geopolitical foundations and are restored as fixed systems. In this manner, *Anti-Oedipus* finds the schizophrenia that is produced within the capitalist machine to be codified and regulated as much as it unleashes energies, desires and intensities: 'Schizophrenia is at once the wall, the breaking through this wall, and the failures of this breakthrough',[7] they claim, 'social machines make a habit of feeding on the contradictions they give rise to, on the crises they provoke, on the anxieties they *engender*, and on the infernal operations they regenerate'.[8]

'Capture' is the term that *A Thousand Plateaus* introduces in order to describe one such contradictory preservation. Signifying the seizure of unity and the appropriation of interiority that takes place in the earliest stages of the state's development, 'capture' points to both a universal process (since it is at work in all states) and an originary moment. Further, this process constitutes a form of 'magic' since the state seems simultaneously both to precede its own appearance and arise out of the capturing of difference:

> the State must have only one milieu of interiority; in other words, it must have a *unity of composition*, in spite of all the differences in organization and development among States.... if we call this interior essence or this unity of the state 'capture', we must say that the words 'magic capture' describe the situation well because it always appears as preaccomplished and self-presupposing.[9]

For social and cultural theory, this process means that the state cannot be fully understood, since it is invented through the capture of exteriorities yet precludes any perception of that which predates the state. 'How is this capture to be explained, then, if it leads back to no *distinct* assignable cause?' Deleuze and Guattari ask, adding that 'theses on the origin of the State are always tautological.... We are always brought back to the idea of a State that comes into the world fully formed and rises up in a single stroke, the unconditioned *Urstaat*'.[10] Their own response to this dilemma is not to engage in a yet another attempt to document the state's prehistory, but to focus on the conceptual violence with which the state apparatus grasps and conceals its hegemony.

According to other work (especially in ethnography, archaeology, and in Marxist historiography) the state develops by taking over ('over-coding') primitive (non-agrarian) communities, and is construed as an imperial force – 'a system of *machinic enslavement*'[11] – that forces early agricultural regimes into submission. Disputing the chronology inscribed in this construction, Deleuze and Guattari (following the work of anti-evolutionist ethnographer Pierre Clastres) claim that such an interpretation of the past – a past composed of pre-imperial, auto-nomous communities which exist prior to the formation of the state – is based upon social and cultural misconceptions. Echoing Derrida's critique of Lévi-Strauss in *Of Grammatology* (which contests the divi-sion between oral communities and modern culture, between the authenticity of speech and the corrupting violence of writing) Deleuze and Guattari argue that the distinctions between different regimes stem from their disparate cultural forms, but this does not mean that these regimes (or the forms they employ) lie entirely beyond the reach of the state apparatus.[12] '*Everything is not of the State precisely because there have been States always and everywhere*', they maintain, 'Not only does writing presuppose the State, but so do speech and language. The self-sufficiency, autarky, independence, preexistence of primitive com-munities, is an ethnological dream'.[13] The state does indeed capture itself – it acquires its unity and interiority – by appropriating exterior regimes, and it also masks this process of invention and prevents adequate speculation on the state's prehistory. This 'miraculating' movement of invention and veiled fabrication means that the state apparatus is not only an intrinsically imperial regime, but that, as far as cultural theory is concerned, its imperialism has a universal quality. The imperialism that ethnography attributes to specific regimes there-fore, according to *A Thousand Plateaus*, touches all cultures at all moments in *known* history.

Such claims might suggest that, for Deleuze and Guattari, inter-cultural violence is uniformly implemented, and a rapid or selective reading of their work could lead to the assumption that the overarch-ing homogeneity of the state and its forms is asserted here. Such a reading would, of course overlook the insistence in both *Anti-Oedipus* and *A Thousand Plateaus* that any act of territorial settlement carries within it an uncertain articulation of spatial rootedness. *A Thousand Plateaus*, for example, describes the state's reterritorializing impulse as one that can only fail in its attempts to conserve the *same* order or to restore the socius fully, since its response to decoding and deterritorial-ization is a neurotic and perverse *re*assertion that produces a different socius, one necessarily transformed by the madness it represses. Deleuze and Guattari are often seen as the hierophants of elective dis-affinities and as critics of an exhausted culture. But, rather than offer-ing a simplistic celebratory of *entirely* transgressive impulses that move *wholly* outside, they argue that the effects of deterritorializing move-ments are to be discerned in the transformations they generate. Although, as they claim in *A Thousand Plateaus*, deterritorialization is 'the movement by which "one" leaves the territory',[14] this movement nevertheless possesses qualitative distinctions and needs to be divided into its 'relative' and 'absolute' forms. Relative departures occur whenever the movement away from a system or apparatus operates alongside a sense of regulated (striated, sedentary) space. Absolute deterritorialization (misleadingly named, since 'the absolute expresses nothing transcendent or undifferentiated') is 'inseparable from correl-ative reterritorializations' and 'is never simple, but always multiple and composite';[15] its departures are formed around already differentiated origins and around multiple (smooth, nomadic) spaces, are irreducible to topological singularities, and enable the production of new spaces and identities.

The failure fully to reterritorialize occurs because exterior forces con-stantly prevent the socius from fully managing schizophrenic flows, from forging a stable and obdurate cultural terrain; for *A Thousand Plateaus*, these exteriorities fall into two types:

> The outside appears simultaneously in two directions: huge world-wide machines branched out over the entire *ecumenon* at any given moment, which enjoys a large measure of autonomy in relation to the States (for example, commercial organization of the 'multina-tional' type, or industrial complexes, or even religious formations like Christianity, Islam, certain prophetic or messianic movements, etc.); but also the local mechanisms of bands, margins, minorities which continue to affirm the rights of segmentary societies in oppo-sition to the organs of State power.[16]

The first of these flows – the limit that defines the essential core of the apparatus, the development of global machines, the spreading of mar-kets beyond the borders of the nation – is, for Deleuze and Guattari, an especially prominent feature of the modern period, and it is with capital's trajectory away from the nation-state (rather than the position of an unruly community that lives within the state's borders) that the 'plateau' devoted to the 'Apparatus of Capture' is most concerned.

Capitalism might well move towards the establishment of a uniform global imperium and its spread might well produce an isomorphism throughout 'diverse social formations', but it does not produce a world-wide homogeneity and, indeed, fails to assert itself as a singular organization: 'all States and all social formations tend to become *isomorphic* in their capacity as models of realization: there is but one centered world market, the capitalist one',[17] they argue. 'But it would be wrong', they continue, 'to confuse isomorphy with homogeneity' because capitalism 'tolerates, in fact requires, a certain peripheral polymorphy.... When international organization becomes the capitalist axiomatic, it continues to imply a heterogeneity of social formations, it gives rise to and organises its "Third World"'.[18] In contrast with the 'heteromorphy' of states that arises from the 'West-East' binary (which for Deleuze and Guattari consists of a distinction between capitalist and socialist 'states of the center'[19]), the 'North-South', 'center-periphery' or 'First World-Third World' division introduces a 'polymorphy' into the state apparatus. Benefiting from capitalism's principle of '*unequal exchange*',[20] the centre finds itself nourished by the economic exploitation of the periphery – the South. At the same time, although 'the general relation of production is capital' in colonial, neocolonial and postcolonial cultures, 'the mode of production' in the Third World 'is not necessarily capitalist'.[21] Capitalism produces an isomorphism between states and 'becomes an axiom providing a substitute for colonization', yet Deleuze and Guattari suggest that this substitution also witnesses the centre's loss of absolute governance, since 'the polymorphy of the Third World States is *partially* organised by the center'.[22]

As much as it draws disparate cultures together, the search for new markets therefore acts to decode and deterritorialize the socius; demanding the expansion of its reach, capital refuses to be enclosed by economic or political barriers and it forces a departure from the regulatory mechanisms of the nation-state – indeed, so crucial to capital is the outside that the state ceases fully to capture itself and no longer acts as capital's primary catalyst. At a certain moment in capitalism's development, a 'threshold' of deterritorialization is reached – a moment when 'it seems that there is no longer a need for a state, for distinct juridical and political domination, in order to ensure appropriation, which has become directly economic'.[23] Such claims might suggest that the state is experiencing an apocalyptic crisis, but for Deleuze and Guattari an absolute rupture does *not* take place when the threshold of global deterritorialization is reached, since the state remains even if it no longer functions in the same way: 'the states change form and take on a new meaning' and become 'models of real-ization for a worldwide axiomatic that exceeds them'.[24] Becoming merely a mechanism for the capitalist axiom, rather than a *sui generis* sovereignty, the nation-state, then, can no longer be conceived in terms of European centres, it undergoes mutations in its departure from Europe, and it ceases to function as a singular force of capture.

By claiming that the nation-state constantly enacts its own deterritorialization – that it exposes its impermanence by turning into a 'model of realization for the capitalist axiomatic'[25] – Deleuze and Guattari provide cultural theory with a concept that has proved to be increasingly influential in recent critical work on the erosion of national frontiers by capital's worldwide exertions. It lies as a palimpsest behind Arjun Appadurai's claim that the centre loses its hold when cultural forms depart from territorial specificity, that 'people, machinery, money, images, and ideas now follow increasingly nonisomorphic paths... the sheer speed, scale, and volume of each of these flows are now so great that the disjunctures have become central to the politics of global culture'.[26] It shapes Manuel de Landa's assertion that the last thousand years of Western history have consisted of 'pidginizations, creolizations, and standardizations in the flow of norms; isolations, contacts, and institutionalizations in the flow of memes; domestications, fertilizations, and hybridizations in the flow of genes; and intensifications, accelerations, and decelerations in the flows of energy and materials',[27] as well as his claim that a bilateral movement of 'stratification' and 'destratification'[28] runs throughout both nature and culture. It informs Gyan Prakash's belief that capital's international flows produce 'new global forms of unevenness, inequality, difference, and discrimination', a process of differentiation that for him 'also renders capitalism open to subaltern pressures'.[29] And even if Timothy Luke does not directly name Deleuze and Guattari, their concept of territorialization-deterritorialization nonetheless resonates in his statement that 'the territorial in-statements of nations simply provide territorialized historical imaginaries... in the global flow of capital, energy, goods, power and power'.[30]

Nomad thought and radicle writing

One set of responses to Deleuze and Guattari's work emphasizes the eclipsing of the nation-state by capital's delocalizing energies, but what makes their work so provocative is the way that it pays attention to the deconstitution of national identity by lines of flight that take place within, as well as beyond, the borders of the nation-state. Incorporated as endo-exteriorities are 'bands, margins, minorities', 'segmentary societies', nomadic movements that resist full incorporation into the social body. However, the idea that the nomad is a restless and wandering drifter and a subject without territory is one that Deleuze and Guattari dispute. Nomadic populations are not migrant populations, they argue, since these groups occupy space in a serial and instrumental manner. Space, for the nomad, is *'open space, one that is indefinite and noncommunicating'*[31]; while this open treatment of space might suggest a disaffection for topological commitment, Deleuze and Guattari stress that the nomad at once dislocates striated space and is spatially situated: 'The nomad distributes himself in a smooth space', they claim, 'he occupies, inhabits, holds that space; that is his territorial principle'.[32] Neither a migrant who departs without returning nor an exiled figure who is forever banished, the nomad is, rather, constituted as an internalized exteriority, inhabiting the state but placed beyond the walls of the *polis*.[33]

As well as showing that segmentary societies inhabit space differently Deleuze and Guattari also claim that nomad thought, in its association with the apparatus of the nation-state, appears to exhibit a sense of racialized rootedness. Nomad thought resists the universalisms of striated, 'classical' thought (which designates 'all the varieties of the real and the true'[34]), but it does reterritorialize space around a self-identical 'race-tribe'. Nomad thought, Deleuze and Guattari tell us:

> does not ally itself with a universal thinking subject but, on the contrary, with a singular race; and it does not ground itself in an all-encompassing totality but is on the contrary deployed in a horizon-less milieu that is a smooth space, steppe, desert, or sea. An entirely different type of adequation is established here, between the race defined as 'tribe' and smooth space defined as 'milieu'.[35]

A potentially problematic conjunction of race and place seems to arise here, and Deleuze and Guattari recognize that the tribe-milieu adequation triggers questions about the difference between cultural identity and cultural exceptionalism. 'What can be done', they ask, 'to prevent the theme of a race from turning into a racism, a dominant and all-encompassing fascism, or into a sect and a folklore, microfascisms?'.[36] The answer lies, according to *A Thousand Plateaus*, in the fact that although the nomadic tribe appears to inhabit a space outside of the *polis*, it is nevertheless shaped by the universalisms that prevail in classical, striated thought:

It is certainly not enough to travel to escape phantasy, and it is certainly not by invoking a past, real or mythical, that one avoids racism. [But]... The race-tribe exists only at the level of an oppressed race, and in the name of the oppression it suffers: there is no race but inferior, minoritarian; there is no dominant race; a race is defined not by its purity but rather by the impurity conferred upon it by a system of domination. Bastard and mixed-blood are the true names of race.[37]

In other words, just as the nomad's position in the state apparatus is one of constitutive disruption, so the state effects a topologizing territoriality in nomadic thought. The fixing of nomadic racial purity is itself a form of deterritorialization-reterritorialization in which nomadic populations lose their past in order to acquire a history and an identity that the state can understand. Intrinsic to this singular trajectory is a process of becoming that both allows the preservation of minority groups and troubles the state's authority. Although born out of a conferred minority status, the nomadic community embraces established versions of 'the real and the true' in order to declare its singular character and, as a result, to maintain its difference from the state apparatus; nomads become 'minoritarian phenomena that could be termed "nationalitarian", which work from within and if need be turn to the old codes to find a greater degree of freedom'.[38] Dominant groups, on the other hand, are unable to share this resistant appropriation: the state, Deleuze and Guattari imply in this passage, can neither fully nor convincingly assert its racial singularity since it is always reforming itself around minorities (such as nomadic populations). If the state seizes anything from the nomad, then, it is the notion of open, smooth space, of horizonless mobility, of non-communicating inhabitation: nomads become a race by being settled by classical thought whereas the state's hybridity is rendered visible by nomadic disruptions.

For *A Thousand Plateaus* the significance of minority groups would therefore appear to lie not in the materiality of their subjection, but in the process of becoming-minor that they can effect upon the majoritarian assemblage. Such an argument is not, of course, without its dangers, and the questions prompted by this text (as well as responses to these questions) are also triggered by similar claims made in Deleuze and Guattari's earlier *Kafka: Toward a Minor Literature. Kafka* develops *Anti-Oedipus'* account of writing as a locus for deterritorialization and reterritorialization, and it anticipates the notion of fascicular writing that emerges in *A Thousand Plateaus*. For *Anti-Oedipus*, writing has, with the emergence of capitalism from the despotic state, taken on the status of an archaic mode of representation: writing belongs to barbarian civilizations because in those societies graphic representation ceases to be distinguishable from oral discourse (a distinction that can be discerned in primitive societies), but acts as a substitute for the voice ('Legislation, bureaucracy, accounting, the collection of taxes, the State monopoly, imperial justice, the functionaries' activity, historiography: everything is written in the despot's possession'[39]). Whereas despotic writing is founded on the idea that communication can take place, with signification functioning as a referential system, capitalist representation detaches itself from the signifier – it becomes 'nonsignifying'[40] and produces signs which act primarily as the agents for the circulation of money. 'Writing has never been capitalism's thing', Deleuze and Guattari write, 'Capitalism is profoundly illiterate. The death of writing is like the death of God or the death of the father: the thing was settled a long time ago, although the news of the event is slow to reach us, and there survives in us the memory of extinct signs with which we still write'.[41] No longer a communicative system that is fixed on the body of the despot – recording legislation, implementing the law, setting down the past – capitalist writing breaks free from its foundations and reveals itself as a simulacrous chain of 'non-signs... nonsignifying signs... flows-breaks or schizzes that form images through their coming together in a whole, but that do not maintain any identity when they pass from one whole to another'.[42]

If *Anti-Oedipus* proclaims writing in general to be one of capitalism's deterritorializing limits, *A Thousand Plateaus* provides a clearer sense of the particular effects of different textual forms. Here, Deleuze and Guattari depart from established directions in textual criticism by treating literature as a non-sequential and non-referential series of associations, rather than as a thematic or expressive medium:

> We will never ask what a book means, as signified or signifier; we will not look for anything to understand in it. We will ask what it functions with, in connection with what other things it does or does not transmit intensities, in which other multiplicities its own are inserted and metamorphosed, and with what bodies without organs it makes its own converge.... Writing has nothing to do with signifying. It has to do with surveying, mapping, even realms that are yet to come.[43]

As well as reiterating their claim that literature operates both as a functioning assemblage and a force of detachment, *A Thousand Plateaus* also refigures *Anti-Oedipus's* differentiation between despotic and capitalist representation in terms of what Deleuze and Guattari believe is an arboreal conception of the relationship between nature and culture. According to this conception, nature's complexity is mirrored in the qualities of the tree: surface traits are manifest and observable, but these are merely the outward expression of a buried and unseen foundation. What nature demands from culture is a form of representation – a 'root-book' – that can speak on behalf of its mute and hidden qualities: such is 'the classical book, as noble, signifying, and subjective interiority'.[44] Of course, for Deleuze and Guattari such a conception – such treatment of writing as a cultural simulacrum that can disclose nature's hidden dimensions – misrecognizes both the function of representation and the reality of nature. The root–book, they argue, functions as a mimetic double, reflecting the world and yet nourishing nature by giving it a recognizable shape. But this process means that nature loses its status as a fixed reality that can be separated from textuality: 'The book imitates the world, as art imitates nature: by procedures specific to it that accomplish what nature cannot or can no longer do'.[45] If nature is not composed of finite essences in the way that Western thought imagines, and if literature's attempt to capture nature is a futile one, then a different form of textuality is needed. Recasting the figure of the root as a signifier of multiplicity ('in nature, roots are taproots with a more multiple, lateral, and circular system of ramification, rather than a dichotomous one'[46]), Deleuze and Guattari, identify what they describe as 'radicle' or 'fascicular' writing – a nomadic writing composed of instalments, rather than possessing an interior completion. This writing, 'to which our modernity pays willing allegiance',[47] they find in Nietzsche's aphorisms, Joyce's alinear language, and Burroughs' cut-up technique.

In *Kafka*, Deleuze and Guattari provide a more detailed sense of this acentred and rhizomatic textuality. *Anti-Oedipus* and *A Thousand Plateaus* trace writing's changing fortunes and describe it as a force of conceptual displacement. But it is in *Kafka* that they consider the effects of literary disruption upon national identity and the nation-state, and they argue that these effects are felt in three ways. First, minor literature is a rebellious legatee, employing a 'withered vocabulary, an incorrect syntax',[48] and deterritorializing discursive conventions by turning against the very forms, styles, structures and principles that it inherits. Second, whereas 'major literature'[49] is primarily interested in relationships between individuals (with social matters 'serving as a mere environment or background'[50]), minor literature places individuals in political situations. Related to this second characteristic is the third trait of minor literature: this literature not only reflects on its social location, but also provides the point of departure for an alternative articulation of community. 'Literature', they argue, 'finds itself positively charged with the role and function of collective, and even revolutionary, enunciation'.[51]

'The impossibility of writing'

The consequences of this non-representational writing for national consciousness are spelt out in a dense and puzzling passage on the narrative disjunctions that flow through minor literature:

> The problem of expression is staked out by Kafka not in an abstract and universal fashion but in relation to those literatures that are considered minor, for example, the Jewish literature of Warsaw and Prague. A minor literature doesn't come from a minor language; it is rather that which a minority constructs within a major language. But the first characteristic of minor literature in any case is that in it language is affected with a high coefficient of deterritorialization. In this sense, Kafka marks the impasse that bars access to writing for the Jews of Prague and turns their literature into something impossible – the impossibility of not writing, the impossibility of writing in German, the impossibility of writing otherwise. The impossibility of not writing because national consciousness, uncertain or oppressed, necessarily exists by means of literature.... The impossibility of writing other than in German is for the Prague Jews the feeling of an irreducible distance from their primitive Czech territoriality.[52]

Kafka here argues that writing is a co-determinant of consciousness and that the act of writing is provoked by the prohibition against community-specific literature. Kafka's work dramatizes a critical ambivalence which can be found in all literary traditions that are assembled around notions of canonicity: the erection of a major language results in a corresponding oppression of minority voices, yet this oppression cannot wholly eradicate subordinated groups; if these groups speak or write at all (as, indeed, they must), they do so from a position of difference within a prevailing linguistic apparatus. Kafka writes, in other words, not as a Prague Jew, but as a writer in German who exposes the '*intensives* or *tensors*'[53] in a major language and who, as a result, begins to challenge the governance of Jewish and Czech literature by the German language.

A number of possible problems in this account of the constitution of (and the forms of deconstitution arising from) minor literature can be identified. Most evident, perhaps, is the question of whether Deleuze and Guattari's claims here border on ontology and essentialism. For example, their assertion that 'A minor literature... is that which a minority constructs within a major language', might imply a chronology in which the minority person, group or community exists prior to the entry into writing. Minorities, according to such a view, would be determined by conditions that are external to textual forces; although subject to representation by major language (and by its corresponding fictional narratives), minorities would nonetheless possess traits and properties (as well as literatures of their own) that are exterior to majoritarian discourse. Réda Bensmaia offers just such a reading of *Kafka*. Minor literature, for him, is the voice of those

> who can begin to speak not only of the violence of colonization, but also of their own differences – the difference between what the state wants them to be and what they themselves want to experiment with; differences between, on the one hand, imperial conceptions of a New World Order that takes into account only the well-understood interests of affluent countries and, on the other, the 'minor' conceptions that naturally belong to peoples continuing to struggle against the underdevelopment that is the legacy of years and sometimes decades of slavery.[54]

Bensmaia's reading of Deleuze and Guattari speaks with a political urgency, but it does so by suggesting that communities possess properties that are intrinsically and exclusively their own Kafka's writing would, following this interpretation of minor literature, form part of a collective enunciation – 'the Jewish literature of Warsaw and Prague' – which is identifiable, predates the arrival of the German language and adequately communicates a self-identical and ontologically secure molarity – 'a primitive Czech territoriality'. Although new forms might well be needed in order to articulate the experiences of oppressed communities, the same character would still be represented in these articulations. Just as Joyce and Beckett write from a minoritarian position that has its origins in their nationality ('As Irishmen, both of them live within the genial conditions of a minor literature'[55]), so Kafka's writing could only have a minority status, regardless of its linguistic and textual properties.

As well as suggesting that minorities possess a distinctive interiority, *Kafka* also seems to claim that insurgence is to be located in a generalized condition of resistance. The deterritorializing effects of minor literature are to be found in an author's 'withered' and 'incorrect' use of a major language, rather than in a text's response to cultural issues:

> Even he who has the misfortune of being born in the country of a great literature must write in its language, just as a Czech Jew writes in German, or an Ouzbekian writes in Russian. Writing like a dog digging a hole, a rat digging its burrow. And to do that, finding his own point of underdevelopment, his own *patois*, his own third world, his own desert.[56]

Texts which neither address the history of European hegemony nor interrogate the continued domination of non-Western cultures by Western values can nevertheless, this passage implies, form part of the struggle against the European nation-state. Colony and metropole here lose their geopolitical specificity, and become narrative sites that can be occupied by both European and non-European writers alike; 'underdevelopment', '*patois*' and 'third world' cease to connote regional or national traits, and instead come to signify a general territorial desertification. It is this delocalized notion of resistance that provokes Leela Gandhi to claim that 'In Deleuze and Guattari's revolutionary manifesto, the third world becomes a stable metaphor for the "minor" zone of nonculture and underdevelopment'.[57]

Claims that the concept of minor literature promotes both an essentialist and a dehistoricizing sense of resistance are, however, complicated by the manner in which Deleuze and Guattari's text (as with their other work) continuously fractures interpretation and speaks with the kind of ambivalence that, for them, characterizes minor writing. While *Kafka* finds itself falling inexorably into a molar inscription of the socius, it also rails against the notion that nationality and community can be determined or fixed. In contrast with their suggestion that a minority predates its entry into writing, Deleuze and Guattari also maintain that cultural identities are formed within regimes of signs. They claim, for example, that minority status is conferred by a prevailing apparatus (certain literatures are 'considered minor'), that fictions are instrumental in the formation of nationality ('national consciousness... necessarily exists by means of literature'), and that linguistic dominance consigns erstwhile narrative forms to a past that is forever lost ('The impossibility of writing other than in German is for the Prague Jews the feeling of an irreducible distance from their primitive Czech territoriality'). Writing, according to these moments, is an originary and irreducible inscription, mediating conceptions of national territoriality and governing any deterritorializing response to the nation-state: as Deleuze states elsewhere, 'A minority never exists ready-made, it is only formed on lines of flight, which are also its way of becoming and attacking'.[58] Formed as an uncertain interior limit, minorities become minor and intervallic when they turn against a major language: both constituted and unclassifiable, Kafka's writing is a minor literature because it signals the undecidable quality of *becoming*-Jewish, and *becoming*-Czech, but never provides readers with the sense that these terms denote a finite territorial belonging.

Similarly, if Deleuze and Guattari appear to exclude non-Western writing from their account of minor literature and its challenge to European majoritarianism, they do so because 'non-Western writing' can no longer, following capitalism's overcoding of global structures, signify a series of discrete aesthetic traditions. An increased isomorphy between nation-states and the establishment of narrative hegemony are direct consequences of European colonialism, and as a result, *Kafka* suggests, non-metropolitan literatures have been shaped by representational codes that arrived with the armies, the missionaries and the administrators of colonial rule. Just as, for Eugene Holland, 'Capitalism can open up the possibility of universal history because its mode of suppressing difference – axiomatization... subverts codes, subjecting them to critique or simply dissolving them',[59] so colonialism generates the conditions for a quasi-universal history of literature. To consider the revolutionary effects of minor literature is necessarily to consider narrative structures that have been shaped by European traditions, even if the texts concerned reside beyond Europe's borders. It is because of this narrative isomorphy that any attempt to return to a lost or pre-colonial textuality could only, for Deleuze and Guattari, result in a confused and misguided nostalgia:

> The revival of regionalisms, with a reterritorialization through dialect or patois, a vernacular language – how does that serve a worldwide or transnational technocracy? How can that contribute to revolutionary movements, since they are also filled with archaisms that they are trying to impart a contemporary sense to? From Servan-Schreiber to the Breton bard to the Canadian singer. And that's not really how the borders divide up, since the Canadian singer can also bring about the most reactionary, the most Oedipal of reterritorializations, oh

mama, oh my native land, my cabin, olé, olé. We would call this a blur, a mixed up history.[60]

While the reassertion of a discrete or local character (as well as the revival of its corresponding discourse – a dialect, patois or vernacular) might appear to resist a major, worldwide language, for Deleuze and Guattari this sentimental regionalism should instead be understood as a sedentary melancholia, one seeking a return to a domesticated topology, to an Oedipalized motherland that is inhabited by virile sons. Rather than arguing that non-European narratives lack national particularity or unwittingly succumb to European forms and structures, Deleuze and Guattari are concerned to show how the literature of cultural dominance fails to cohere in the way that European critics often imagine.

Kafka therefore anticipates *A Thousand Plateaus* by arguing that the challenge segmentary societies offer to the nation-state lies not in an identitarian assertion, but in the process of becoming-minor that they incessantly enact upon the striated space of the nation.[61] If the very existence of minorities troubles entrenched typologies, this does not mean that they inhabit a static and self-identical position of exteriority. Rather than forming determinable groups, minorities are 'a line of becoming or fluctuation';[62] eluding the 'axioms' that would determine an identifiable quantity or property, minorities are 'nondenumerable, nonaxiomizable sets, in short, "masses", multiplicities of escape and flux'.[63] And because minorities form nonaxiomizable sets, the changes they provoke would not result in the ascension of the subjugated to a position of dominance, but would render uncertain those cultural classifications (such as sexual and racial identity) through which majoritarian governance is maintained:

> Nonwhites would receive no adequate expression by becoming a new yellow or black majority, an infinite denumerable set. What is proper to the minority is to assert a power of the nondenumerable, even if that minority is composed of a single member. That is the formula for multiplicities. Minority as a universal figure, or becoming-everybody/everything.... Woman: we all have to become that, whether we are male or female. Nonwhite: we all have to become that, whether we are white, yellow, or black.[64]

Passages such as these have been, and continue to be, among Deleuze and Guattari's most contentious. For Alice Jardine, the (non-)notion of becoming-woman is seen to affect and be effected by men, with women left as 'A silent, mutable, head-less, desire-less, spatial surface necessary only for *His* metamorphosis'.[65] Similarly, Christopher Miller argues that Deleuze and Guattari's summons to 'become nonwhite' is addressed to a shared condition of whiteness, and tacitly censors political transformations that have been made in the name of black-ness: 'Becoming-woman, becoming-animal, becoming-minoritarian and becoming-"third world"', he argues, 'is a masquerade invented expressly for white male majoritarian humans to play; it is a form of exoticism'.[66] Disputing such responses to the concept of becoming woman, Rosi Braidotti and Elizabeth Grosz also suggest an alternative sense of how becoming nonwhite functions in Deleuze and Guattari's writing. Braidotti agrees that their work pays little attention to some elementary issues in feminism ('In order to announce the death of the subject, one must first have gained the right to speak as one'[67]), but she argues that if 'there cannot be social change without the construc-tion of new kinds of desiring subjects as molecular, nomadic, and multiple', then one task of feminism must be 'to resist the recoding of the subject in/as yet another sovereign, self-representational lan-guage'.[68] Drawing attention to often-ignored remarks in *A Thousand Plateaus*, Grosz points out that the reassertion of gendered identity is, for Deleuze and Guattari, both an essential and a critical consequence of majoritarian universalisms: 'It is', they assert in *A Thousand Plateaus*, 'indispensable for women to conduct a molar politics, with a view to winning back their own organism, their own history, their own subjectivity'.[69] But simply recouping Deleuze and Guattari for identity politics is not, according to Grosz, the most valuable aspect of their work. Their contribution should instead, she claims, be found in the movement away from entrenched notions of corporeality: 'They provide an altogether different understanding of the body than those that have dominated the history of Western thought in terms of the linkage of the human body to other bodies, human and nonhuman, animate and inanimate'.[70]

For both Braidotti and Grosz, becoming-minor does not point to a platitudinous celebration of difference but neither, more importantly, can it serve the interests of dominant groups or majoritarian thought. Rather, becoming-minor entails both the reassessment of minor groups, categories, or identities and the disruption of the economy that authorizes divisions between dominant and minority. Becoming-woman or nonwhite is becoming reactive – a negation of negation that involves a revaluation of specific minority communities, as well as a challenge to the nomenclature or 'rigid segmentarity'[71] within which supposedly immutable differentiations are inscribed. The concept of becoming-nonwhite is, then, one that disrupts agonic distributions of racial and cultural identity, one that leaves the state unable convincingly to shape itself and its subjects into a stable stratum. Whereas the European nation-state has set itself upon a dual foundation (both determining that which falls within its borders and establishing itself as a universal order) it also, Deleuze and Guattari insist, finds itself undone by the bidirectional movement of minorities and capital that are central to its functioning. 'All of thought' they argue 'is a double becoming, rather than the attribute of a Subject and the representation of a Whole'.[72]

The neighbourhood of concept

Becoming nomadic, the state's self-presupposing capture, capitalism's worldwide polymorphy, narrative and national decodings are concepts that emerge between *Anti-Oedipus*, *Kafka*, and *A Thousand Plateaus*. Deleuze and Guattari's last collaboration, *What is Philosophy?*, returns to and develops these concepts, but it does so while claiming that the process of conceptual invention is itself a compellingly non-nationalitarian one. Echoing *Anti-Oedipus*, for example, *What is Philosophy?* traces the state's unity to a process of regional appropriation that also transforms the state: 'The *imperial spatium* of the State and the *political extensio* of the city are not so much forms of a territorial principle as a deterritorialization that takes place on the spot when the State appropriates the territory of local groups or when the city turns its back on its hinterland'.[73] Echoing *A Thousand Plateaus*, *What is Philosophy?* claims that capital's global drift triggers the obsolescence of the nation-state as a sovereign order: 'capitalism functions as an immanent axiomatic of decoded flows (of money, labor, products). National states constitute the "models of realization" of this immanent axiomatic'.[74] And, like *Kafka*, *What is Philosophy?* situates the (non-)representational as a creative alternative to Western majoritarianism: 'Europeanization does not constitute a becoming but merely the history of capitalism, which prevents the becoming of subjected peoples. Art and philosophy converge at this point: the constitution of an earth and a people that are lacking as the correlate of creation'.[75]

While *What is Philosophy?* certainly echoes other work by Deleuze and Guattari it is primarily concerned with an issue which, although analogously explored by Deleuze in his own work on Anglo-American literature, appears only briefly in *Anti-Oedipus*, *Kafka*, and *A Thousand Plateaus*. Responding to Nietzsche's preoccupation with the relationship between knowledge and territoriality, Deleuze and Guattari consider whether thought is embedded in national contexts, asking 'Can we speak of Chinese, Hindu, Jewish or Islamic "philosophy"?'.[76] In order to answer this question, Deleuze and Guattari turn to *The Will to Power*'s efforts to dissociate philosophy from its Hellenic roots by drawing a distinction between 'the philosopher' and 'the Sophist'. For Nietzsche, the Sophist ('Anaxagoras, Democritus, the great Ionians') belongs to Hellenism but also exposes the dereliction of early Greek thought and breathes the last sigh of a tired culture. Such a decline begins, during this period, because greater association with other cultures comes to threaten Hellenic values and the sense of cultural autonomy becomes attenuated: 'The *polis* loses its faith in the uniqueness of culture, in its right to rule over every other *polis*', Nietzsche writes, 'One exchanges cultures, i.e., "the gods" – one thereby loses faith in the sole prerogative of the *deus autochthonus*'.[77] Born out of this transition is the 'philosopher' who is 'the *reaction*'[78] – a figure who seeks to reinaugurate the socius by altering its relationships with other cultures. This philosopher, for Nietzsche, 'sees the decay in the decay of authority: he seeks new authorities (travels abroad, into foreign literatures, into exotic religions –)'.[79]

A similar reading of the passage from the Sophist's transcendental principles to the philosopher's reinvention of the city are very much in evidence in *What is Philosophy?*. Echoing *The Will to Power*, Deleuze and Guattari describe the transition from imperial regimes to the Greek *polis* as a movement from transcendence to immanence:

> In imperial states deterritorialization takes place through transcendence... The territory has become desert earth, but a celestial Stranger arrives to reestablish the territory or reterritorialize the earth. In the city, by contrast, deterritorialization takes place through immanence: it frees an Autochthon, that is to say, a power of the earth that follows a maritime component that goes under the sea to reestablish the territory.[80]

Charting this departure of the *deus autochthonus* is, however, only of passing interest to Deleuze and Guattari: rather than dwelling on the transition from the celestial to the maritime, *What is Philosophy?* focuses instead on Nietzsche's characterization of the philosopher as the agent of a wider cosmopolitanism.

In terms of economic history, they claim, Greece grew under the shadow of 'archaic eastern empires',[81] but it was sufficiently distant from the centres of those empires to develop different modes of commerce. The growth of these other markets 'along the borders of the Orient'[82] resulted in migration from the East: artisans and merchants arrived in Greece – 'strangers in flight, breaking with empire and colonised by people of Apollo'.[83] It is this combination of international commerce on the margins of imperial governance with the arrival of 'strangers' from Greece's borderlands that forms the matrix from which philosophy is born, since this nascent way of thinking is nourished by the associational life that is peculiar to Greece:

> What do these emigres find in the Greek milieu? At least three things are found that are the de facto conditions of philosophy: a pure sociability as milieu of immanence, the 'intrinsic nature of association' which is opposed to imperial sovereignty;... a certain pleasure in forming associations, which constitutes friendship, but also a pleasure in breaking up the association, which constitutes rivalry;... and a taste for opinion inconceivable in an empire, a taste for the exchanging of views, for conversation.[84]

Accompanying this reformation of the Greek socius is the development of a specific type of intellectual activity which, according to Deleuze and Guattari, is characterized by conceptual invention. Imperial regimes rely upon figures ('Chinese hexagrams, Hindu mandalas, Jewish sephiroth, Islamic "imaginals", and Christian icons'[85]) in their representations of celestial transcendence, and they comprehend the world through 'pure abstraction'; the Greeks, in contrast, create concepts to understand the plane of immanence. Co-relative, inessential, athetic, and ultimately incomprehensible, concepts are formed in combination with other concepts and here there are no positive terms, only 'zones of indiscernibility' and an 'exoconsistency': 'the concept itself abandons all reference so as to retain only the conjugations and connections that constitute its consistency. The concept's only rule is internal or external neighborhood'.[86] Generated by a particular milieu and characterized by concepts without independent or *a priori* qualities, philosophy is, therefore, a distinctively Greek form of intellection that begins *de novo*. The question 'Can we speak of Chinese, Hindu, Jewish or Islamic "philosophy"?' therefore needs to be answered with care: if philosophy consists of thinking that 'can be populated by figures as much as by concepts',[87] then it certainly does not belong to a specific culture. If, on the other hand, philosophical thought comes into being through 'the effect of the concept', then Chinese, Hindu, Jewish, or Islamic thought of the same period should more appropriately be termed 'prephilosophical'[88] or 'antephilosophical'.[89]

Such an argument appears to see Deleuze and Guattari once again looking to the West in order to understand cultural traditions and their transformation. Just as *Kafka* seems, on the surface, to locate both major language and the deterritorializing effects of minor literature solely within a European orbit, so *What is Philosophy?* seems at once to track the interior constitution of Greece and to attribute a universal quality to the intellectual developments associated with this constitution. Both Greek and non-Greek cultures are, readers of *What is Philosophy?* might infer, placed *sub specie eternitatas*: non-Greek thought has significance only as a precursor to the Greek concept, and the classification of other intellectual traditions as 'prephilosophical' and 'antephilosophical' suggests a uniform scale which would allow the measure of civilization and progress to be taken. However, *Kafka* disconcerts the impression that it is only the 'withered vocabulary' of European writers that exemplifies minor literature (by showing that the capitalist axiomatic splits apart the European/non-European polarity), and *What is Philosophy?* similarly works to contest the impression that philosophy inhabits a stable and determinable region.

What could be construed as an unavowed Eurocentrism in *What is Philosophy?* rapidly turns into a genealogy that locates identity in terms of a radical impropriety: while echoing Husserl by arguing that 'Philosophy is a geophilosophy'[90] and locating the invention of the concept in a specifically Greek milieu, they also draw attention to the divided inception of thought and nation, challenging what they see as a misguided search for a 'necessary principle that would link philosophy to Greece'.[91] Work by Hegel and Heidegger provides Deleuze and Guattari with examples of the attempt to root philosophy in particular region, though it is Heidegger's conflation of the German thinker and the Greek philosopher that comes in for particular criticism in *What is Philosophy?*:

What remains common to Heidegger and Hegel is having conceived of the relationship of Greece and philosophy as an origin and thus as the point of departure of a history internal to the West, such that *philosophy necessarily becomes indistinguishable from its own history.* However close he got to it, Heidegger betrays the movement of deterritorialization because he fixes it once and for all between being and beings, between the Greek territory and the Western earth that the Greeks would have called Being.[92]

'Perhaps this strict professor was madder than he seemed', they later remark, 'He got the wrong people, earth, and blood'.[93] In contrast with such a definitive sense of an unsullied and enduring Western character, Deleuze and Guattari argue that although the birth of the concept is assignable to a particular culture, it cannot be ascribed to a discrete national essence or to a pure and invariant origin: 'philosophy was something Greek', but it was 'brought by immigrants'.[94] And where Heidegger appears to find in art the reaffirmation of an unadulterated nationality, Deleuze and Guattari find uncertain, minor affiliations: 'the race summoned forth by art or philosophy is not the one that claims to be pure but rather an oppressed, bastard, lower, anarchical, nomadic, and irremediably minor race'.[95]

'Even the skies become horizontal'

What is Philosophy? reproaches Heidegger in particular, but it is also careful to point out that the concept has triggered a series of specifically European forms of national reterritorialization. Within classical Greece itself they find conjunctions between the birth of a milieu and the formation of an empire: for example, the alliance of Greek states that defeated the Persian fleet in the Bay of Salamis sought to expand its orbit by encompassing other states, such as those in the Aegean. The result of this geocentrism, Deleuze and Guattari observe, is that 'the deepest bond existed between the democratic city, colonization, and a new imperialism'.[96] Later developments in Europe have, according to *What is Philosophy?*, attempted to revive such a conjunction of the democratic city and colonial endeavour. But whereas Greece certainly sought to widen its borders, European empires have far outstripped their precursor's colonial appetites by establishing an isomorphic world market:

> A world market extends to the ends of the earth before passing into the galaxy: even the skies become horizontal. This is not a result of the Greek endeavor but a resumption, in another form and with other means, on a scale hitherto unknown, which nonetheless relaunches the combination for which the Greeks took the initiative – democratic imperialism, colonizing democracy. The European can, therefore, regard himself, as the Greek did, as not one psychosocial

type among others but Man par excellence, and with much more expansive force and missionary zeal than the Greek.[97]

Conceptual invention, then, may be traced back to particular conjunctions that occurred in Greece, but Europe has sought to sedentarize concepts, to striate them in notions of the real and true, and to turn them into property.[98] Contemporary enterprise culture has purloined and commodified the concept ('the most shameful moment came when computer science, marketing, design, and advertising... seized hold of the word *concept* itself'[99]), and *What is Philosophy?* also recognizes that philosophy as a discipline has itself contributed to this taming of the concept's unruly indiscernibility. Again taking their cues from Nietzsche (as well as Kant's '"geography" of Reason'[100] in the *Critique of Pure Reason*), Deleuze and Guattari document the geophilosophical distribution of this domestication, and they show how seventeenth-century France, eighteenth-century England, and nineteenth-century Germany have variously sought to arrest the itinerant concept. French thought, they claim, is dominated by a civilizing impulse and is populated by conceptual taxonomists who extract intellectual profit from both the known and the unknown, from both metropolitan knowledge and peripheral or 'uncivilized' thought: the French philosophical persona is 'like the inventory of habitable, civilizable, knowable or known lands that are summed up by an awareness or cogito.... The French are like landowners whose source of income is the cogito'.[101] Whereas French thought displays a certain mobility, German philosophy constantly seeks a return to the Greek concept, refuses to relinquish 'the absolute', and wishes to expel the 'anarchy' and 'barbarism' that has become resurgent in post-Hellenic Europe: 'what the Greek possessed Autochthonously, German philosophy would have through conquest and foundation'.[102] Different again, for Deleuze and Guattari, is English thought. English thinkers have a nomadic quality, they roam unencumbered 'over the old Greek earth'[103] and their ideas are formed around 'custom and convention',[104] rather than around the cogito or the absolute. But English thinkers are also philosophical pirates, acquiring concepts by 'inhabiting' the ground on which those concepts develop and valuing concepts only because they have been captured – 'they only believe in what is acquired'.[105] For Deleuze and Guattari, then, specific directions in European philosophy can be attributed to the various processes of reterritorialization that are experienced by the Greek concept: philosophy is constantly 'reterritorialized on the national state and the spirit of the people'[106] and is 'marked by national characteristics or rather by nationalitarianisms'.[107]

Against such nationalitarian overcodings, Deleuze and Guattari's history of the originary cosmopolitanism of philosophy turns into what can only be an uncertain account of the contingent and undecidable. Rather than endorsing an entirely Eurocentric historiography, suggesting that both Western and non-Western cultures can be situated within a single and linear temporality, or implying that creative thought is planted firmly in Greek soil, *What is Philosophy?* works against the positivism that has characterized historical discourses, and it challenges attempts (by disciplinary thought) to transform the concept into an instrument of reason, an object of 'contemplation, reflection, or communication'.[108] Systems of thought may well enter into alliances with capitalism and the European nation-state, but Deleuze and Guattari also find in philosophy the resources for challenging the reterritorialization of global culture around either nationalitarianisms or market forces. Resituating philosophy as the moment between the deformation and reformation of structured thought, as unmarketable disjuncture ('what saves modern philosophy is that it is no more the friend of capitalism than ancient philosophy was the friend of the city'[109]), and as an incessant line of flight, Deleuze and Guattari find in it the conditions for a departure from national identification: 'Becoming stranger to oneself, to one's language and nation', they ask, 'is not this the peculiarity of the philosopher and philosophy...?'.[110]

Some commentators – including Hardt and Negri – maintain that this concept of disjuncture leaves theory only with the sense of the social as an ungraspable event, where identity turns in to an amorphous postidentitarian space, and where cultural transformation produces a vacuum of inconceivable otherness. Such a response to *Anti-Oedipus*, *Kafka*, and *A Thousand Plateaus* cannot be sustained, however, since these texts develop a series of non-predicative theories – nomadism, becoming-minor, global polymorphy, smooth space absolute deterritorialization, and so on – which begin to name the movements of exteriority that cannot be incorporated into the nation-state's codings. Indeed, given that Hardt and Negri's notion of 'Empire' engages in the impossible act of naming the non-systematic flows of capital and power, it too must take its place alongside these non-propositional theories.[111] This process of conceptual invention does not emerge from a decadent rejection of cultural norms or an impulsive spurning of intellectual good conduct. Instead, as Nancy observes in respect of Deleuze, this work 'effectuates a philosophical real.... It is a philosophy of nomination and not of discourse. It is a matter of naming the forces, the moments and the configurations, not unravelling the meaning'. [112] Seeking to facilitate the arrival of other forms of knowledge, Deleuze and Guattari's collaborative work puts names to these forces, movements, and configurations, but in *What is Philosophy?* they insist that these names emerge from a process of creation that cannot be captured by striated thought: it is this nomadic thought that disconcerts the West's nationalitarian foundations, it is this conceptual invention that produces 'new concepts for unknown lands'. [113]

4
'Atopic and Utopic': Kristeva's Strange Cosmopolitanism

According to one inveterate caricature, poststructuralism consists of a coherent, if unruly, school of thinkers who essentially promote the same agenda: complacently celebrating polymorphism, indulging in an insipid and misguided assault on the 'the economy of the same', revelling with a carnivalesque excess in the dissolution of the sovereign subject, clamorously affirming terminal culture are seen to be its principal concerns. When viewed in terms of this caricature, Kristeva's recent work seems to strike an oddly conciliatory, if not utterly pacific, note: here, it is conspicuously not the case that two millennia of tradition are to be swept away in a tide of vertiginous antihumanism, and neither is Western culture hardened into a monolith that is shattered by the overwhelming force of its innumerable contradictions. Of course, such an image of poststructuralism provides only the most jejune reduction of critique to fixed and polarized positions, and Kristeva shows how unhelpful this caricature is, not only by insisting that a critical revaluation of tradition is needed (indeed, her work has always concerned itself with such a revaluation), but also, more specifically, by claiming that the tradition of universalist thinking in the West demands a sharper reassessment. Such a reassessment constantly returns in Kristeva's recent writings; here, the concepts of the foreigner, cosmopolitanism, and hospitality are seen to allow a move beyond restricted notions of place, region, or milieu, and for Kristeva they offer alternatives to the ideas about European identity that are often found in universalist thought.

Kristeva's recent work may well turn more directly towards the concepts of the foreigner, cosmopolitanism, and hospitality, but her earlier work has certainly not ignored questions of national identity or cultural difference. At the most elementary level, as Anna Smith points out, Kristeva shows how poetic language renders the writing and reading subject estranged, alienated, forever banished from itself: 'poetic language', Smith writes, 'is a *fire of tongues*. It has an infinite, ecstatic quality that eludes the mastery of human consciousness. The landscape of literature then, is inhabited by a foreignness that deflects the traveller and divides us from ourselves. We become, in other words, exiles'.[1] Exile may well be played out and put on display by poetic language, but this literary *signifiance* is little more than the exposure of a general linguistic condition. Departing from Idealist and Romanticist transcendentalisms, rejecting Saussurean accounts of the synchronicity of the sign, and contesting psychoanalytic tendencies to posit the body as an immanent presence, Kristeva's account of semiotic anteriority traces the limit of representation and invokes a series of pulsions that leave the subject endlessly in process. What is also signalled here is the notion of a place beyond any assigned topos, a site exceeding territorial determination; with the arrival of predicative language this semiotic externality becomes colonized by the empire of the sign.

Less oblique are the remarks on nationality in 'Women's Time'. Following Nietzsche, this essay famously draws a distinction between 'cursive time' and 'monumental time'.[2] The first of this couple plots the emergence, sedimentation, and morphology of identities within a particular symbolic setting, whereas the second discloses the irreducibility of the social to the singularities of nation or culture, and it reveals instead the shaping of identity by multiple histories. Kristeva illustrates this division with the example of 'European women' – a classification that allows the position of women in Europe to be charted, although, crucially for Kristeva, this typology also relies upon a transnational epistemology: 'they will not be only... "women of Europe" but will echo in a most specific way the universal traits of their structural place in reproduction and its representations'.[3] Monumental time does not, then, simply provide an alternative sense of history, it more importantly reveals that the nation has ceased to offer a plausible narrative of its own internal coherence and no longer operates as *the* organizing principle of collective belonging. Echoing *Anti-Oedipus*'s claim that capitalism moves irrevocably towards an isomorphic global imperium, 'Women's Time' opens with a paean to the demise of the nation:

> The nation – dream and reality of the nineteenth century – seems to have reached both its apogee and its limits when the 1929 crash and the National-Socialist apocalypse demolished the pillars that,

according to Marx, were its essence: economic homogeneity, historical tradition and linguistic unity. It could indeed be demonstrated that the Second World War, though fought in the name of national values... brought to an end the nation as a reality: it was turned into a mere illusion which, from that point forward, would be preserved only for ideological or strictly political purposes, its social and philosophical coherence having collapsed.[4]

It is this collapse of the nation as a reality that sanctions the readings of cultural identity and difference that Kristeva develops in *About Chinese Women*. Here, Kristeva documents the trip that she, along with others associated with *Tel Quel*, made to China in 1974. The opening exergue of this text describes how this trip engendered feelings of unadulterated foreignness whilst this group was under the Chinese gaze: 'An enormous crowd is sitting in the sun: they wait for us wordlessly, perfectly still. Calm eyes, not even curious, but slightly amused or anxious: in any case, piercing, and certain of belonging to a community with which we will never have anything to do'; 'I feel like an ape, a martian, an *other*. Three hours later, when the gates of the exhibit are opened to let our cars pass through, they are still there, sitting in the sun... calm, distant, piercing, silent, gently releasing us into our "strangeness"'.[5] Despite this sense of an overriding difference, and despite the impression that Chinese culture has an inscrutable quality, Kristeva nevertheless believes that some form of understanding can be reached. Seeking to 'measure the distance that separates me from Huxian',[6] she argues that it is possible, in an ethically vigilant reading, to place the processes of sexual differentiation that have left European women 'foreign to the social order'[7] alongside the covering over of China's matrilineal origins. Clearly, such an account is as unable fully to access Chinese history as it is incapable of entirely relinquishing European values, but it would nonetheless effect changes to the 'universalist conceptions of man and history'[8] that have governed European thought. Two buried histories, two hidden temporalities – both subsisting in an 'outside time', both outside of symbolic temporality – become more visible here. What allows Kristeva to draw both groups together is neither a common femininity nor a general biological state, but a shared condition of repression and difference which can be glimpsed through the cracks that are spreading over the surface of Western 'monotheistic capitalism'.

At the very moment that Kristeva turns away from universalist conceptions that have prevailed in Western culture, then, she simultaneously turns towards another version of universalist thinking, one which attempts both to interrupt the ordering of sexual difference and to unsettle the regimented structuring of cultural difference. Such a rethinking of universalist traditions she later pursues in greater detail in *Strangers to Ourselves* and *Nations without Nationalism*.[9] Both texts explore the complexities that lie embedded in theoretical constructions of the nation – complexities which, she argues, have been neglected by those who look to canonical writing in order to fortify the idea that nationality is a natural form of collectivity or the social expression of an unsullied ethnicity. At the same time, however, Kristeva also begins to rework her onslaught on the function of role and status of national formations. If 'Women's Time' and *About Chinese Women* suggest that the nation is rapidly becoming an indefensible anachronism, then *Strangers to Ourselves* and the essays collected in *Nations Without Nationalism* see Kristeva moderating what appears, in her earlier writing, to be a wholesale offensive on the place of the national idea in the functioning of Western culture. 'I am convinced', she writes in *Nations Without Nationalism*,

> that contemporary French and European history, and even more so that of the rest of the world, imposes, for a *long while*, the necessity to think of the *nation* in terms of new, flexible concepts because it is through the nation that the economic, political, and cultural future of the coming century will be played out.[10]

'A polyvalent community'

In *Strangers to Ourselves*, the production of these 'new, flexible concepts' is initiated by a genealogy of 'the foreigner': Kristeva here charts the ways in which Western cultures have been shaped around groups that are placed outside of or at a remove from those seen as native inhabitants, and she traces the route through difference that has led to the figuring of a distinctive European character. Many of Kristeva's attempts to reshape this legacy hang on what appears to be an elementary question: 'is a society without foreigners possible?',[11] and both here and in *Nations Without Nationalism*, she concludes that the foreigner is not the distant and different figure who enters the space of the nation from without, but instead 'lives within us'[12] and is '*our* uncanny strangeness'.[13]

Strangers to Ourselves arrives at this conclusion after surveying the place of the foreigner in Western intellectual history, from Aeschylus to Freud. Central to this account are a range of Enlightenment thinkers and political figures – Fougeret de Monbron, Guy-Jean-Baptiste Target, Anacharsis Clootz, and Thomas Paine – who variously resist attempts to restrict immigrants' political rights, and who relocate those designated as strangers in terms of a more generalized understanding of humanity. These figures contribute to a moment in which ideas about national identity were experiencing significant revision, and they effect a 'permanent shattering'[14] of the concepts that have contained both the domestic citizen and the foreigner. However, if there is one narrative above all others that counters the Enlightenment exnomination of the foreigner, then for Kristeva this is to be found in Montesquieu's work. Kristeva repeatedly turns to Montesquieu when tracing the development of an embryonic universalism which, for her, introduces a notion of cultural totality that is compellingly cosmopolitan: according to *Nations Without Nationalism*, Montesquieu's idea of 'the nation as *esprit général...* is one of the most prestigious creations of French political thought',[15] and *Strangers to Ourselves* echoes this sentiment by claiming that he offers 'a new concept of politics, understood as an attempt to harmonize what is irreducible through an interplay of diversified systems and stratums... His "modernism" is to be understood as a rejection of unified society for the sake of a coordinated diversity'.[16]

Commentators usually cite Montesquieu's influence upon the French Revolution and his standing as a founder of the social sciences when seeking to situate his place in intellectual history. For example, in the introduction to his edition of Montesquieu's 1748 *The Spirit of the Laws*, Franz Neumann points out that many seize upon Montesquieu's claim that liberty is secured both through the departure from monarchical despotism and through the splitting of political power into several institutions. 'His sympathies', Neumann states,

> were for a monarchy... tempered by a *corps intermédiaire*, by 'intermediary powers'... composed of the Parliaments, aristocracy, corporations, etc. An independent judiciary, crucial in his system for the preservation of life, liberty, and property against arbitrary acts, is to be secured by the venality of the judicial offices.[17]

Both Emile Durkheim and Louis Althusser recognize the significance of Montesquieu's support for the separation of state power, but they are more interested in the sociological dimensions of *The Spirit of the Laws*. Durkheim praises what he sees as the development, in this text, of an

early positivist historiography: 'Montesquieu's science... deals with
social phenomena and not the mind of the individual.... The author's
chief aim is to know and explain what exists or has existed.... He is
concerned, not with instituting a new political order, but with defining
political norms'.[18] These norms, for Montesquieu, are to be located
neither in the realm of conscious intention (with law arising out of
reasoned consent), nor in the sphere of human nature (with man's
essence preceding and determining the social); rather, he 'declares the
whole system of laws, past and present, to be "natural"', but 'natural'
here signifies 'the "nature" not of man but of the social organism'.[19]
Freedom, according to this model, would arise when the different parts
of this organism work in harmony with each other, and not from the
governance of society by one person or group of people.

One of Althusser's early essays similarly welcomes the methodological advances made by *The Spirit of the Laws*. Montesquieu's contribution, Althusser argues, lies in his challenge to utopian idealism, in his
separation of 'the material of political facts' from abstract notions of
natural law, which are 'nothing but disguised value judgements'.[20]
Anticipating both Hegel and Marx, Montesquieu seeks to describe the
elementary principles that are at the core of all social organisms: his
work, Althusser maintains, promotes the idea of a universal history
that is populated by states which, although different in shape, have a
definable totality: 'With Montesquieu', Althusser writes,

> the totality, which was an idea, becomes a scientific hypothesis,
> intended to explain the facts. It becomes the fundamental category
> which makes it possible to think, no longer the reality of an ideal
> state, but the concrete and hitherto unintelligible diversity of the
> institutions of human history. History is no longer that infinite
> space in which are haphazardly scattered the innumerable works of
> caprice and accident, to the discouragement of understanding,
> whose only possible conclusion is the insignificance of man and the
> greatness of God. This space has a structure.[21]

Responses such as these situate *The Spirit of the Laws* as an innovative,
but nonetheless rationalist, text: it is through scientific investigation that
the internal logic of different social formations may be identified, and it
is through the scrutiny of political history that liberty (albeit within the
constraints of the social) may be defined and realized. These, however,
are not the issues that Kristeva prioritizes, and neither are they the conclusions that she reaches in her reading of Montesquieu's volume.

Like Althusser, Kristeva finds Montesquieu's concept of cultural totality to be an important one. In contrast with Althusser, however, Kristeva points out that this concept of totality is traversed by a series of singularities that are often ignored by commentators on *The Spirit of the Laws*. Montesquieu's text classifies social systems according to their mode of political governance – republican, monarchical, or despotic – and these systems are (to an extent) shaped by the combination of diverse constitutive features, such as climate, topography, quality of soil, size of population, and territorial dimensions. 'If it be true that the temper of the mind and the passions of the heart are extremely different in different climates', Montesquieu writes, 'the laws ought to be in relation to the variety of those passions and to the variety of those tempers'.[22] But as much as each social apparatus is affected by its material setting, it is also, for Montesquieu, formed around cultural forces: 'Mankind are influenced by various causes: by the climate, by the religion, by the laws, by the maxims of government, by precedents, morals and customs; whence is formed a general spirit of nations'.[23] *The Spirit of the Laws* therefore places the totality of the social at the intersection of two different orders: settling on neither a geopolitical determinism nor an anthropocentric rationalism, Montesquieu's notion of totality is, as Kristeva observes, one marked by a divided unity, 'encompassing *nature* and *culture... men* and *institutions; laws* and *mores;* the *particular* and the *universal; philosophy* and *history'*.[24]

Kristeva's reading of *The Spirit of the Laws* foregrounds the processes of mediation that work against monocausal accounts of the nation's genealogy: nationality is here seen to be arranged serially across time and space, with local and historical factors producing cultural specificity, rather than emerging as a deviation from, or corruption of, an ideal collectivity. At the same time, however, she also draws attention to the way in which an idealist universalism *is* operative in Montesquieu's account. Although Montesquieu identifies the various factors that constitute diverse cultural formations, *The Spirit of the Laws* does not conclude that different societies are wholly separate, or that analysis of them is prevented by an irremediable difference. Montesquieu looks instead to the expansion of trade in the eighteenth century – and to the erosion of national frontiers that results from the spreading of markets – and sees in this extension the opportunity for a restitution of mankind's *esprit général*. Human sociability provides the foundation for the moderation of political power and can bring about social emancipation; crucially, this sociability is not limited by national boundaries. Kristeva:

This *fully social…* reaches its climax when Montesquieu's thought tackles the *totality of the species*. His thinking is then weighed down with fatalistic determinism (particularly climatic) and conceives the political fabric of the globe on the basis of the sociability and 'general spirit' that govern the human species finally restored to its actual universality through the modern expansion of trade. The nation's burden, so often acknowledged, is then transposed in order to be absorbed at the heart of a *borderless* political philosophy dominated by the concern for politics understood as the maximal integration of mankind in a moderate, attainable ideality.[25]

As borders begin to disappear, so too do the categories of citizen and foreigner. What is important for Kristeva, however, is that Montesquieu not only promotes an idealism in which 'nation-states must give way to higher political systems'.[26] He also avoids the kind of transnational universalism that many (often those in postcolonial studies) associate with Enlightenment thought. Montesquieu certainly believes that liberty will arise out of the growing realization of mankind's *esprit général*, but this process is only possible through a progressive decentralization of political power, and with the development of a non-integrative and internally divided totality. The nation-state may well be superseded by 'higher political systems', but these systems are composed of various collectivities that are themselves formed around a series of singularities. The *esprit général*, in other words, speaks not with a clear and univocal voice, but is a polyphonic expression, as dissociated from its essence as it is a manifestation of an ideality; built around the further fragmentation of an already bifurcated political order, this totality has always been without centre or unity.

If *Strangers to Ourselves* underlines the refiguring of the nation that necessarily follows Montesquieu's *esprit général*, then *Nations Without Nationalism* draws attention to the continuing role that the nation can continue to occupy after its metamorphosis. Contrasting the 'texture of many singularities'[27] that informs Montesquieu's notion of a transnational humanity with those mystical nationalisms (such as Herder's *Volksgeist*) that root the character of the people firmly in the soil of the nation, Kristeva argues that Enlightenment concepts of national identity (especially those associated with French thought) can breathe new life into an old and tired idea, while at the same time avoiding the pitfalls of European particularism.[28] Rather than hailing the demise of the nation, *The Spirit of the Laws* can trigger a productive revivification of the idea of the nation, and central to this reactivation is a departure from the idea that nationality signifies an enduring and essential regional character; instead, Montesquieu allows us to rethink national identity as contingent and open-ended. Such a revisionist strategy clearly does not advance the sort of political nihilism or cultural anarchism that is often associated with poststructuralism: rather, Kristeva here suggests that although nations are ceasing to function as they once did (and, indeed, may be facing their obsolescence), they nevertheless continue to play a role in the emergence of less regimented social and symbolic orders. If the concept of 'the nation as *esprit général* (with the heterogeneous, dynamic, and "confederate" meaning that Montesquieu gives to a political group) is one of the most prestigious creations of French political thought',[29] then for Kristeva it is because this idea 'brings together the national and the cosmopolitan without for that matter erasing national boundaries – which remain a historical necessity for the coming century at least'.[30] Neither announcing the arrival of a new, non-national, global order nor declaring that the nation persists as a determining and resolute power, a critical cosmopolitanism therefore intervenes between structured dwelling and unregulated dispersion, ambivalently acknowledging the continuing force of the nation while also pointing to an unknowable and unthematizable 'polyvalent community'.[31] Such an 'atopic (foreignness) and utopic (a concord of people without foreigners, hence without nations) position' for Kristeva offers 'a means to stimulate and update the discussion on the meaning of the "national" today'.[32]

Ius cosmopoliticus

By regarding cosmopolitanism not as the macropolitical present but as a burgeoning force that is radically transforming the role of the nation, *Strangers to Ourselves* and *Nations Without Nationalism* stand at the vanguard of a critical cosmopolitanism that has been gathering momentum since the late 1990s. For many associated with this concept, a rigorously theorized approach to cosmopolitanism can allow us both to reflect on the reshaping of modernity by globalizing forces and to address counter-hegemonic interventions by anticolonial and postcolonial nationalisms. Pheng Cheah, for example, cautions against precipitate declarations of transnationality, and argues that a new cosmopolitanism – which he phrases as 'the cosmopolitical' – needs both to recognize the ways in which transnationalism has shaped the past as much as it is affecting the present, and to appreciate how popular nationalisms have rallied those struggling against neocolonial forces:

in the cosmopolitical today, even activist cosmopolitanisms are in a conflictual embrace with the popular nationalisms that are imperative in the postcolonial South. These popular nationalisms cannot afford to refuse the resources and gifts of aid offered by transnational networks. However, given their irreducible inscription within the material linkages of global capital, these giving cosmopolitanisms can also unintentionally undermine popular attempts to renationalize the compradorized state.[33]

Whereas Cheah stresses the greater care that cosmopolitical thought needs to exercise over the reconstitution of the nation-state by progressive nationalisms, the editors of *Public Culture's* special issue on cosmopolitanism emphasize the productive flexibility of this concept. What is urgent and distinctive about this idea, they argue, is its indeterminate quality: resisting conclusive interpretation, it slips between cultural traditions (since it is aporetically informed by multiple intellectual histories) and audaciously embraces a protean logic. For them, 'A cosmopolitanism grounded in the tenebrous moment of transition is distinct from other more triumphalist notions of cosmopolitical coexistence'.[34] Importantly, this mobile and multivalent cosmopolitanism is not so much produced by the West looking askance at its own intellectual history as it is the outcome of a minoritarian repetition of authoritative discourses: 'The cosmopolitanism of our times', they argue,

> does not spring from the capitalized 'virtues' of Rationality, Universality, and Progress; nor is it embodied in the myth of the nation writ large in the figure of the citizen of the world. Cosmopolitans today are often the victims of modernity, failed by capitalism's upward mobility, and bereft of those comforts and customs of national belonging. Refugees, peoples of the diaspora, and migrants and exiles represent the spirit of the cosmopolitical community.[35]

Elsewhere, Bhabha similarly challenges neoliberal tendencies to equate cosmopolitanism with a multiculturalism that views transcultural community as harmonious and consensual cohabitation. Such a multiculturalism, he points out, has been imposed upon colonized cultures from above, whereas 'vernacular' cosmopolitanisms can unlock alternative histories of colonialism, each recording 'not simply its major events but its small, forgotten voices'.[36] If this cosmopolitanism written from below for Bhabha embodies a nomadic and hybridized postcoloniality, then for James Clifford the consequences of cosmopolitanism are a modernity cut adrift from its positivist moorings. Questioning the significance that Cheah gives to progressive nationalisms ('The hope that "popular" nationalisms will ultimately be different from other nationalisms is surely utopian'[37]), Clifford points to cultural formations that are not wholly governed by national codes. What he calls 'Fourth World' or 'discrepant' cosmopolitanisms (such as tribal groups) may well 'work within and against national structures', but they are not produced by those same structures; instead, for Clifford, this cosmopolitanism 'undermines the "naturalness" of ethnic absolutisms, whether articulated at the nation-state, tribal, or minority level'.[38]

Divergent though these accounts might be, they nevertheless share Kristeva's belief that cosmopolitan thought offers a route out of both pathological nationalisms and phobic inscriptions of 'the foreigner'. Like Kristeva, they also see themselves as legatees to Kant's work on immigration, hospitality, and world peace. However, while some responses often warn against the notion of a neutral and civilized totality that Kant appears to endorse, Kristeva maintains that the 'moral universalism'[39] of the Enlightenment is decisively transfigured in Kant's writing on the constitution and legislation of the international community. Kant's cosmopolitanism, she maintains, contests the collapsing together of nationality, ethnicity, self-identity, racial character, bordered interiority, and territorial belonging.

Two essays – 'Idea for a Universal History with a Cosmopolitan Purpose' of 1784 and 'Perpetual Peace: A Philosophical Sketch' of 1796 – see Kant dissociating moral norms from their regional setting, and situating them instead within a common context. In the second of these essays, Kant builds the foundation for rethinking social formations in terms of *a priori* laws which extend beyond the borders of the state, and which provide the foundation for reshaping human culture as a universal community. Upon this foundation he assembles a series of articles which would effect peace between states and institute an worldwide federation of republican states, and he regards these as the outcome of the natural progress of human history: 'The mechanical process of nature', he argues in 'Perpetual Peace', 'visibly exhibits the purposive plan of producing concord among men, even against their will and indeed by means of their very discord'.[40] Such speculations on the dynamic interplay of the agonistic and synthetic are prefigured in 'Idea for a Universal History', where Kant maintains that the purposive and systemic quality of nature can be tracked through human history.

Beginning with Greece and Rome, he argues, political history has developed episodically: in it we can 'discover a regular process of improvement in the political constitutions of our continent (which will probably legislate for all other continents)'.[41] Moreover, he argues,

> we must always concentrate our attention on civil constitutions, their laws, and the mutual relations among states, and notice how these factors, by virtue of the good they contained, served for a time to elevate and glorify nations (and with them the arts and sciences). Conversely, we should observe how their inherent defects led to their overthrow, but in such a way that a germ of enlightenment always survived, developing further with each revolution, and pre-pared the way for a subsequent higher level of improvement.[42]

War, commerce, the fact that all areas are inhabitable: these reveal to Kant that nature is driving people ever more into contact and conflict with each other. What is needed, and what 'Perpetual Peace' offers, is a set of rules that act progressively to mitigate dispute and disharmony, and for Kant these rules are to be derived from reason – the highest and most autonomous of all human cognitive faculties. Reason pro-vides people with a sense of their perfectibility, and reason grants people the capacity to work towards a global legal framework that can overcome the 'savage and lawless freedom'[43] that has promoted the interests of particular individuals or groups.

This concept of a transnational community is one that Kristeva finds compelling, but what need to be emphasized, she argues, are several decisive traits that are particular to Kant's universalism. He certainly finds the principle of community to be a universal one, but the states that contribute to and constitute this worldwide association must, he insists, remain divergent. This divergence emerges partly as an expres-sion of the fundamental character of man, which for Kant presents itself as a schizophrenic 'unsocial sociability':[44] social systems, accord-ing to 'Idea for a Universal History', are born out of an tremulous vacillation between the constraints of interdependence and man's self-interest, between man's 'inclination to *live in society*' and his 'tendency to *live as an individual*'.[45] The anxiety that results from such a divided ontology is responsible for aesthetic and cultural production, he argues ('All the culture and art which adorn mankind and the finest social order man creates are fruits of his unsociability. For it is compelled by its own nature to discipline itself, and thus, by enforced art, to develop completely the germs which nature implanted'[46]), but this ambivalence also demands laws that operate at the universal level – a 'law-governed external relationship with other states'[47] is needed before man's unsociability can be fully and conclusively tamed.

For Kristeva, this notion of cosmopolitan law is significant because it seeks to establish a worldwide legislature that oversees all regions without at the same time turning cosmopolitan federation into a uniform global order. But while the existence of certain organizations (most obviously, the Council of Europe, the European Union, and United Nations) suggests that such a federation has arrived and is a present reality, Kristeva believes that the cosmopolitanism envisaged by Kant is one that is yet to come:

> Kant's text inscribed, at the outset of a political ethics and a legal reality that are still to be carried out, the cosmopolitan concept of a mankind finding its full accomplishment without foreigners but respecting the right of those that are different. The notion of *separation* combined with *union* was to clarify such a practical cosmopolitanism that nature foresees and men carry out.... *separation* and *union* would guarantee universal peace at the core of this cosmopolitanism.[48]

Cosmopolitanism here is conspicuously not the same as Europeanization, and neither is it a synonym for Westernization. Indeed, Kristeva observes, Kant's notion of universal reason plainly challenges the idea that the West alone is in command of rationality, and we can draw upon it when questioning imperial practices that have sought to arrogate authority exclusively to a European centre. Expansionist policies are seen only as self-interest rewritten for the international stage, and they are 'far removed from that ideal'[49] of universal justice: for Kant, 'the inhospitable conduct of the civilized states of our continent, especially the commercial states, the injustice which they displaying visiting foreign countries and peoples (which in their case is the same as conquering them) seems appallingly great'.[50] While certain directions in Enlightenment thought do indeed see European culture as the height of civilization, or lend themselves to an assimilationist ethic, Kristeva therefore argues that Kant's idea of reason does not buttress the Enlightenment's Eurocentrism since it troubles territorial expansion and often works against European interests.[51]

Kristeva's reading of Kant's universalism tacitly responds to those who would find the principle of reason to be shaped entirely by a Eurocentric and a colonial sensibility. As convincing as this might be on one level (since it divests the Enlightenment of its self-styled cultural particularity), Kristeva nevertheless fails to address what are, for others, critical questions that are prompted by Kant's work. Quite apart from the succour that Kant appears to give to the supposition of European legislative pre-eminence ('a regular process of improvement in the political constitutions of our continent... will probably legislate for all other continents'), the enunciatory position implied in his universal history certainly begs Derrida's question 'But who, we?'. Anyone asking this question might point out that the pronouns 'we' and 'our' tend to speak of a violent inclusivity, one maintaining the outlandish status of the foreigner at the very moment that community is affirmed. Indeed, Derrida himself comes close such a conclusion in his reading of 'Perpetual Peace'. Focusing on Kant's third 'definitive article' for enduring peace – 'Cosmopolitan Right shall be limited to Conditions of Universal Hospitality'[52] – Derrida points out that although cosmopolitan hospitality for Kant appears to be both universal and limitless, the rights of residence that should be given to foreigners are qualified and contingent. Hospitality is a right, for Kant, because it reflects the inalienable condition of the human person: if all people equally share the same character, then exclusive regional occupation would betray natural law. 'Kant's philosophical project', as Allen W. Wood describes it,

> is truly cosmopolitan in its intent, not limited by any geographic or cultural borders. Its articles are meant not merely as precepts of a *ius gentium*, applying to the relations between sovereign states, but beyond this also as principles of a *ius cosmopoliticum*, which regards *all* peoples of the earth as a 'single universal community'.[53]

However, since this universal character does not automatically find itself expressed in state legislation, treaties between states are needed to facilitate the transfrontier movement of people: although rights of visitation are fundamental and incontestable for Kant, rights of residence require negotiation. This slippage – from natural law to state legislation – is one that concerns Derrida, and not only because of the way that humanity's universal condition can only come into being (and, consequently, disappears) when supplemented by juridical systems. Derrida's concern instead rests on the assertion of a state sovereignty that underlies the legislation of cross-border traffic: 'hospitality' Derrida argues, 'is dependent on and controlled by the law and the state police'.[54] The hospitality that is so fundamental to Kant's cosmopolitanism therefore turns out to do little more than outlaw hostility towards newcomers. In order to tackle this problematic construction of a restricted hospitality, wherein an unreserved hospitality both provokes and is proscribed by the law, Derrida proposes that unconditional and juridical laws need to interrogate each other more forcefully:

> It is a question of knowing how to transform and improve the law, and of knowing if this improvement is possible within an historical space which takes place *between* the Law of an unconditional hospitality, offered *a priori* to every other, to all newcomers, *whoever they may be*, and the conditional laws of a right to hospitality, without which *The* unconditional Law of hospitality would be in danger of remaining a pious and irresponsible desire, without form and without potency, and of even being perverted at any moment.[55]

By arguing that abuses conducted in the name of the state are not to be answered with an empty utopianism, 'On Cosmopolitanism' shares with *Strangers to Ourselves* a vigilant resurrection of Enlightenment universalisms. On the other hand, the shortcomings that Derrida identifies in Kant's account of natural and cosmopolitan law seem to be of little concern to Kristeva. Certainly, Kristeva's championing of a post-Enlightenment cosmopolitanism – the *dramatis personae* of which are, above all, Montesquieu and Kant – appears once again to leave non-European intellectual traditions on the margins of political theory, and counter-narratives of the nation remain peripheral to cultural intervention. Modelled as it is on a European legacy, Kristeva's cosmopolitanism implies that this heritage alone can provide a passage out of the entrenched and pathological disavowal of the migrant, the exiled, the alien, the foreigner. Popular nationalisms play no part in this transformative process, and although Kristeva is keen to unearth the nomadism and hybridity that are buried in a supposedly uniform and settled tradition, she nonetheless reassigns a frontiered singularity to this tradition by seeing it as both the locus of the old and the source of the new.

Just as worrying as this obscure and monoculturalist normativity, however, is that Kant's rush to embrace the law is not convincingly confronted by Kristeva. Derrida's claim that the cardinal significance of the law lies in its aporia, and that the task of cosmopolitan thought is to intervene between an illimitable hospitality and the juridical regulation of the foreigner, finds little support in Kristeva's concept of a split cosmopolitanism. In *Strangers to Ourselves*, unconditional hospitality seems to disappear, and in its place there are 'a political ethics and a legal reality' that are both cosmopolitan and 'still to be carried out'.

But here, as in 'Perpetual Peace', it would appear that a heightened reason and an enhanced legislative system are needed in order to usher in a cosmopolitan future; rather than representing the limit to symbolic order, as it does for 'On Cosmopolitanism', Kant's separation/union double ultimately leaves regulatory institutions firmly in place. The danger here is one that Derrida alerts us to: if a cosmopolitan future can only come into being by way of structured rights, then hospitality must remain subject to conditional laws. If, as Kristeva argues with regard to Montesquieu, 'national boundaries... remain a historical necessity for the coming century at least',[56] then these conditional laws of hospitality would have to respect the sovereignty of state systems.

Strophe/antistrophe

Recent thinking about cosmopolitanism and hospitality points both to conceptual weaknesses in Kristeva's conclusions about the transfiguration of the nation and the foreigner, and to an interest only in counter-Enlightenment universalisms that develop in the West. But what *Strangers to Ourselves* and *Nations Without Nationalism* do offer are subtle responses to earlier accusations that Kristeva romanticizes the difference of other cultures while at the same time leaving the supposed consistency and civilization of the West unchallenged. Spivak's 'French Feminism in an International Frame' is perhaps the best-known work which takes Kristeva to task for failing to develop such a challenge. For Spivak, a 'macrological nostalgia' can be found in *About Chinese Women*, since Kristeva's text at once sentimentalizes the East (by embracing dubious anthropological theses on the social and sexual heterogeneity, as well as the matrilineal and matrilocal foundations, of Chinese pre-history) and implicitly views the West as an even monotheistic capitalism:

> The 'Indo-European' world whose 'monotheism' supports the argument of the difference between China and the West is not altogether monotheistic. The splendid, decadent, multiple, oppressive, and more than millennial polytheistic tradition of India has to be written out of the '*Indo*-European picture in order that this difference may stand... Kristeva thus speaks for a generalized West.[57]

A Critique of Postcolonial Reason sees Spivak continue to question the insular vision of Europe that she finds in Kristeva's work. Spivak here cites Kristeva's comments (made in 'My Memory's Hyperbole') on the role of the US and Europe in the face of a rising Third World:

This challenged giant [the United States]... may, in fact, be on the point of becoming a David before the growing Goliath of the Third World. I dream that our children will prefer to join this David, with his errors and impasses, armed with our erring and circling about the Idea, the Logos, the Form: in short, the old Judeo-Christian Europe. If it is only an illusion, I would like to think it may have a future.[58]

This rallying call is, Spivak declares, 'bewilderingly Eurocentric',[59] and Kristeva's assertions here certainly appear to confirm the impression – initiated by *About Chinese Women* – that her cultural taxonomy is rooted in a fixed and adversarial dichotomy.

Strangers to Ourselves and *Nations Without Nationalism* begin to challenge the impression that might be drawn from these pieces: departing from a sentimentalized archaeology of an Eastern (and matrilineal) difference and disputing the ways in which the West has been constructed as a monolith, these texts turn towards cardinal moments in European thought and culture, attempting in the process to reveal the ambivalent, uncertain, and internally conflictual character of this tradition. *Strangers to Ourselves* and *Nations Without Nationalism* are not, then, just interested in rereading work that has informed modern notions of international justice, or with establishing how ideas of universal peace can contribute to a theoretical and political restructuring of the nation-state. Rather, Kristeva's texts are concerned with the way that this uncertain character stretches backwards, as an inaugurating force, as well as one which shapes the future: turning towards the West, these texts seek to expose the exteriority that has always been at the heart of European identity.

One concern of *Strangers to Ourselves* is the way in which early cosmopolitan thought is informed by Hellenic universalisms that defend Greek principles. For example, anticipating Deleuze and Guattari's claim that with Greece's democratic imperialism 'even the skies become horizontal',[60] Kristeva regards Stoic ethics as part of a flattening, assimilative, and autocratic *sensus communis*:

> Thus founded on *oikeiosis*, on conciliation, that universalist ethics leads one, on the political plane, to challenge separate city-states and substitute a tolerant cosmopolitanism. *Megapolis*, the large polis, is an ideal brought out during the imperial era, and it includes the entire universe, from citizens to the stars.[61]

Cosmopolitanism would therefore seem to be motivated by an ethnic narcissism in which pragmatic self-protectionism is disguised as inter-cultural hospitality. At the same time, however, the cosmopolitan impulse that begins in national self-interest does not, Kristeva observes, effect a wholly normative or phobic encounter with the for-eigner. Indeed, she argues, certain articulations of the cosmopolitan ideal sometimes counter the notions of civilized and rational conduct that are at the heart of the democratic polis. In Zeno's *Republic*, for example, there are traces of a Stoicism that rejects controlled self-governance, favouring instead a libertarian ethic that is based upon unregulated self-interest and the heightening of pleasure. When reading this text, Kristeva states,

> One feels that cosmopolitanism emerges from the core of a global movement that makes a clean sweep of laws, differences, and prohibitions; and that by defying the polis and its jurisdiction one implicitly challenges the founding prohibitions of established society and perhaps of sociality itself; that by abolishing state-controlled borders one assumes, logically and beforehand, an over-stepping of the prohibitions that guarantee sexual, individual, and familial identity. A challenge to the very principle of *human associ-ation* is what is involved in cosmopolitan utopia.[62]

Here, the subject is privileged over the polis: rather than envisaging a utopia in which one culture acquires authority by arrogating to itself a universal standing, this version of the cosmopolitan ideal sees regional, cultural, and sexual boundaries falling as the individual rises to pre-eminence. As much as the category of the foreigner is a trou-bled and troubling one in Greek culture, Kristeva also, then, finds the notion of an untainted sociality to be inconsistently and unsatisfact-orily articulated.

For Kristeva, this uncertain articulation of community and belonging is exemplified in Aeschylus's *The Suppliants*, a tragedy recording the mythical journey of Danaüs and his fifty daughters (the Danaïdes) from Egypt to Argos. Unhappy with the fate of his daughters – to be married to the fifty sons of his twin brother, Aegyptus, and with the political and military implications of this mass union – Danaüs and his daughters initially find asylum in the Peloponnesian city of Argos, but are then discovered by Aegyptus and forced into marriage with their cousins. Angry with this outcome, Danaüs instructs his daughter to kill their husbands on their wedding night; all except two comply – those who do find themselves condemned in Hades to an eternity of pouring water into a broken vessel. Readings of the Danaïdes myth often focus on its closing moment: Montaigne, Shelley, Browning and Hume are among those who seize upon the image of the daughters consigned forever to their interminable and subterranean task, suggesting that this myth should be read allegorically as a conceit in which human and divine retribution are collapsed together, or as a trope for incessant and futile labour in the secular world. Aeschylus's coding of this myth selectively narrates the daughters' plight, offering only an account of the Danaïdes' flight, their reception in Argos, their discovery by Aegyptus, and ending with the chorus entreating Zeus to 'Save me from cruel subjection to a man I hate':[63] what this text stresses is the (albeit short-lived) act of deliverance that is effected by the Argives' hospitality. The Chorus's opening song shows the daughters' own articulation of their plight: 'we come/Not under band for guilt of blood,/Not driven out by a city's sentence:/Escape is our choice,/Our hope of escape from lust of men,/From abhorred and impious union with Aegyptus sons'.[64] Later in the play, Danaüs instructs his daughters on how properly to petition for the Argives' hospitality:

Now quickly prepare white suppliant leaves, sign of Zeus sacred, held
　　　　　　　　　　　　　　　　　　in the left hand,
Mournful, respectful, answer needfully
The strangers; tell distinctly of an exile
Untainted by murder. Let no boldness
Come from respectful eye and modest features.
Not talkative nor a laggard be in speech:
Either would offend them. Remember to yield:
You are an exile, a needy stranger,
And rashness never suits the weaker.[65]

So successful are these acts of suppliance that Danaüs and his daughters win civic freedom in Argos, but, more importantly, they also gain protection by the martial and legal resources of Argos: 'We are free to settle here, subject/Neither to seizure nor reprisal, claimed/neither by citizen nor foreigner',[66] Danaüs declares, conveying Argos's ruling on the Danaïdes' immigrant status. Concerning itself neither with the daughters' crimes nor with their fate in Hades, then, Aeschylus's *The Suppliants* instead represents the Danaïdes as the victims of tyrannical rule and as respectful observers of Greek ritual who petition for hospitality according to established principles of border protocol.

Critics often find in *The Suppliants* an affirmation of reason, as well as an assertion of divine authority. H.D.F. Kitto, for example, argues that Aeschylus's play shows how human and divine are intimately tied together: 'Aeschylus asserts here, as elsewhere, that there is a supreme power; that is to say, there is a unity in things, some direction in events, which imply a supreme power; and this he identifies with Zeus'.[67] For others, Aeschylus's play demonstrates how the advanced polis can interact rationally with, and show hospitality towards, travellers from abroad who share the same sense of civilized conduct; those foreigners who do not are seen to betray both considered morality and international protocol ('foreigners must learn to use greater respect',[68] the King of Argos exclaims at the arrival of the Herald of Aegyptus). Sanctioned by divine authority and legitimated by reasoned order, propriety, ethics, and justice appear to belong to an incontestably universal system of value; emphasizing the Argives' treatment of the Danaïdes as much as the daughters plight, *The Suppliants* suggests that the judicious treatment of others is central to the mature state. Here, there seems to be no place for the disruptive effects of cultural difference; rather, it is the willed undertaking of suppliance by the foreigner and the generous granting of hospitality by the native citizen that is meaningful for Aeschylus.

Kristeva's interest in the Danaïdes' flight from Egypt (and in Aeschylus's rendering of this departure) lies in the daughters's lineage, and in the question of whether their classification as foreigners is an adequate or sustainable one. Central to Aeschylus's account is the role of the King of Argos, who not only listens to the Danaïdes's petition but also carries their campaign to the Argive citizens. In working on the daughters's behalf, *Strangers to Ourselves* observes, the King of Argos takes on the role of the 'proxenus' – 'the middleman between the polis and those belonging to a foreign community, providing a remedy to their statutory incapacity'.[69] As immigrants from Egypt, the Danaïdes are therefore required formally to lobby through the person of the proxenus; the outcome of this process is, however, a remarkable one for Kristeva. Whereas successful suppliants may have enjoyed residential privileges, they were nevertheless subject to different types of taxation and were usually denied the right to own property. The Danaïdes, in contrast, appear not to receive the same treatment as other travellers from abroad, and instead become more fully incorporated into the Argive polis than their status as foreigners would suggest.

The reason for this strange treatment is to be found, Kristeva argues, in the daughters' ambiguous national identity. Outwardly Egyptian women – immigrants who find shelter in the Greek polis – the

Danaïdes are also, according to mythological history, descendents of the Argive priestess Iō (who, as the object of Zeus's amorous affections, is metamorphosed by his jealous wife Hera into a heifer, constantly troubled by a gadfly, and forced to wander from Argos to Egypt). This heritage suggests to Kristeva that Aeschylus's account of the Danaïdes myth is by no means straightforward, one simply documenting a flight from injustice and sexual violence that results in further injustice and sexual violence, or merely charting a unidirectional voyage from homeland to exile. Rather, Aeschylus's *The Suppliants* draws attention to a double coding of nationality, since the daughters's descent from Iō and the outcome of their entreaty reveals them to be at once Greek and Egyptian, both natives of and foreign to the host nation. 'The Danaïdes were exceptionally well incorporated', Kristeva maintains, 'and that only because of their double nature, *astoxenoi*, at the same time citizens because of their Argive descent *and* foreigners because they came from Egypt'.[70] One of the earliest texts to deal with questions of national identity, *The Suppliants* therefore finds it difficult to show a culture at home with itself, and it fails to provide the image of disinterested Greek benevolence towards foreigners that readers might otherwise be tempted to find in Aeschylus's tragedy.

Aeschylus's play, in Kristeva's reading, turns into a metonym of a culture that is beginning to refine both its own self-consciousness and a sense of those outside of Greece's borders. But as much as it is concerned with showing how 'the foreigner' has experienced the law of the community in different ways, *Strangers to Ourselves* also draws a decisive conclusion from this genealogy: foreignness, rather than constituting an incomprehensible and inscrutable otherness, should instead be recast as an immutable trait of national identity. The notion that the state or the nation can provide the subject, the family, or the indigenous community with a generalized and stable collectivity rapidly collapses here. Inhabiting the nation-state's most venerated principles, foreignness turns into a primary and determining feature of Europe's emergence; rather than approaching from a distance, the force of the foreigner within has always threatened the unity and self-determination of a people, community, or state. Representing an inaugural moment in the development of the frontiered state, *The Suppliants* exposes the discourse of cultural association as an anxious discourse. Cosmopolitanism – the irreducibly foreign constitution of the state's centre – no longer inhabits a distant or future horizon, but is an inalienable alienation, a condition of pure contamination that is woven into the very fabric of European culture.

Mourning and melancholia

Derrida's 'On Cosmopolitanism' would suggest that the hospitality portrayed in *The Suppliants* should be resignified as conditional hospitality, for the Danaïdes are required to perform acts of supplication in order to find a place among the Argives, and their remarkable treatment is a consequence of their remote consanguinity. More pressing than the question of what Aeschylus's narrative might reveal about unconditional hospitality, perhaps, is Spivak's assertion that a 'macrological nostalgia' surfaces when Kristeva turns to questions of national identity and cultural difference. There are, clearly, crucial differences between the arguments developed in *Strangers to Ourselves* and *Nations Without Nationalism*, and those advanced in *About Chinese Women*: Kristeva's later reflections on the fusion that founds European identity certainly depart from the notion that Eastern diversity acts as a counterpart to Western sameness – a notion that Spivak infers from *About Chinese Women*. This difference notwithstanding, however, a certain nostalgia can still be discerned in Kristeva's reading of *The Suppliants*, as well as in the theory of the foreignness inaugurating European forms of collectivity that she derives from this text.

In an interview, Kristeva remarks that 'I am very attached to the idea of the woman as irrecuperable foreigner',[71] and *Strangers to Ourselves* finds Aeschylus's recounting of the Danaïdes myth significant because it discloses the place of women as the earliest foreigners: 'It is noteworthy', she states, 'that the first foreigners to emerge at the dawn of our civilization are foreign women'.[72] Central to the Danaïdes' plight, but of only passing interest to Aeschylus's narrative, is a woman who is both outside of the polis and beyond reason: Iō's madness leads her 'not on a journey back to the self, as with Ulysses... but toward a land of exile, accursed from the start'.[73] Iō is important to Kristeva, then, because she exposes the way in which women have been construed as foreign to the community's circumscribed interiority, but her status as the Danaïdes' ancestor also dramatically reshapes their classification as suppliants from overseas. As well as this genealogical relationship, there is also a causal correlation between Iō's exile and the Danaïdes' flight from Egypt: both departures take place as a flight from marital union and sexual legitimacy. This conjunction reinforces the sense of the daughters' exteriority, since they arrive from beyond the borders of the city-state, but even when adopted by the Argives they remain outside of legally sanctioned sexuality. For Kristeva, then, the daughters 'were foreigners for two reasons: they came from Egypt and were refractory to marriage. Remaining outside the community of the citizens of Argos, they also refused the basic community constituted by the family'.[74]

Additionally, and in more anthropological terms, a more profound issue surfaces when the mythopoetic significance of kinship systems and their narration in *The Suppliants* are considered. For Kristeva, this myth constitutes a defining moment in the history of kinship regulation, since it represents 'an age-old time when an endogamous society became exogamous'.[75] Rather than simply showing the necessity for, and trauma resulting from, such a transition, the Danaïdes myth also, Kristeva argues, highlights the collocation of violence with the origin of the exogamous family. When resisting the marital injunctions passed down from Aegyptus, Danaüs's daughters display the hostility towards their kin that is required if legitimate sexuality is to be confined to alliances outside of the bloodline. This myth, Kristeva claims, 'through the very ambivalence it ascribes to those foreigners, recognized the necessity for the violence of passion (or, on the social plane, the validity of extirpation, or wrenching away, of foreignness itself) as foundation for the basal family alliance'.[76] Both antagonism and foreignness are essential to this system, then, and it is women who are seen to possess both qualities.

However, two problems need to be identified in this reading of *The Suppliants*, and in the significance that Kristeva attaches to Aeschylus's text. The first, and less significant, problem is one of hermeneutic inconsistency; textual evidence sanctions Kristeva's argument that foreignness inhabits the economy of the Western state, yet this evidence is not always seen to be sufficient. *The Suppliants* supplies Kristeva with an exemplary narrative of exile and hospitality because the daughters's status as refugees is specifically derived from their standing as women. But in order to emphasize the Danaïdes' ambiguous regional identity, Kristeva finds herself stepping outside of Aeschylus's text, and looking instead to other narratives of estrangement. It is Iō's banishment that results in the Danaïdes' Egyptian identity, and it is Iō's erstwhile homeland that eventually welcomes the daughters, but her story plays almost no part in Aeschylus's text. As a result, then, Kristeva has to look beyond *The Suppliants* in order to track the ambiguous genealogy of the Danaïdes that, she argues, is central to this narrative.

The second (and related) problem concerns the general definition of textuality that is at work in *Strangers to Ourselves*. On the one hand, Kristeva suggests that the bifurcated foundations of European culture can only be accessed by way of structured textuality. While this textuality may have certain gaps, aporia, and ambiguities, it nevertheless provides the sole resource for conceptualizing the past. Appearing to endorse Derrida's notorious claim that 'The sign is always the supplement of the thing itself',[77] Kristeva suggests that positivity is irremediably coded within a discursive apparatus, and the task of the critic is to expose how this apparatus both privileges the proximate and works against the truths that it appears to establish. Enveloped in representations of the foreigner and the cosmopolitan, *Strangers to Ourselves* thus warns against thetic descriptions of cultural difference:

> Let us not seek to solidify, to turn the otherness of the foreigner into a thing. Let us merely touch it, brush by it, without giving it a permanent structure. Simply sketching out its perpetual motion through some of its variegated aspects spread out before our eyes today, through some of its former, changing representations scattered through history... An otherness barely touched upon and that already moves away.[78]

Nations Without Nationalism similarly rails against those cultural typologies that are founded on the idea of an original and enduring national character. 'A defensive hatred, the cult of origins easily backslides to a persecuting hatred',[79] she insists, 'when I say I have chosen cosmopolitanism, this means that I have, against origins and starting from them, chosen a transnational or international position, situated at the crossing of boundaries'.[80]

Such remarks echo the cautionary note that is struck in the first section ('From Our Side') of *About Chinese Women*. Anxious to avoid anthropology's empiricist aspirations, this text repeatedly underlines the epistemic specificity of Kristeva's observations, and it stresses the provisionality of her conclusions. The lenses through which the Tel Quel group view China are, she states, shaped by '*two thousand years of history*', and

> *understanding China will involve much more than fitting these lenses over the reality of China as it is given to us by sinology, by contemporary history, or by our own observations. To do so during our journey through China would mean that the reality of China is accessible through our models, our habits, that it lends itself to our way of seeing. I'm not saying that this reality is invisible to the Westerner, who is condemned forever to the relativity of his knowledge. I'm saying only that we must adjust our glasses before trying to look close up at what's going on on the other side.*

> *In the meantime, the notes that follow are nothing but a first hesitant step in that direction.*[81]

Later, this extended metaphor disappears as Kristeva notes that her distorted vision of Chinese culture is determined by symbolic codes and systems. Understanding China involves not so much a scopic self-reflexivity as an '"aesthetic" mode of reasoning' which eliminates

> straight away the problem of an 'objective truth'... it shifts people to a symbolic situation in literature or in the past, selected according to the influence it continues to exert in the present. And it is there, in that symbolic, archetypal situation, that the dramas of passion, ideology, and politics that underlie the present traumatic event which concerns us and which we seek to understand (in our own terms) are called into play and begin to unravel, as in a psychodrama, a pre-psychoanalytic 'happening'.[82]

The continuation of this '"aesthetic" mode of reasoning' in *Strangers to Ourselves* would imply that the birth of the West can never be properly discerned, but must always be regarded from a distance. Rather than revealing the alterity of the stranger, then, *The Suppliants* can only reveal an inaugurating moment that is already divided from itself, and has always been marked by internal separation. And, although this non-recuperative reasoning can draw attention to the power relations that govern the symbolic values attached to community and difference, it can never fully speak of the foreigner.

On the other hand, and just as Spivak claims in respect of *About Chinese Women*, it can be argued that Kristeva's concept of the foreigner *does* seek to capture and solidify difference in positive terms. Briefly abandoning the grammatological caution that elsewhere qualifies its observations, *About Chinese Women* declares that the difference of Chinese writing is readable, and that it can be read as an unsettling *signifiance*:

> The logic of Chinese writing (a visual representation, the mark of a gesture, a signifying arrangement of symbols, logic, and certain syntax) presupposes, at its base, a speaking, writing individual, for whom what seems to us today a pre-Oedipal phase – dependency on the maternal, socio-natural continuum, absence of clear cut divisions between the order of things and the order of symbols, predominance of the unconscious impulses – must have been extremely important.[83]

The 'macrological nostalgia' of which Spivak writes is plain to see here. Before systematized writing, before the censoring order of symbols, before socio-sexual prohibitions are internalized, there is a subject-in-process – a subject whose drives are expressed in an arche-writing that is closer to the performativity of speech than it is to systematized signification.[84]

Despite the major differences between *About Chinese Women* and *Strangers to Ourselves*, a similar association of cultural difference with semiotic pre-Oedipality is evident in both texts. Kristeva's reading of *The Suppliants* does not merely move beyond Aeschylus's text in order to trace the Danaïdes' difference. It also attempts to escape textuality itself. Or, more precisely, it attempts to move beyond the symbolic apparatus of the European nation-state: if, when they stand before the Argive citizens, the daughters trigger a series of cultural – *European* – concepts and institutions (the exogamous family, notions of the foreigner and interior community, transfrontier protocol, hospitality, and so on), then whatever precedes their arrival enters the province of Europe's pre-history. But despite its pre-symbolic status, Kristeva nevertheless seeks to give this pre-history a name and to identify its various characteristics. Not only is the foreignness of foreigners recognizable to Kristeva ('there are those who waste away in an agonizing struggle between what no longer is and what will never be... there are those who transcend: living neither before nor beyond, they are bent with a passion'[85]), but the moment of pure maternality that is embodied by Iō also begins to fall within the orbit of Kristeva's genealogy. As a consequence, the Argos inhabited by Iō is seen to correspond directly with post-Danaïdean Argos; while predating 'the birth of our civilization', Iō's Greece suddenly loses its extra-discursive status, and becomes at once a time before time and a definable origin. The hermeneutic inconsistency that can be discerned in *Strangers to Ourselves* therefore reflects a phenomenological contradiction: while seeking not to reify the foreigner, Kristeva's 'touch' nevertheless places cultural difference in the grip of language.

Strangers to Ourselves and *Nations Without Nationalism* offer a bravura rereading of the universalist thrust of European intellectual history, and both texts show how canonical writers and thinkers (sometimes obliquely) challenge the tradition that they are often thought to endorse. Kristeva's contribution to debates about the role and future of the nation-state lies in her intractable attention to the ambiguous coding of identity in European writing; it is this emphasis on the strange and generative cosmopolitanism of Western culture that sees an apparent Eurocentrism slide rapidly into a rigorous and radical anti-

Eurocentrism. But other questions need to be asked of Kristeva's claims about this divided and uncertain tradition. In addition to the question of how a progressive development of conditional hospitality might impede the fracturing effects of unconditional hospitality, there is also the question of whether a pre-European and pre-symbolic exteriority can lose its enigmatic quality and become subject to a recuperative symbolic order. Her reading of Aeschylus's *The Suppliants* compellingly explores the concatenation of 'women' and 'the foreigner' that is central to the West's logic of disavowal. But by siting this text at the dawn of civilization, while also tracing the source and origin of this first light, Kristeva impossibly construes difference as a readable and articulable polysemia, rather than as a dissemination that leads, ultimately, to the inscrutable and the ineffable.

5
'In the Shadow of Shadows': Spivak, Misreading, the Native Informant

In the closing pages of the 'Philosophy' chapter in *A Critique of Postcolonial Reason*, Spivak voices her admiration for Deleuze and Guattari's reading of Marx. This reading, she argues, crucially recalibrates the value of 'value' in Marxism by situating both nature and capital in the order of desiring-production, turning the source of the human into a machinic structure that is coded (though one which, as Chapter 3 shows, resists interpretation in the moment that it is decoded). Contributing to this reassessment are, Spivak argues, often-neglected remarks in *Anti-Oedipus* that subtly rewrite Marx's notion of the Asiatic Mode of Production by seeing in it a mutability that other accounts fail to discern. Deleuze and Guattari's rewriting most visibly challenges organicist tendencies in ethnography by claiming that all regimes are constituted by a disruptive and disjunctive collision of fragments, rather than by the progressive coding of a coherent and continuous socius. For Spivak, however, their account of the Asiatic Mode of Production also lends itself to a rethinking both of capital's insatiable wanderlust and of the disempowerment it engenders for its victims: 'Deleuze and Guattari are not specialists of Asia. Yet, because they have, in my judgment, applied a broad intuition of value-production and coding to a study of globality, they are able to hint at an approach to a "third world" full of "agents" of coding'.[1] Deleuze and Guattari's 'broad intuition' is significant, then, because it allows theory more persuasively to regard capitalism not as a necessary – transient – moment that brings history to people without history (those belonging to the Asiatic Mode), but as a system that overcodes other regimes by seeking (not always successfully) to hold down the unruly differences that work against capitalism's interests.[2]

Spivak's appreciation for Deleuze and Guattari's rewriting of Marx emerges from her claim that authoritative philosophical work has been built around the figure of the 'native informant' – a figure who, she argues, inaugurates the idea of the human but who is, at the same time, written out of existence (or 'foreclosed'[3]) by European narratives. *A Critique of Postcolonial Reason* identifies a series of cases that illustrate this process of foreclosure, including Kant's notion of man which she (unlike Kristeva) finds constructed around the idea of an uncivilized non-European non-subject, and Hegel's benevolent 'Euro-teleological normativity'[4] which, she maintains, treats Indian literature as a deviation from, rather than an instrument in, the progress of history. Marx's notion of the Asiatic Mode of Production is similarly formed against a backdrop of non-European identity, but although Marxism has in other respects provided anti-colonial and resistance movements with a conceptual framework for contesting Europe's colonial intrusions, even here cultural difference appears to slide into historical distance.

The Asiatic Mode of Production has proved to be a thorny idea to grasp, and its problematic heritage is often attributed to its under-theorized status in Marx's writing. For Spivak, however, this Mode of Production has become overdetermined in the Marxist lexicon, with its lack of initial definition triggering a heterodox range of subsequent definitions. Significantly for Spivak, these definitions have pointed both to historical anteriority and to geographical peripherality: seen by some as a synonym for primitive communism (thus leaving the Asiatic Mode frozen permanently in a moment of precapitalist primordiality), this mode for others characterizes systems which are in synchronous simultaneity with, but wholly external to, European capitalism (a view that still denies the Asiatic Mode historicity by placing it outside of a normative and developmental temporality). That the theory of the Asiatic Mode of Production provides Marx with an alibi for conceiving imperialism as a global imperative has been documented at length. For Spivak, however, this concept should not simply be treated as a metonym of nineteenth century historiography, but needs to be situated more profoundly as a lacuna that is essential to a certain idea of the European. Regardless of the differences between both readings of this Mode, it is, she argues, a 'theoretical fiction'[5] which appears only spectrally, and yet underwrites Marxism's narrative of political economy.

A mute declaration

If the Asiatic Mode of Production represents an untheorizable limit in Marx's thinking, it does not follow that such a limit should, in order to heal this damaged body of work, be fully theorized, or that this native informant could be written back into full presence. Certainly there are, for Spivak, problems with how Marx understands European history and capitalism's progressive provisionality, but these would not be solved in any attempt to restore the Asiatic Mode as a symmetrical or contiguous consciousness. Instead, her reading turns away from any simple reversal of the regime of identification that she discerns in Marx's notion of Europe; her deconstructive reading of Marx,

> would not see a non-European norm standing over against this dynamic of aberrations that wrote history. It would rather suggest that this other perspective undoes the strict opposition between norm and aberration and makes post-revolutionary social engineering, on the basis of a proven authentic (European, not Asiatic) origin, as fraught as any positivization of the indeterminate.[6]

Here, Spivak recalls a motif that is often associated with her work, the idea that the subaltern cannot convincingly be conceived as a lost, yet recuperable, presence. Working through this idea in several essays that now occupy a canonical place in postcolonial studies, Spivak maintains – with some consistency – that the restoration of a peasant, native, or subaltern consciousness needs to be contested in the resistance to colonial history. Such a challenge she finds, in some of her earlier writings on textuality and knowledge, in the work of the Subaltern Studies group: this group are frequently treated as revisionist historians who set out to recover the lost consciousness of the subjugated subaltern, but for Spivak such an apparently recuperative initiative needs to be understood as part of an insurgent foundationalism, since this group suggests that 'subaltern consciousness is never fully recoverable, that it is always askew from its received signifiers, indeed that it is effaced even as it is disclosed, that it is irreducibly discursive'.[7] In this manner, Chakrabarty argues that 'the practice of subaltern history would aim to take history, the code, to its limits in order to make its unworking visible'.[8]

More frequently cited is 'Can the Subaltern Speak?,' which continues in this mood by arguing that the search for an authentic subalternity is a doubly misguided enterprise. Not only is this essay, 'committed to the notion that... a nostalgia for lost origins can be detrimental to the exploration of social realities within the critique of imperialism',[9] it also observes that the diversity of subject-positions under colonialism needs to be recognized: 'One must... insist that the colonized subaltern *subject* is irretrievably heterogeneous'.[10] 'Can the Subaltern Speak?'

traces this heterogeneity through the practice of widow self-sacrifice *(sati)*, in which Hindu women immolated themselves on their dead husbands' funeral pyres. For Spivak this tradition illustrates the double narration and dual displacement of women in India, since *sati* has been regulated both by patriarchal customs in India and by British colonial law. On the one hand, there is what Spivak terms 'the Indian nativist argument'[11] which sets out to establish the objectives of those women who performed *sati* and concludes that these women were thinking agents who wanted to die for their husbands. On the other hand, in 1829 the British implemented laws prohibiting the act of *sati*, laws which promote notions of human nature and universal civilization, and which locate Europeans as 'White men saving brown women from brown men'.[12] Since both practices mean that the voices of women disappear in the very moment that they are inscribed, the history of *sati* must be understood as the history of a double repression: rather than adequately representing Hindu customs or recovering the intentions of those women who committed *sati*, history must instead be treated as a series of essentially prosopopoeic, catachrestic, and discriminating master-narratives that have 'worlded' the world of Hindu women in their own interests.

Spivak's rewriting of 'Can the Subaltern Speak?' as part of the 'History' chapter in *A Critique of Postcolonial Reason* is notable not just because it allows Spivak to re-assert her argument that any challenge to the epistemic violences of colonialism and postcoloniality needs scrupulously to negotiate sentimental notions of an authentic and untroubled ethnicity. There is also rupture in this repetition, since this essay's return is accompanied by some subtle modifications in Spivak's characterization of the subaltern. Where her earlier version emphasizes the inexpressibility and inscrutability of the subaltern ('The subaltern as female cannot be heard or read'; 'The subaltern cannot speak. There is no virtue in global laundry lists with "woman" as a pious item'[13]), *A Critique of Postcolonial Reason* is more guarded in the conclusions it draws from the overcoding of women's experiences (such as those of the Rani of Sirmur or Bhubaneswari Bhaduri) under colonialism. Indeed, Spivak states that 'I was so unnerved by this failure of communication that, in the first version of this text, I wrote, in the accents of passionate lament: the subaltern cannot speak! It was an inadvisable remark'.[14]

Spivak's remark was inadvisable for a number of reasons. *A Critique of Postcolonial Reason* continues to contest the idea that historical excavation can unearth the buried remains of a once-intact identity, and

Spivak here reiterates her elementary claim that colonized women's multiple coding forces them – more than others – from history's putative luminosity: 'As we approach Sirmur', she states, 'we move from the discourses of class and race into gender – and we are in the shadow of shadows'.[15] Despite this obscurity, however, she argues that even if colonized women's speech has been silenced by different authorities, the act of committing *sati* is itself a mute declaration: Bhubaneswari Bhaduri is, then, 'a figure who intended to be retrieved, who wrote with her body. It is as if she attempted to "speak" across death by rendering her body graphematic'.[16] That this inexpressible intention can be traced is hinted at by Spivak in both the earlier and later versions of her essay: 'Between patriarchy and imperialism subject-constitution and object-formation', she writes, 'the figure of the woman disappears, not into a pristine nothingness, but into a violent shuttling that is the displaced figuration of the "third-world woman" caught between tradition and modernization'.[17] Remarks such as these underline the idea that, although refused access to the forms of subjectivity that are open to Hindu men, and although governed by a colonizing force that speaks on her behalf, the voice of the subaltern woman can be traced through the history of effacement that has silenced her. The place of 'third-world women' needs to be seen as a vacillating one which allows their voices to be heard not as the sigh of an oppressed creature, but as a silently communicative 'aporia between subject and object status'.[18] Where the earlier version of this essay emphatically claims that subaltern women have been utterly excluded from speech, both versions nevertheless offer a hauntology of the repressed, the echoes of whose voices can be heard only as a soundless utterance.

A Critique of Postcolonial Reason is concerned to clarify the extent to which the subaltern can be characterized because the claim that colonized women's voices have been stifled could, despite Spivak's constant qualifications, lend itself to a sentimentalizing and restitutive identity politics. For instance, an unhelpful distinction between colonized and colonizer might, she feels, remain after her 'inadvisable remark' that the subaltern cannot speak. If such a distinction holds, Spivak warns, then the postcolonial critic is condemned either to the impossible pursuit of an oppressed ethnicity's lost consciousness, or to descend into further silence about subaltern muteness. A more compelling approach would be one which recognizes the heterogeneous character of both the subaltern and the colonized, and which admits to the constitutive interdependence of both groups. And, against the wishes of some in postcolonial studies, such an understanding of colonialism would establish a sense of how counter-memory must negotiate its own debt to discursive practices established by colonialism and postcoloniality: 'I think it is important', she writes, 'to acknowledge our complicity in the muting, in order precisely to be more effective in the long run. Our work cannot succeed if we always have a scapegoat. The postcolonial migrant investigator is touched by the colonial social formations'.[19]

To assert that the subaltern cannot speak could, by the same token, imply that dominant groups are invested with an expressive self-identicality, but Spivak's revised version more precisely argues that distancing and distortion are common to both subaltern and colonial identities. What *A Critique of Postcolonial Reason* argues for is not a distinction between self-articulation and muteness, but between Europe's authoritative assignment of cultural presence to itself and its corresponding allocation of a deviant or deficient quality to the subaltern. Finding themselves forever coded, both the dominant and the subaltern are rendered impossible despite the identifications that speech apparently makes possible; silence here becomes a condition of all speech, and a secret remains perpetually at the heart of all disclosure. What this means for Bhubaneswari Bhudari is that she is not entirely silent, just as colonial and patriarchal discourses cannot convincingly speak themselves or maintain their authority by a simple discursive fiat. 'I am able to read Bhubaneswari's case', Spivak points out, 'and therefore she *has* spoken in some way.... All speaking, even seemingly the most immediate, entails a distanced decipherment by another, which is, at best, an interception. That is what speaking is'.[20] Bhubaneswari Bhudari is not, then, on the other side of speech, but finds herself situated on the margins of cultural discourses which shape themselves precisely through the act of peripheralizing women such as her.

Spivak after Derrida

The critique of the sovereign subject that motivates 'Can the Subaltern Speak?' therefore persists and is extended when rewritten for *A Critique of Postcolonial Reason*. The concept of the native informant allows Spivak to continue to warn against the harnessing of a weakly theorized nostalgia to anti-colonial struggle, against hasty declarations of a resistant difference, and against rash pronouncements on an activism beyond theory. But this (non-)concept also develops the notion of subalternity by allowing the relationship between hegemony and resistance to be re-evaluated with greater theoretical complexity than her earlier work might suggest: on the one hand, the concept of the native informant troubles one-dimensional and unidirectional accounts of colonial dominance (since it always returns to haunt those narratives which identify the human subject in European terms); on the other hand, this concept can provide counter-colonial theory with an alternative to the melancholic invocations of enduring ethnicity that have prevailed in nationalist discourses.

Challenging both the failings of postcolonial criticism and the epistemic violences of colonialism and postcoloniality is a prominent concern in Spivak's work, but this critique also draws in thinkers who might otherwise be taken for her allies. Clearly, the benevolent universalisms of certain directions in feminist criticism have attracted her attention, but she shows how even the most anti-humanist thought sometimes preserves the self-identity of the subjugated subject. In this manner, *A Critique of Postcolonial Reason* restates her already famous reservations about 'Intellectuals in Power', an exchange between Foucault and Deleuze: 'just as some "third world women's" critique romanticize the united struggle of working-class women, these hegemonic radicals also allow undivided subjectivity to worker's struggles'.[21] 'Can the Subaltern Speak?' finds a compelling alternative to Foucault and Deleuze's 'postrepresentationalist vocabulary' that 'hides an essentialist agenda'[22] in Derrida's vigilant refusal to endorse the logocentric foundations of anti-ethnocentric thinking. 'I must' she states when concluding 'Can the Subaltern Speak?', 'acknowledge a long-term usefulness in Jacques Derrida which I seem no longer to find in the authors of *The History of Sexuality* and *Mille Plateaux*'.[23] The significance of this acknowledgment takes on new dimensions, however, when it fails to survive the revisions that occur for *A Critique of Postcolonial Reason*.

Spivak has never been reluctant to declare the solidarity that she feels with Derrida's work, and a range of Derridean lineaments inform her account of the elaborate orchestration of power in colonial and postcolonial systems. In '*Glas*-Piece: A *Compte Rendu*', one of her earliest pieces on Derrida, the full extent of this identification with Derrida's ideas begins to take shape. Reading Derrida's ambidextrous and bipolar *Glas*, Spivak here reflects on how Derrida mimetically interlaces his own signature with those of Hegel and Genet: infecting Hegel's deliberations on the family by laying open their many fissures and parasitically draining Genet's writing of its disseminatory force, *Glas*'s two adjacent columns also revive these bodies of work by folding them together and inseminating them with the other voices of

Nietzsche, Heidegger, and Derrida himself. 'Derrida himself' does not, however, escape unscathed in this dual act of dispersion and insemination, but is instead rendered essentially incomplete and scattered as the phantasy he has always been. *Glas* can be read, Spivak states, 'as a fiction of Derrida's proper name turning into a thing, of an autobiographical autotherapy or interminable self-analysis against the duping of self-sovereignty, crypting the signature so that it becomes impossible to spell out'.[24] The autopoeisis of *Glas* does not, as it might appear to do, unveil the secret name of a Derrida we all want to know; rather, it discloses – and thus disfigures – the figuring of autonomous authorship and turns against the graphing of the proper name. Echoing de Man's claim that autobiography is the replacement of a self that never existed,[25] as well as presaging her assertion that 'autobiography is a wound where the blood of history does not dry',[26] Spivak finds in *Glas* an assault on the subject's sovereignty that she pursues with greater vigour in 'Can the Subaltern Speak?' and *A Critique of Postcolonial Reason*.[27]

More recently, Spivak has continued to underline what she sees as the crucial role that Derrida's ideas should play in any advanced critique of cultural power. 'Deconstruction and Cultural Studies' turns to the concept of teleiopoeisis that Derrida develops in *Politics of Friendship*, rather than to *Glas's* auto-affective and self-defeating autopoeisis; here she points to the 'new politics of reading'[28] that lies in the idea that complicity informs resistance, and argues that deconstruction can prompt a rethinking of cultural studies' positivism. For Derrida, the compound term 'teleiopoeisis' carries a critical ambiguity; it signals the way in which a certain logic works as a *parti pris*, seeking rhetorically to programme its own conclusions in advance. (Derrida's example here is taken from Nietzsche's *Beyond Good and Evil*: '"Alas! If only you knew how soon, how very soon, things will be – different –"'[29]). But while teleiopoiesis operates as a 'future-producing'[30] act, it simultaneously works performatively as an event, detaching the futurity of the future from the present in the very moment that this coming difference is inscribed. The proximate becomes distanced, and what is disavowed becomes desired:

> As soon as one needs or desires one's enemies, only friends can be counted... and here madness looms. At each step, on the occasion of every teleiopoetic event. (No) more sense [*Plus de sens*]. That which is empty and that which overflows resemble one another, a desert mirage and the ineluctability of the event.[31]

Conveying this madness, according to *Politics of Friendship*, is the adverb 'perhaps' that runs through Nietzsche's text. Signifying only contingently, 'perhaps' functions to presage what is to come (the *'arrivant'*), but without assigning a predicative quality to the possible. This concept of the inconceivable, Derrida insists elsewhere, is 'a way of replacing the logic of necessity, the logic of dialectics, with a relationship to the future, to what is coming, to what could come to us under the modality of the maybe'.[32]

Shuttling between the speculative and the undecidable, teleiopoiesis is yet another instance of the impossible possible that for Derrida gestures towards the foolishness of the 'perhaps'. This, Spivak submits, can help to reshape and open up the concerns of Cultural Studies. At the most general level, such a structural shift would seek to prevent issues, critics, texts, or artefacts from hardening into a disciplinary orthodoxy. And this shift would bring about a further conceptual transformation by avoiding the attempt to determine cultural systems that (contradictorily) accompanies pronouncements on the social as simulation: 'To ignore this limit' that is pointed to by the deconstructive 'perhaps' 'is to transcendentalize systems, including "social constructions"'.[33]

More specifically, these changes would demand a departure from the extrinsicality to which Cultural Studies sometimes aspires, whereby analysis and critique are seen to be uncontaminated by the institutions, processes, and power that are under scrutiny. This transformation would not simply constitute a loosening of methodological principles or a move away from positivism; rather, Spivak argues that Cultural Studies' transdisciplinarity can allow it to reach different conclusions than the subjects that constitute it, especially Area Studies, Anthropology, Comparative Literature, and History. In particular, she claims, Cultural Studies can interrogate the uncritical metropolitanism that has informed these modes of cultural analysis and commentary:

> Cultural Studies must open up from the inside the colonialism of European national-language based Comparative Literature and the Cold War format of Area Studies, and infect History and Anthropology with the 'other' as producer of knowledge. But from the inside, acknowledging complicity. No accusations. No excuses. Only, learning the protocol of those disciplines, turn them around, laboriously.[34]

Declarations like these appear to do little more than endorse familiar deconstructive tropes (it is necessary to read homeopathically, to inhabit a structure in order to make it tremble, to speak the language of the master in order to displace the economy of mastery, and so on – derived, often, from a selective and solitary reading of *Of Grammatology*), but Spivak's claim here extends beyond reasserting an elementary call for strategic immanence.[35] The version of catachresis that she offers in 'Deconstruction and Cultural Studies' is one in which the figure who haunts metropolitan knowledge is 'the other' – the native informant – as 'producer of knowledge'; establishing the metropolis in the moment of being effaced by the metropolis, this phantasm exposes the exnomination of subaltern difference that enables the incorporation of colonial Europe. Tracing this figure for Spivak entails attention to teleiopoietic procedures: highlighting the miraculating ruse that collapses together the performative and the constative, Spivak points out that both subjectivity and national identity are often certified by a permanence which arrives almost invisibly (and always violently) in the moment of their constitution. The task of Cultural Studies should be to expose this paralogistic narrative wherever it arises, and deconstruction in general, and the notion of teleiopoiesis in particular, would allow the cultural critic to reveal the distancing of difference that works against metropolitan inscriptions of origin and end. However, rather than seeking to disclose a hidden subject or monumentalize a buried ethnicity, deconstructive Cultural Studies would recognize the limits to historical documenta-tion and sidestep an ossifying exposition of the past by placing its account of the generative subaltern para-subject in the domain of a non-transcendentalizing 'perhaps'. 'Derrida', Spivak argues in 'Resident Alien', 'has opened hospitality onto teleopoesis – a structure of touch-ing the distant other that interrupts the past in the name of the future rupture that is already inscribed within it'.[36]

'*Glas*-Piece' and 'Deconstruction and Cultural Studies' provide just two examples of the call to theoretico-political responsibility that Spivak finds in Derrida's writing. Both essays also illustrate the equivo-cating way in which her work answers this call: '*Glas*-Piece' reflects on *Glas's* myriad threads that tie Hegel to Genet and weave together reason and madness; 'Deconstruction and Cultural Studies' in contrast witnesses a Spivak whose thinking is punctuated by a series of Derridean locutions and motifs. In one sense, these differing strategies allow Spivak to avoid imposing a monocritical account on the material she explores, and the notion that deconstructive readings partially inhabit the text under consideration is certainly reflected in the poly-valence of her writing styles. However, while these multiple articula-tions might lend themselves to a voguish critical pluralism, potential problems with this shifting theoretical mode do – as Spivak herself admits – need addressing. Quite apart from the possibility that an uninterrogated notion of agency lies behind the motivation and selection of the critical techniques offered here, there is also the possibility that the critical attitudes adopted in '*Glas* Piece' and 'Deconstruction and Cultural Studies' might betray the spirit of deconstructive theory by turning it into a theoretical model or critical method. Didacticism, it might be argued, is still at work in her reading of particular texts; in spite of her protestations ('to read all these open ended lines of writing at the same time calls for a different style of reading'[37]), '*Glas*-Piece' retains a pedagogic function (indeed, her claim that 'An essay of this length cannot speak of the many riches of Derrida's discourse on Hegel's discourse of the family'[38] suggests that an extended piece could unravel the enigma of Derrida's discourse). That this 'piece' finds itself trapped between exegesis and deconstruction is captured in Spivak's subtitle, with '*compte rendu*' ambivalently coding her response to *Glas* as both an iterative review and a summative overview.

Purloining Derrida's concepts provides Spivak with an alternative route into deconstruction, but this too falls foul of a similar betrayal. Just as Julian Wolfreys voices misgivings about the institutionalizing of deconstruction as deconstructiv*ism* ('deconstruction cannot be practised because there is not an aspect of Derrida's work which, when translated, can be turned into a theory which can then, in turn, be put into practice as a method for reading'[39]), so Spivak identifies problems with work – her own included – which is telegraphically informed by Derridean questions, tropes, neologisms, idioms, and concepts. The danger here, she points out in an essay on the place of deconstruction in America, is that such a treatment reduces Derrida's work to a repertoire of concepts that are transported across textual and contextual boundaries. 'I seem', she remarks, 'to fall back these days on miming a procession of figures rather than following an argument. This is, I realize in amused despair, a sort of thematization that annuls deconstruction yet once again'.[40] This problem is not one of exegetical transparency but one of thematic transposition: the ability to mime 'a procession of figures' would only be possible if those figures possessed an independence and a unicity that would allow them to be wholly detached from the moment and circumstance of their articulation. While Derrida certainly finds the notion of contextual delimitation to be a problematic one,[41] he is just as insistent that theoretical displacements are structured and framed by the scene of their emergence. Ventriloquizing such concepts as autopoeisis, teleiopoiesis, or perhaps would seem to run counter to this insistence, and it suggests that Derrida's work offers a free-floating critical argot that can be thematized and recalibrated for – without, at the same time, being disfigured by – a range of theoretical demands.

Spivak does indeed acknowledge the 'annulment' of deconstruction that occurs with conceptual transposition, but a further danger – one to which she does not draw our attention – becomes apparent when the precise theoretical demands that saturate her thinking are considered. Some commentators on the relationship between poststructuralism and postcolonial theory place Spivak among those who politicize deconstruction by forcing its allegedly abstracted critique of metaphysical marginalia into debates concerning the social function of colonial and postcolonial signifying systems. Thus, for Stephen Morton, 'Spivak expands Derrida's deconstructive thinking beyond the framework of western philosophy, and sets it to work in diverse fields ranging from "Third World" women's political movements to postcolonial literary studies and development studies'.[42] By transferring Derridean motifs in the way that it does, Spivak's work might suggest that an appropriative translation of Derrida's ideas is needed so that they can speak to theorists whose concerns lie with questions of colonialism, postcoloniality, and the emerging operations of global capital. If, as she has observed on several occasions, translation is 'necessary but impossible'[43] – if it is not just an act of affiliation, affirmation, devotion, or a relationship between equivalents but is also an act of disaffiliation, denial, and treachery – then her work might be viewed as a postcolonial recoding of an otherwise unrelated conceptual intervention. Yet another version of catachresis, Spivak's translation of Derridean concepts into a postcolonial vocabulary would seem to imply that deconstruction lacks just such a theoretical vector. Spivak lends credibility to this impression when she claims that 'the postcolonial as the outside/insider translates white theory as she reads, so that she can discriminate on the terrain of the original. She wants to use what is useful'.[44]

Misreadings

Spivak's account of her relationship with deconstruction, and of the ways in which Derrida's work might contribute to theories of postcoloniality, becomes complicated when she considers Derrida's competencies as a commentator on Marx and Marxism, There are, she admits, moments in Derrida's writing which could respond more precisely to the critique of national identity by non-Western Marxism. 'At the

Planchette of Deconstruction is/in America', for example, points to work by Asian Marxists who have been reading Marx against the grain of 'the predictive Eurocentric scenario' and whose work opens 'the space of a "new International"'. Since he does not consider this work, Spivak asks, does Derrida miss an opportunity to break with restricted – European – visions of an alternative future?

> I am aware that Derrida always speaks of a *Western* metaphysics because he does not wish to overstep the boundaries of what he knows and what writes him. The messianic and metempsychosis are thus not aberrant. But if one proposes a *"new International"*, should one not perhaps cast a glance at the fate of these other sustained efforts?[45]

Misgivings are expressed here, but remarks such as these also highlight the fact that divisions between Derrida's work and theories of colonialism, postcoloniality, and globalization cannot be maintained. Indeed, a significant part of Spivak's work seeks to throw light upon 'an unknown "postcolonial" Derrida',[46] and the slippages and transpositions that are to be found in her 'own (mis)interpretation of Derrida'[47] take place between allied versions of cultural intervention – both of which expose and explore the auto-affection that is central to Europe's miraculating self-invention – and not between the discrete theoretical terrains of a partitioned typology (deconstruction/postcolonial theory).

In one of her earliest essays on Derrida and Marx, the 1987 'Speculation on Reading Marx: After Reading Derrida', Spivak anticipates this account of deconstruction's consequences for political theory by challenging the assumption that 'deconstruction' and 'Marxism' are proper names that designate fixed, finite, and separate fields of inquiry. Her focus here is a footnote in 'White Mythology' that reflects on the notion of 'the proper' – the proper name, self-proximity, self-possession, propriety, cleanliness, truth, and so on – in *The German Ideology*. This footnote takes Marx to task for leaving metaphysical concepts of property (such as bodily properties) uninterrogated, but it also claims that the resources for redressing this unwitting metaphysicality can be found in Marx's text; for Derrida, this critique 'opens, or leaves open, the questions of the "reality" of the proper'.[48] For Spivak, this analysis of the ambiguities that underpin Marx's materialism can be extended to his concept of labour-power: what Marx's readers often fail to acknowledge, she argues, is that if capitalism invents the body of the labouring class, then this class must be characterized by a radical impropriety. The source of resistance to capitalism should not, then, be located in the 'proper labour' of a class that needs to overcome its alienation, but should instead emerge from the improper logic that is central to capitalism's identifications. Marx's conclusions about this matter 'are not clearly drawn', she maintains, since:

> We remain caught within the opposition *Fremdarbeit* (alienated labour) and *Eigenarbeit* (proper labour) – work for the capitalist and for oneself. Here Derrida allows us to see that the condition for the possibility of this opposition is *Eigenarbeit's* own 'impropriety' or inadequation to itself.... Marx's well-known conclusions, even when the in- or super-adequation of labour-power to the body is most clearly articulated, is one of opposition, not complicity.[49]

However, as much as 'At the *Planchette* of Deconstruction' and Speculation on Reading Marx' are concerned to establish connections between deconstruction, Marxism, and postcolonial theory, this attempt at reconciliation undergoes a dramatic shift in both tone and direction when Spivak claims that Derrida's remarks on Marx (at least, until the appearance of *Specters of Marx*) extend little further than a series of scattered associations. 'Limits and Openings' lists some of these 'many analogies and references'[50] to Marx; these include *Limited Inc.* (where 'one finds analogies between normative language taxonomies and capitalism and its crisis-management'), 'The *Retrait* of Metaphor' (in which 'Heidegger's metaphoric practice itself is described in economic terms'), 'Restitutions to the Truth in Pointing' (where 'criticism is presented in terms of use-, exchange-, and surplus-value'), and 'Economimesis' (where 'the naturalization of political economy by Kant is presented in terms of the God-poet relationship'[51]). Typifying Derrida's reflections on the relationship between capital and value, these essays suggest to Spivak that the Marxist problematic figures in his work 'only by a clandestine metonymy'[52] which authorizes itself by discreetly parrying Marxist interventions in the very moment that it appears to confront them.

Intrinsic to this succession of 'abdications and postponements'[53] lies what is, for Spivak, an elementary misreading of Marx's theory of value; in spite of her petition for alternative critical strategies in 'Deconstruction and Cultural Studies' ('No accusations. No excuses'), Spivak's 'Limits and Openings of Marx in Derrida' and her later 'Ghostwriting' both bring a series of allegations to bear on Derrida's misapprehension of the links between capital and value. Evidence for this misunderstanding can be found, she argues, in *Limited Inc.*, where Derrida collapses Marx's notion of use-value into Heidegger's account of Being. At stake in both theories is a claim to originary properties, and for both thinkers these first principles remain scarred by their incorporation into systematized exchange. Both carry out their own versions of the phenomenological reduction: both arrive at a sense of what remains after the veil of superficial appearance is drawn aside, and both seek to expose a substratum that lies beneath layers of sedimented impressions. For Spivak these two theoretical fictions – use-value and Being – are, however, irreducible to each other in the way that Derrida suggests, since use-value is always marked by the intentionality of the user: for Marx, the phenomenality of the object cannot be deduced from its use in the way that it can be for Heidegger, and it is a sign of Marx's theoretical sophistication that for him 'There is no such thing as subtracting use-value from a thing'.[54] Puncturing the surface of being, for Heidegger, allows a dark and primordial light to shine through; piercing the artifice of exchange-value does not, according to Marx, disclose a utility that indexes the materiality of a pure object. Use-value, Spivak therefore insists, is a 'slippery idea' that does not point to 'a thing in its nakedness',[55] but instead reveals only a more basic structure of commodification.

'Limits and Openings' is concerned to question those moments in Derrida's work when Marxist discourse props up interventions that are not primarily concerned with the subtleties of Marx's thinking, and one example of this can be found in his citing of 'surplus-value' when gesturing towards a generalized relationship beyond intentional consciousness. The problem here for Spivak is not just that Derrida appropriates Marx's concepts for his own ends. Rather, these occasional detours into Marxist vocabulary signal a larger misunderstanding of political economy, and especially of capital's transnational appetites. Turning to Derrida's reflections on the future of Europe in *The Other Heading*, Spivak picks out his claim that 'capital' in Valéry's *La liberté de l'esprit* is laden with polysemia: for Derrida,

> Valéry puts to work the regulated polysemy of the word 'capital'. This word compounds interests, it would seem; it enriches with surplus-value the significations of memory, cultural accumulation, and economic or fiduciary value. Valéry assumes the rhetoric of these tropes, the different figures of capital referring to each other to the point where one cannot nail them down into the propriety of a literal meaning.[56]

As in 'Speculation on Reading Marx', Spivak here salutes the non-proprietary route that Derrida follows through this polysemia, and, she argues, it allows theory to hear Marx's disparate voices. On the other hand, as much as this non-heuristic reading allows Marxism to move beyond the entrenchments of a canonized orthodoxy, it nonetheless for her shows that a disregard for Marxist concepts continues in Derrida's writing, and this in spite of his pronouncement that it is necessary to reread Marx ('It will always be a fault not to read and reread and discuss Marx'[57]). Specifically, value is once again misconstrued here, she maintains, since Derrida fails to finesse the theory of surplus-value in the way that Marx does. Not only does he fall short of addressing the strict sense in which surplus-value denotes the difference between the labour-power that actuates commodity production and the exchange-value that is attached to the commodity produced. He also sees absolute surplus-value as 'the infinite source of more and more value',[58] rather than as the value that is created when the working day is lengthened.

A closer reading of *Capital* would, Spivak insists, have allowed Derrida to advance more convincing conclusions about the Eurocentrism that, according to *The Other Heading*, operates in Valéry's vaunting of France's cultural capital. Spivak admits that Derrida's version of absolute surplus-value – construed, as it is, in terms of capital's universalizing impulse – certainly allows us to realize that territorial violations lie embedded in European culture:

> In the event, Derrida makes a good point, the best that intellectuals with strong leftist sympathies but not sufficient knowledge of the Marxian project can make these days: that Europe's 'memory' as itself has colonialism inscribed in it; keeping contemporary Europe 'pure' cannot escape that memory.[59]

But she also maintains that such conclusions offer little more than a sweeping call for rememorizing European history as colonial history. What the theory of absolute surplus-value can offer – presumably with a 'sufficient knowledge of the Marxian project' – is a more detailed account of how capitalism extends surplus-value by striving for new markets while at the same time restructuring the working day and stretching the constituency of productive labour. Had Derrida reread *Capital* in the way that *The Other Heading* itself counsels, Spivak argues,

> it would not have been difficult to launch a more rigorous critique of Valéry's Eurocentric 'idealism' – to have noticed that because the search for ever *more* absolute and less relative surplus-value contin-

ues unchecked in the post-Fordist New Europe – the feminization of superexploitation rages in the sweatshops of that very Turin where Derrida's words were pronounced.... If *Capital* had indeed been reread, he would have known that this global feminization of super-exploitation is determined precisely by the gendering of sexual difference all over the world and Europe gains from it.[60]

While a deregulation of critical and theoretical methods can allow a plethora of meanings to spill out of Marx's text, for Spivak such eccentric readings allow the signifier of Marx's text to become wholly detached from its signified. By diluting the force of Marx's interventions, Spivak asserts, Derrida's Marxism ceases to provide a satisfactory method either for mapping capital's transnational trajectories, or for understanding the increasing feminization of the workforce.

Between hauntology and ontopology

If 'Limits and Openings' insists that the concept of 'use-value remains the unquestioned possibility' of deconstruction, but that Derrida's 'politicoeconomic vocabulary'[61] has often inhibited the actualization of this possibility, then Spivak's later 'Ghostwriting' maintains that Derrida's restricted understanding of political economy continues in *Specters of Marx*. Opening with a short avant-propos on her 'relationship to "deconstruction"',[62] Spivak declares that this bond has become 'more intimate, more everyday, more of a giving – away, and in – habit of mind'.[63] At the same time, these prefatory remarks also anticipate what is to follow by looking back to '*Glas*-Piece', revisiting the mimicry – the affirmation-negation coevality – that is intrinsic to Derrida's reading of Hegel and Genet, and which extends into Spivak's reading of *Glas*. Again, this ambivalence is played out in the way in which 'Ghostwriting' both applauds the left-leaning convictions of *Specters of Marx* and expresses Spivak's frustration with Derrida's Marxism. But 'Ghostwriting' does not simply update Spivak's earlier claims about the shortcomings of Derrida's Marxism. One of the striking traits of 'Ghostwriting' is that it is more outspoken about what remains implicit in 'Limits and Openings': despite its complexity, Spivak tellingly argues in this later essay, Marx's work nevertheless offers a stable and definable corpus that is open to unequivocal interpretation.

According to 'Ghostwriting', the basic lessons in Marxism that are left unheeded by Derrida specifically concern subaltern women and the insurgent struggles that make capitalism tremble. When thinking about exactly which ghosts appear in Marx's writing, Spivak insists that the body of the working woman is one that, for him, inhabits the shifting corpus of the revenant, yet neither the increasing centrality of women to the processes of productive work nor women's reproductive labour are tackled in *Specters*. Whereas Derrida's 'hauntology' stresses the messianic *arrivant* and a community that cannot be anticipated, Spivak argues that 'the reproductive body of woman has now been "socialized" – computed into average abstract labor and thus released into what I call the spectrality of reason – a specter that haunts the merely empirical, dislocating it from itself'.[64] Similar problems for Spivak surround the critique of ontopology that lies behind the concept of the new International. This notion sets out to shake the foundations of the (Europhilic) nation-state by placing national community out of joint with itself and challenging the 'axiomatics linking indissociably the ontological value of present being (*on*) to its situation, to the stable and presentable determination of a locality, the *topos* of territory, native soil, city, body in general'.[65] For Spivak, however, the concepts of ontopology and the new International are based on a weak understanding of the complex movement of capital. Derrida does indeed name ten plagues of the new global hegemony,[66] but, she insists, he collapses together different functions of capital, confuses different notions of value, and as a consequence fails to examine the complex interconnectivity of these plagues:

> Derrida cannot see the systemic connections between the ten plagues of the New World Order... because he cannot know the connection between industrial capitalism, colonialism, so-called postindustrial capitalism, neocolonialism, electronified capitalism, and the current financialization of the globe, with the attendant phenomena of migrancy and ecological disaster.[67]

Fixing on the territorializing logic that strictly roots identity in locality, Derrida's concept functions in *Specters* as an antonym for the (inconceivably) atopic and unlocalizable. The trouble with this concept for Spivak, however, is that it allows theory no position from which to consider counter-hegemonic activity. If the main thrust of *Specters* is to allow the difference of the New International to disconcert both European exceptionalism and more general forms of ethnocentrism, then Derrida's text seems once again to render voiceless those engaged in resistance writing and thinking. Spivak:

> The subaltern are neither 'nationally rooted' nor migrant; their intra-national displacement is managed by the exigencies of inter-national capital.... Their struggles reflect a continuity of insurgency which can only too easily be appropriated by the discourse of a come-lately *New* internationality in the most extravagantly public-ized theoretical arenas of the world. Subalternity remains silenced there.[68]

Clearly, then, Spivak is less than enthusiastic about some of the concepts that are central to *Specters*. Between the notions of hauntology and ontopology the subaltern drops out of sight: *Specters*, 'Ghost-writing' insists, fails to see the systemic interplay of capitalism's various forces, but at the same time attributes too much systematicity to a subaltern idiom that here becomes yet another unheard utterance.

Estates and exegesis

Spivak's reservations do indeed leave questions hanging over Derrida's readings of Marx. When voicing these reservations, however, she makes a number of surprising claims, and sometimes slips into the sort of discourse that seems improbable in a theorist so closely associated with deconstruction. On some occasions, the vocabulary that she employs in her response to Derrida is recriminatory. Thus, while she states in the Foreword to *Outside in the Teaching Machine* that she feels an '(always respectful) impatience'[69] towards Derrida's characteri-zation of Marx, this impatience is phrased less-respectfully elsewhere. 'Limits and Openings', for example, states that Derrida 'confuses'[70] Marx's arguments, and that his understanding of surplus-value demon-strates 'an embarrassing lack of awareness of Marx's use of the term'.[71]

On other occasions (and very much tied to the accusation that Derrida's appreciation of Marx is confused and embarrassing), an appeal to exact exegesis radiates out of Spivak's rejoinder. When in 'Limits and Openings' she states that 'Marx's ethicoeconomic counsel, in its detail, should be digested, incorporated, and thus inscribed in the body of the feminist and antiimperialist struggles',[72] Spivak turns away from the more deconstructive argument that she elsewhere promotes, and transcendentalizes Marx by implying that his counsel is consti-tuted as a permanent critique, one that is not reshaped by the contexts in which it finds itself. Such a digestion, incorporation, and inscription would certainly see feminist and antiimperialist struggles learning the protocol of Marxist critique. But the notion that, in order to speak to these struggles, Marxism is obliged mutually to digest, incorporate, and be inscribed by feminist and antiimperialist struggles seems not to be an issue here. In contrast with the plurivocity of *Glas* that Spivak celebrates earlier, Marxism here turns into an analysable cryptonymy – a static and enduring thematics that intervenes unilaterally. It is for this reason, as Moore-Gilbert observes, that 'Her relationship to Marxism is... difficult to fix. On the one hand she confesses to Sara Danius and Stefan Jonsson, "I'm not really a Marxist cultural critic", while to Robert Young she asserts, "I'm an old-fashioned Marxist"'.[73]

In 'Ghostwriting' Spivak's appeal to core themes in Marxism is made more forcefully. Part of this essay is written in a confessional mode: several times she states that her misgivings about Derrida's reading of Marx arise out of her own sense of proprietoriality towards Marx. Her unhappiness with *Specters* surfaces because she 'so desperately wanted Derrida to get Marx rightish',[74] but she then wonders whether these reservations are triggered by a clandestine craving for interpretive directness, asking 'Am I a closet clarity-fetishist when it comes to Marx?'.[75] 'Ghostwriting' frequently suggests that this may indeed be the case. Echoing her other writing, including 'Responsibility' and *A Critique of Postcolonial Reason*, this essay argues that an ethical response to the past is one which regards history as a hauntology, not as a bare and recuperable facticity: 'You crave to let history haunt you as a ghost or ghosts, with the ungraspable incorporation of a ghostly body, and the uncontrollable, sporadic, and unanticipatable periodicity of haunting.... It is not, then, a past that was necessarily once present that is sought'.[76] Working against such an alternative historiography, however, this essay also asks 'Is it just my proprietorial reaction to think that you can't catch any specter of Marx if you don't attend to the ghost's signature?'.[77] Implying that it is possible somehow to seize the 'ungraspable incorporation of a ghostly body', to treat Marx as the source and guarantor of his own utterance, Spivak therefore appeals to two conflicting forms of proprietoriality: she lays claim to the interpretation of a textual corpus that is also in full possession of itself.

Given that Spivak constantly alerts us to the unreliability of the confessional mode, it would be prudent to remain skeptical during those moments when she comes clean about her proprietoriality towards Marx. Certifying her possession of Marx is Spivak's signature, but this essay also cautions that signatures are not to be trusted: recalling the earlier '*Glas*-Piece' (which maintains that *Glas* encrypts the signature to the extent that it 'becomes impossible to spell out'[78]) and echoing Derrida's 'Signature Event Context' (which argues that 'a written signature implies the actual or empirical nonpresence of the signer'[79]), the opening pages of 'Ghostwriting' suggest that we should be vigilant during such confessional moments. According to the double logic of the signature, Spivak's true feelings can only be concealed at the very moment of their revelation: were we, as a consequence, not to trust Spivak's self-avowed proprietoriality, then her reservations about Derrida's 'confused' and 'embarrassing' reading of Marx would take on a different character. Indeed, when Spivak's compacts her work into phrases like 'all communication is infected by *destinerrance*'[80], she again complicates the legitimacy of such candid moments in her own writing.

Surprisingly, perhaps, Derrida finds no such equivocation in 'Ghostwriting'. His 'Marx & Sons', a somewhat uncharacteristic essay, assesses and responds to a series of commentaries on *Specters of Marx*. These commentaries – by, among others, Ahmad, Hamacher, Jameson, Macherey, and Negri – for him mostly engage responsibly with the readings that he offers: 'Nearly all seek to analyse, understand, argue – to elucidate, not to obfuscate. Nearly all seek to discuss rather than insult (as one so often does today, to avoid asking oneself painful questions), to object rather than belittle or, in cowardly fashion, wound'.[81] Nearly all, but not quite all, for Derrida also declares his unhappiness with certain commentators' 'prioprietorial'[82] claim to Marx's legacy. Embodying this sense of interpretive ownership is Eagleton ('One can only rub one's eyes in disbelief and wonder where he finds the inspiration, the haughtiness, the right. Has he learned nothing at all? What proprietary rights must be protected... To whom is "Marxism" supposed to belong?'[83]), but he also discovers this tendency in Spivak's 'Ghostwriting'. Derrida's unhappiness with Spivak stems partly from what he sees as a series of misreadings in her essay; these are due, he states, to 'her unbridled manipulation of a rhetoric' and to a distortive ventriloquism – 'so massive a falsification' – which turns his critique of the stasis of the political into an injunction not to repoliticize.[84] There is, of course, a chance that Derrida is not venting frustration in the way that he appears to here: his work disinters the buried misprisions, manipulations, and falsifications that are at work even (especially) in the most neutral of commentaries, so these accusations might expose nothing more than traits that are covertly at work in all critical activity. But the tenor of the remainder of the essay, in which Derrida declares

his admiration for Jameson's and Ahmad's thorough and careful readings of *Specters of Marx*, would suggest that 'Marx & Sons' is – remark-
ably for Derrida – unequivocally calling for more equivocating critical
interventions than those offered by Spivak.

What lies behind this displeasure is not just a sense of professional
injury on Derrida's part. Rather, his frustration with 'Ghostwriting'
erupts from this essay's demand for truthful exegesis; this demand, he
argues, is rooted in the notion that the right response to Marx precedes
the act of interpretation. Not only does Spivak seek to define the parameters within which acceptable readings of Marx can take place, she
also – prioprietorially – suggests that these parameters can be determined in advance of any encounter with Marx's writing. The implications of this prior appropriation are what Derrida rails against in 'Marx
& Sons'. If Spivak's account of Derrida's confusion is a valid one, then
critics like her will always have been the heirs to Marx's legacy; within
such an economy other readers would therefore have to submit their
readings for imprimatur by this estate.

Further reflection on this disagreement could pick out the discourse
of their contretemps, pointing out the ways in which it borders inflammatory invective: 'One of the things that jar in *Specters* is Derrida's
constant correcting and patronizing of a "silly" Marx';[85] 'Some of her
errors stem from an outright inability to read'.[86] To some readers, such
phrasing might suggest that this dispute has deteriorated into a conflict
between personalities, rather than forming part of a scholarly exchange
on the question of validity in interpretation. Rapaport is one such
reader: in 'Marx & Sons', he claims,

> Derrida has even shown a loss of temper that reveals quite a lot
> about his personal investment in deconstruction as an intellectual
> movement whose legitimacy is not to be called into question. In
> fact, in 'Marx & Sons' he even lashes out against Spivak in what I
> take to be a rather apparent misunderstanding of 'Ghostwriting': the
> view that because she criticizes Derrida, she must be situating
> herself wholly in opposition to him. In fact, she has advanced her
> critiques, which are entirely in line with her previous writings, not
> in order to embarrass Derrida, but to show where his critical
> emplacements are vulnerable to attack.[87]

But although Derrida's excoriation of Spivak for her failure to read is
open to dispute, his retaliation does raise questions about her reaction
to *Specters'* confusion. Certainly, some irony would be at work if Spivak

misreads Derrida's failure to read Marx, and this would enervate the force of a number of her objections. For example, the concept of ontopology is a troubling one for Spivak. This concept, she argues, construes culture as a monolithic dominance, but when describing this process an interesting slippage seems to occur: she initially claims that 'The criticism of "ontopology"... can only see the unexamined religious nationalism of the migrant or national', but then later writes that 'to see all activity attached to the South as ontopologocentric, denies access to the news of subaltern struggles against the financialization of the globe'.[88] Finding insight in Derrida's blindness, Spivak's initial point here is that *Specters* cannot consider the full effects of counter-hegemonic movements, but she then implies that even though he equates minority movements with a hegemonic reassertion of territorialized ethnicity, his work does not necessarily lead to this narrow response.[89]

Conclusions

Thumbnail sketches often characterize Spivak's work as a multivalent and polyvocal body of texts which lock together Marxism, feminism, and deconstruction in a rigorous reassessment of cultural systems. But, as other commentators have observed of her earlier writing, there are imbalances in this composite treatment of different critical modes: as much as Spivak at times associates her thinking with Derrida's, at other times she argues that Marxism offers greater insight into global power than the critical strategies provided by deconstruction. What starts as a disruptive polysemia, Young argues, turns into a terminal monocritique:: 'For all the carefully constructed disparateness of her work, for all the discontinuities which she refuses to reconcile, Spivak's Marxism functions as an overall syncretic frame. It works... as a transcendentalizing gesture to produce closure'.[90]

Such a 'transcendentalizing gesture' persists in her recent comments on deconstruction and Marxism, and although she continues to declare her solidarity with Derrida, she is nevertheless equally prepared to voice her misgivings about his work. Her criticisms of Derrida are not just targeted at his relative inattention to the counter-hegemony of subaltern groups – this criticism is perhaps the most provocative one for those who draw upon deconstruction when theorizing colonialism and postcoloniality. Rather, Spivak claims that Derrida's careless reading of value metonymically points to his inability to understand postcoloniality, capitalism's global hegemony, and transnational resistance

movements. This conclusion is a remarkable one for a cultural commentator with Spivak's allegiances, and not only for the reason that it
departs from the encomium that she often exhibits towards Derrida.
This conclusion is also remarkable because she can only arrive at it by
turning away from the notion of theoretico-political interpretation
that she promotes elsewhere, and by endowing Marx's writings with a
stable and static substance. What Derrida's misreading of Marx means
for Spivak, in other words, is that the critique of European epistemic
systems now demands a departure from Derrida as much as it does
from, for example, Deleuze or Foucault. The Foreword to *Outside in the
Teaching Machine* underlines this sentiment: characterizing her relation
to deconstruction by ventriloquizing Derrida's 'The Force of Law', she
states here that 'As I have repeatedly acknowledged, all my work is a
forcing of deconstruction(s) into an "impure, contaminating, negotiated, bastard and violent... filiation"'[91]. However, this contaminating
negotiation of deconstruction becomes one that speaks from the
uncontaminated interiority of Marx's text. 'Deconstruction', she states,
'is among the things that have to be catachretized',[92] but she seems to
infect an already tainted theoretical articulation – to render deconstruction impure – by grafting purity onto it.

Challenging what she sees as Derrida's unjustifiably revisionist treatment of Marx's writing, Spivak problematically suggests that the true
sense of Marx's writing can be discovered. Not only does this entail
recuperating textuality as an archive of enlightening texts – a recupera-
tion that Spivak contests elsewhere – it also suggests that the ideas
offered by Marxism provide *the* paradigm for perceiving exactly how
postcoloniality and global culture operate. No longer is it the case for
her that cultural power is confronted most effectively by transdisciplin-
ary and transtheoretical work; instead, it is Marxism that steps in
where other cultural theory fails. The critical feedback that is generated
by this surprisingly non- (perhaps even anti-) deconstructive manoeuvre is one that threatens to overwhelm Spivak's status as theorist of
postcoloniality, and it begs at least two questions. If Marx's theory of
absolute surplus-value offers an accurate method for analysing and
understanding the position of women workers in relation to capital's
transnationality, does it therefore allow us to hear the muted voice of
the subaltern? Alternatively, if – as Spivak herself submits – a deconstructive mode of conceptual invention is needed in order to loosen
the bonds of an exclusionary positivism, then is a more disconcerting
infringement of interpretive othodoxies and analytical propriety
needed in her response to Marx after Derrida?

6
'To Move Through – and Beyond – Theory': Bhabha, Hybridity, and Agency

Spivak, the previous chapter has shown, remains unconvinced that Derrida's challenge to ontopological thinking can provide cultural theory with a compelling critical strategy. For her, Derrida's critique of ontopology is symptomatic of his wider inattention to the particularities of postcoloniality: it implicitly monumentalizes all inscriptions of nationality and treats all insurgent narrative as a uniform repetition of hegemonic discourse. Offering a weak account of capital's transnationality, Derrida's concept also allows us to look only to dominant accounts of belonging, and it would therefore seem to leave all subaltern enunciation beyond theory's compass. Bhabha's *The Location of Culture* expresses similarly misgivings about Derrida's willingness to consider postcolonial resistance. Here, Bhabha certainly draws upon some of Derrida's ideas in order to challenge narratives of fixity that have been central to colonial conceptions of non-Western cultures; one of the debts that he declares most prominently is the one owed to Derrida's 'The Double Session', an essay that extends the notion of supplementarity to Plato's theory of mimesis in the *Philebus*. Plato here distinguishes between an original and its reproduction, but according to Derrida this dichotomy collapses because in the *Philebus* original truth (the source of painting) is itself described as a form of representation ('painting, that degenerate and somewhat superfluous expression, that supplementary frill of discursive thought, that ornament of *dianoia* and *logos*... functions as a pure indicator of the essence of a thought or discourse defined as image, representation, repetition'[1]). Just as *Of Grammatology* finds writing to be instrumental to the fulfilment of presence (rather than being the appurtenance or additive surplus described by Rousseau), so 'The Double Session' finds the unique origin (and its correlates, such as essence, interiority, ideality, and so on) as much as mimesis to be a discursive practice marked by repetition, dehiscence, and division. Following in the tracks of Derrida's reading of *Philebus*, Bhabha argues that similar dividing practices have persisted throughout European thinking, and can be seen in the discursive procedures that are intrinsic to colonial articulations. Characterizing the inconsistent and incoherent naming of the colonial subject in European narratives, Bhabha writes: 'The black is both savage... and yet the most obedient of servants...he is the embodiment of rampant sexuality and yet innocent as a child; he is mystical, primitive, simple-minded and yet the most worldly and accomplished liar and a manipulator of social forces'.[2] Clearly, in such cases, there is no racial quality that can be attributed to original essences; instead these examples reveal that colonial perceptions are formed around conflictual images and representations – copies of copies, disjointed and split assignations – rather than cohesively referential significations.

More than this, for Bhabha, the ambivalence of colonial discourse produces an inadvertent disclosure of its 'rules of recognition'[3] since it is only through the repetition and reinstitution of discriminatory codes that colonial authority is possible. It is only by repeatedly naming and renaming the difference of the colonized subject that the metropolitan centre can identify itself; emerging by a process of differentiation and disavowal, European colonial identity is possible only through its impossibility:

> The colonial signifier... is... an act of ambivalent signification, literally splitting the difference between the binary oppositions or polarities through which we think cultural difference.... Splitting constitutes an intricate strategy of defence and differentiation in the colonial discourse. Two contradictory and independent attitudes inhabit the *same place*.... Splitting is... a form of enunciatory, intellectual uncertainty and anxiety that stems from the fact that disavowal is not merely a principle of negation or elision; it is a strategy for articulating contradictory and coeval statements of belief.[4]

Bhabha therefore follows in the footsteps of Derrida's reading of Plato, insisting that the regime of truth that informs colonial authority is a neurotically heterological one; just as in the *Philebus* representation ceases to be a mere 'ornament of *dianoia* and *logos*' (and instead comes to exemplify the repetition at the heart of *logos*), so for Bhabha colonial enunciation find itself experiencing an internal agonic struggle, constantly splitting original coherence apart, and, as a result failing fully or finally to fix itself in terms of a stable identity.

At the same time, however, Spivak's assertion that Derrida's ideas need to be transposed (in order to consider the place of women in the 'Third World' or to identify teleiopoetic tendencies in the European foreclosure of the native informant) finds itself echoed in Bhabha's suggestion that Derridean concepts, tropes, and critical strategies can only lend themselves to the critique of colonial and postcolonial regimes if they are transported across theoretical terrains. In *The Location of Culture*, for instance, we read that Derrida's concern with the relationship between Western metaphysics and Eurocentrism extends only to a 'passing remark':

> My insistence on locating the postcolonial subject *within* the play of the subaltern instance of writing is an attempt to develop Derrida's passing remark that the history of the decentred subject and its dis-location of European metaphysics is concurrent with the emergence of the problematic of cultural difference within ethnology. He acknowledges the political nature of this moment but leaves it to us to specify it in the postcolonial text.[5]

What Bhabha suggests here is that the close relationship between decentred subjectivity and ethnological critiques of ethnocentrism is treated in an overly-concise manner in 'Structure, Sign, and Play in the Discourse of the Human Sciences' (the essay to which he refers in the above passage), and the consequence of this concision is that such 'remarks' by Derrida need to be taken up and extrapolated by post-colonial critics. Other readers of Derrida might point out that this sug-gestion can be sustained only if 'Structure, Sign, and Play' is detached from one of its companion pieces, *Of Grammatology*. Scrutinizing the ways in which ethnography's anti-ethnocentrism is informed by an ethnocentric reliance on the idea that the speaking subject is authen-tically self-present, *Of Grammatology* plays a significant role in postcolo-nial challenges to European (and Eurocentric) conceptions of identity – a role that is obviated in Bhabha's passing reference to Derrida's 'passing remark'. Furthermore, Bhabha here is not simply reluctant to explore in detail the deficiencies that he finds in Derrida's account of affinities between the critique of subjectivity and theories of cultural difference. The passage above also sees Bhabha modifying his initial claim (that Derrida fails to consider the full implications of the alliance between the subject's dislocation and notions of cultural difference) when he argues that Derrida's main shortcoming is a failure to provide postcolonial *literary* studies with particular textual readings. Bhabha's suggestion that a schism exists between two bodies of work – that Derrida's work stands apart from and does not adequately engage with postcoloniality – is therefore tempered by his subsequent assertion that Derrida is concerned solely with debates about, rather than representations of, cultural difference.

A similar hesitation can be found in Bhabha's reading of 'The Double Session', where he appears more forcefully to argue that Derrida's ideas require transposition from schematic questions of interpretation to a more situated interrogation of cultural power. Thus, understanding how English colonial authority has operated through an ambivalent 'double inscription' for Bhabha

> demands a departure from Derrida's objectives in 'The double session'; a turning away from the vicissitudes of interpretation in the mimetic act of reading to the question of the effects of power, the inscription of strategies of individuation and domination in those 'dividing practices' which construct the colonial space – a departure which is also a return to those moments in his essay when he acknowledges the problematic of 'presence' as a certain quality of discursive transparency.[6]

Again, Bhabha's phrasing is inflected with hyperbole. He might well 'turn away' from Derridean concerns (here, *Dissemination*'s notion of writing as the fissured inscription of reality-effects) in order to read discriminatory narratives of Englishness and colonial governance. But to see this as an deviation from, or a selective rebuttal of, Derrida's political limitations (rather than as the more specific detour into the literature of English colonialism) would be to arrive at hasty and ill-considered conclusions about the extent to which Bhabha extends and politicizes Derrida's ideas. Once again, the substance of Bhabha's criticism turns out to be that Derrida falls short of offering precise readings of particular enunciations and identifications – that he 'fails to decipher the specific and determinate system of address'[7] – rather than the implied and quite different charge that Derrida fails to consider the differential distribution of power and authority over colonial and postcolonial networks.

If Bhabha equivocates in his responses to the interpretive scope of 'Structure, Sign, and Play' and *Dissemination*, the same vacillation is not in evidence when he turns to the concept and critique of ontopology that is offered in *Specters of Marx*. This concept, Bhabha observes, concerns itself with how recent signifying practices – new information technologies and the emerging patterns of communication they engender – are not simply resulting in the contraction of global culture, nor initiating an unprecedented community of neighbourly nation-states. Instead, Derrida shows how these practices are provoking a crisis in established articulations of national belonging. 'Their particular force', Bhabha argues in 'Day by Day... With Frantz Fanon', 'lies in disturbing the assumptions of a *national ontopology*: that is, the specific binding of identity, location and locution/language that most commonly defines the particularity of an ethnic culture'.[8] A subtle shift in Bhabha's Derridean affiliations occurs here: unlike Derrida's earlier writings (which are seen to provide postcolonial theory with principles that become operative only when transposed), *Specters of Marx* is welcomed because it offers critical resources that directly confront 'postcolonial and post-cold war inter-ethnic unrest and xenophobic nationalisms that haunt the history of the present'.[9] And yet, this commitment notwithstanding, Bhabha believes that *Specters of Marx* still tends towards 'the spectral and the schematic':[10] although he begins here to situate Derrida on the fringes of postcolonial theory, he is not entirely convinced that the concept of ontopology is sufficiently far-reaching,[11] or that it pays attention to how determinations of national belonging are rewritten by those who find themselves cast into the outer reaches of the nation-state's identifications. According to Derrida's temporality, 'the displacement anterior to the imaginary of national rootedness counteracts the ontopological tendency';[12] this might well disrupt the myths of origin that form and inform national consciousness, but for Bhabha it is also necessary to explore the transformations that occur when migrant and minority groups repeat these narratives:

> I want to focus on the enunciative and identificatory processes in the narrow passage *in-between* the discourse of rootedness, and the 'affect' of displacement. My interest lies in the transient intersection where the claims to national culture within the ontopological tradition (the presentness of the past and the stability of cultural or ethnic ontology) are touched – and are translated by – the interruptive and interrogative memory of the displaced or displaceable populations that inhabit the national imaginary – be they migrants, minorities, refugees or the colonised.[13]

Superficially, then, Bhabha seeks to supplement Derrida's ideas, but without turning postcolonial theory into a substitution for deconstruction; at the very least, the idiom he assumes when setting out to broaden deconstructive thinking is less recriminatory than the one adopted by Spivak. If, for Spivak, Derrida's weakness lies in his refusal to address capital's systemic structuration, or a failure to consider international voices in the emergence of global culture, then, for Bhabha, Derrida's deficiency lies merely in a disinclination to read the literature of colonial and postcolonial governance. As Bart Moore-Gilbert observes, 'Bhabha calls for the habitual attention of deconstruction to dissemination and *différance* to be reconfigured, so that it is focused... on how signification is affected by particular sites and contexts of enunciation and address, more specifically those pertaining to the peculiar conditions of (neo-)colonialism'.[14] Scratch this surface, however, and comparable misgivings become evident. Like Spivak (and echoing the claim, made by commentators like Parry and Ahmad, that postcolonial theory politicizes deconstruction's understanding of culture), Bhabha implies that transitional work is needed in order to force deconstruction to overcome its reluctance to enter debates about colonialism and postcoloniality. And just as Spivak finds minority voices beyond the scope of Derrida's analysis of ontopology, so Bhabha too suggests that Derrida is not interested in how minority voices disrupt cultural taxonomy or trouble entrenched inscriptions of the nation.

Hybridity and discrimination

When Bhabha declares in the above passage that he wants 'to focus on the enunciative and identificatory processes in the narrow passage in-between the discourse of rootedness, and the "affect" of displacement', he restates his commitment to issues and concepts that have persistently (though not necessarily consistently) informed his work. Focusing on the interstices that depolarize the separation of foundational monoliths ('the discourse of rootedness') from those who are repressed and dominated ('the "affect" of displacement') is certainly a primary concern for Bhabha. But this focus does not mean that Bhabha has returned fully to the notion of colonial mimicry that is often associated with his earlier essays, or that he has entirely abandoned the concept of cultural hybridity towards which many of *The Location of Culture's* main arguments gravitate.

Hybridity remains important to Bhabha because it allows him both to challenge hegemonic conceptions of cultural identity and to question tendencies in postcolonial theory to perceive strict and unyielding divisions between a metropolitan centre and a colonial periphery; these divisions for him treat the centre as unilaterally possessing

power, and see the marginalized as inert, dispossessed, and disarticulated. For Bhabha this fixed and essentializing dichotomy – partly
derived, he suggests, from a misreading of Said's *Orientalism*[15] – is
inadequate to the task of understanding the complex and overlapping
relationships that shape both the internal and the external contours of
the nation; instead of treating cultural identity in terms of static, rigid,
Manichean dichotomies, or in terms of indigenous ethnicities and
enduring native cultures, postcolonial theory can begin to expose the
displacing effects that are produced by, and return to haunt, colonialism's discriminating sensibility.

Bhabha sees this notion of hybridity as one developing out of and
extending Fanon's account of the psychological effects that French
colonialism produces in colonized Antilleans.[16] Traumatized by the
recognition that the white colonizer does not share his self-image,
the 'black man', Fanon argues, finds himself burdened by a state of
'corporeal malediction':[17] refused entry in to the whiteness that is
vaunted by colonial culture, and yet unable to embrace the blackness
that he embodies, the colonized person exposes the contradictions of
assimilationist rhetoric by revealing the essentially split nature of
racial-epidermal identification. Crucially for Fanon, this psychic conflict needs to seen be as a defining characteristic of white colonizing, as
well as black colonized, identity: just as the colonized Antillean loses
the sense that he possesses an inherent selfhood (and instead comes to
see his subjectivity as something that is determined by the white gaze),
so the French colonizer implicitly depends on 'the black man' for his
superiority, civilization, and whiteness. Although parity by no means
exists in this asymmetrical distribution of power and privilege, what is
common to the populations that inhabit French colonialism is a breakdown in the distinction between two racial types; neither Antillean nor
French identity can be seen as having a separate or internal character,
and it is colonialism's hidden dialectic that leads Fanon to conclude
that 'The Negro is not. Any more than the white man'.[18] For Bhabha,
this dislocation of an entrenched racial sensibility both reveals the
ambivalence of colonial identifications, and (less explicitly) points to
the idea that cultural identities traverse and transform each other.
With Fanon's writing, Bhabha states in *The Location of Culture*, 'That
familiar alignment of colonial subjects – Black/White, Self/Other – is
disturbed with one brief pause and the traditional grounds of racial
identity are dispersed whenever they are found to rest in the narcissistic myths of negritude or white cultural supremacy'.[19] A similar sentiment is at work in 'Day by Day... With Frantz Fanon':

Fanon has introduced us to a dialectic disjunction between the discourse of historical, nationalist exemplarity and the temporality of the 'emergent everyday', in order to put before us, precisely, the possibility of thinking our way towards a national-internationalism (*trans*nationalism? globality?) without ethnic nationalisms.[20]

As well as these palpable resonances with Fanon's analysis of the French colonial psyche, Bhabha's theory of hybridity also echoes other psychoanalytically informed approaches to Western thought and culture, such as Deleuze and Guattari's claim that Europe schizophrenically produces disruptive energies, desires, and intensities in the moment that it codifies and regulates itself.[21] Within this irresolvable ambivalence, colonial axiomatics depend upon naming both the colonizer's sameness and the colonized's distinctiveness: 'The field of the "true"', Bhabha writes, 'emerges as a visible sign of authority only after the regulatory and displacing division of the true and the false'.[22] The structure of this regime of truth means that the gaze of the colonizer finds its authority in the same instant that it splits itself asunder, since the difference of the colonized becomes recognizable only if it is somehow decodable by the colonizer's conceptual economy. If (as the literature of colonization attests) the colonizer believes that such a decoding is possible – if it is possible for some form of recognition to take place – then the colonized's otherness is not and has never been an absolute one. Hybridity, Bhabha insists, is an essential feature of the colonizer's singularity because it is the disavowal of the colonized's strangeness that smoothes the passage of the colonizer's emergence; without this disavowal – without the dreaded act of taking the colonized's difference to heart – the colonizer could not exist. Demonstrating the decentring and damaging consequences of this uncanny constitution should, he argues, form an important part of counter-colonial activity:

Resistance is not necessarily an oppositional act of political intention, nor is it the simple negation or exclusion of the 'content' of another culture, as a difference once perceived. It is the effect of an ambivalence produced within the rules of recognition of dominating discourses as they articulate the signs of cultural difference and reimplicate them within the differential relations of colonial power – hierarchy, normalization, marginalization and so forth. For colonial domination is achieved through a process of disavowal that denies the chaos of its intervention as *Entsellung*, its dislocatory presence in order to preserve the authority of its identity in the teleological narratives of historical and political evolutionism.[23]

What is provocative about Bhabha's revision of hybridity, however, is that he does not just disclose an uneasy ambivalence at the heart of the cultural unity that colonizing nations assign to themselves. He also – perhaps more contentiously – claims that hybridity provides the colonized with a theoretical and political resource for fighting the rules of recognition that form the bulwark for colonial authority. Bhabha's words on this matter have become familiar, but they are worth citing again:

> Hybridity is the sign of the productivity of colonial power, its shifting forces and fixities; it is the name for the strategic reversal of the process of domination through disavowal (that is, the production of discriminatory identities that secure the 'pure' and original identity of authority). Hybridity is the revaluation of the assumption of colonial identity through the repetition of discriminatory identity effects. It displays the necessary deformation and displacement of all sites of discrimination and domination. It unsettles the mimetic or narcissistic demands of colonial power but reimplicates its identifications in strategies of subversion that turn the gaze of the discriminated back on the eye of power.[24]

An undisclosed hybridity thus lies at the core of colonial practices, and ambivalent strategies are repeatedly deployed in order to mask the fractures that are effected by this hybridity. But for Bhabha, disclosure of this impropriety does not end with the declaration that 'Hybridity is heresy',[25] with describing how colonial authority works against itself, or with showing how notions of cultural purity necessarily break down after being installed as part of a hegemonic order. Revealing that contamination is essential to a colonizing culture's self-identification, hybridity also provides the resources for an active challenge to colonial rhetoric by throwing into sharp relief both the exclusions that are central to determinations of national character and the unsustainability of those determinations. Just as the colonizing culture finds its narcissistic image dislodged during the act of self-enunciation, so the colonized culture loses its status as a wholly disavowable alien object: 'The paranoid threat from the hybrid is finally uncontainable', Bhabha argues, 'because it breaks down the symmetry and duality of self/other, inside/outside'.[26] Interrupting colonial binaries and lifting the veil on identity's permanent polymorphosity, hybridity brings about an illicit and exorbitant reversal of discrimination because the colonized subject can no longer be seen as the foreigner who is utterly disempowered, disenfranchised, or disarticulated by colonialism's authoritative discourse. As Nikos Papestergiadis explains, 'For the non-western to enter the West it must do so in the guise of the cultural hybrid: the non-western westerner'.[27]

Evidence of this reversal – if evidence is needed – arrives in *The Location of Culture* in the form of 'the English book' which finds itself estranged when transported to Delhi, as well as in those texts – *Heart of Darkness, A Passage to India, Casablanca, An Area of Darkness, Handsworth Songs, Beloved, The Satanic Verses*, 'Contemporary Sri Lankan theatre... the Anglo-Celtic canon of Australian literature and cinema... the South African novels of Richard Rive, Bessie Head, Nadine Gordimer, John Coetzee'[28] – which intervene in colonialism's differentiating logic and dramatize its contradictions.[29] Of course, Bhabha is not alone in arguing that these contradictions can mobilize interventionist practices. For Jean Bernabé, Patrick Chamoiseau, and Raphaël Confiant, authors of the manifesto *In Praise of Creoleness*, when the French seized parts of the Caribbean they triggered a disjunctive interaction of national and cultural traditions that now provides the basis for interrogating France's continuing authority as a colonial nation:

> Creoleness is the *interactional or transactional* aggregate of Caribbean, European, African, Asian, and Levantine cultural elements, united on the same soil by the yoke of history. For three centuries the islands and parts of continents affected by this phenomenon proved to be the real forges of a new humanity, where languages, races, religions, customs, ways of being from all over the world were brutally uprooted and transplanted in an environment where they had to reinvent life.... Creoleness is 'the world diffracted but recomposed', a maelstrom of signifieds in a single signifier: a Totality.[30]

As much as Bernabé, Chamoiseau, and Confiant turn to originary displacement in order to rewrite mythic and racially hierarchical codings of the social, others question whether such a focus on hybridity can provide postcolonial studies with a sufficiently rigorous or politically empowering approach to cultural power. Ania Loomba, for example, views Bhabha's emphasis on hybridity as geopolitically insensitive, arguing that it inclines towards a universalism that cannot see the particular configurations and consequences that are produced by colonial rule: 'ironically', she claims, 'the split, ambivalent, hybrid colonial

subject projected in his work is in fact curiously universal and homogeneous – that is to say, he could exist anywhere in the colonial world....
He is internally split and agonistic, but undifferentiated by gender,
class or location'.[31] The charge that Bhabha is inattentive to class and
gender is one repeatedly made by his critics, and because these issues
are not at the forefront of his writing, it would seem that he is happy
to leave this allegation hanging over his work.[32] However, to extend
this accusation, and to allege that he ignores spatial and geopolitical
distinctions, is a less plausible undertaking. Just as, for Kristeva,
Montesquieu's notion of an *esprit général* points to humanity's divided
unity, so Bhabha's notion of hybridity represents a return to universalist thought, one that also distorts universalism's synoptic gaze by refusing to view transcultural affinities as a recognizable totality. Again,
Bernabé, Chamoiseau, and Confiant are instructive here: although
Creoleness is a shared condition, they also insist that it directly contests the principles and propositions upon which universalist thinking
is based. 'There are', they maintain, 'a Caribbean Creoleness, a Guy-
anese Creoleness, a Brazilian Creoleness, an African Creoleness, an
Asian Creoleness and a Polynesian Creoleness, which are all very different from one another but which all result from the matrix of the same
historical maelstrom'.[33] In other words, the concept of Creoleness –
like Bhabha's concept of hybridity – intercalates the opening between
human uniformity and ethnic particularity, challenging the fixity that
is attributed to these categories in work on race and culture, and pointing to the overlapping and interlocking relationships that exist
between space, subjectivity, and the social.

'Between the Western sign and its colonial signification'

More convincing are the series of questions that Young finds provoked
by Bhabha's work. When Young's *Colonial Desire* examines notions of
hybridity and their place in racial theory, it is not concerned with
potential shortcomings in Bhabha's work: aside from charting the
dangers that result from the botanical and anthropological morphology
of the term 'hybridity' (a term which, he points out, has been variously
deployed to deny or denigrate inter-species and inter-racial reproduction – a morphology that Bhabha does not take into consideration),
Young's book does not dwell on theoretical problems or contradictions
that might operate in Bhabha's resignification of it. Instead, for Young,
the concept of hybridity allows Bhabha to challenge identitarian
assumptions about racial distinctions, and to force postcolonial studies

to confront 'the mechanics of the intricate processes of cultural contact, intrusion, fusion and disjunction'.[34] What is unclear about *Colonial Desire* is whether Young here embraces Bhabha's notion of hybridity, or whether he is disinclined to rehearse many of the questions that he raises in *White Mythologies*, one of the earliest and most influential assessments of the subtle tones in Bhabha's work.

White Mythologies identifies what it sees as a series of gaps, inconsistencies, and contradictions in the itinerant accenting that Bhabha's gives to several concepts, especially mimicry, ambivalence, and hybridity. The last of these encounters difficulties, Young claims, because Bhabha seems to be undecided about exactly which cultural forces produce hybridity, and about how hybridity might empower countercolonial resistance. For Young, this indecision does not simply mean that Bhabha fails to arrive at a definitive conclusion about the source and status of hybridity; rather, this indecision arises because Bhabha is unable satisfactorily to reconcile the incompatible interpretations of hybridity that he puts forward. Writing in respect of Bhabha's 1985 essay 'Sly Civility', Young asserts that 'Bhabha finds himself obliged to make two contradictory arguments: while there is always an ambivalence at work within the discourse of colonial instruction, that ambivalence is at the same time the effect of its hybridization in the colonial context'.[35] Ambivalence, Young claims here, is seen by Bhabha both as an inalienable trait of colonial discourse (a discourse which, in other words, corrupts itself at the moment of cultural intrusion and territorial conquest) and as the (often hidden) syntheses that are the outcome of appropriation by colonized populations. This confusion, Young goes on to argue, hints at national and ethnic singularities that can be aetiologically grasped: Bhabha's theory of hybridity

> suggests the articulation of two hitherto undifferentiated knowledges – implying a pure origination of both Western and native cultures which Bhabha's earlier point disallows. Perhaps this is one reason why the hybrid, which seemed of such crucial theoretical and political significance in 'Signs Taken for Wonders', subsequently drops silently out of sight.[36]

As Young observes, the notion that either Western or colonial knowledges have an indivisible and determinable foundation would undoubtedly go against many of the claims that Bhabha makes elsewhere about cultural hybridity. But evidence to support the assertion that such a contradiction exists is a little thin on the ground: although

'Sly Civility' is at times unclear about the source of colonial ambivalence, this lack of precision does not necessarily support the conclusion that Bhabha contradicts himself on the matter of cultural unity and its corruption by colonial hybridization. The passage to which Young refers, but does not quote, when describing this contradiction is one of the more ambiguous ones in Bhabha's essay. Responding to John Stuart Mill's belief that good government in India is tied to the documentation of colonial administration, Bhabha writes:

> Between the Western sign and its colonial signification there emerges a map of misreading that embarrasses the righteousness of recordation and its certainty of good government. It opens up a space of interpretation and misappropriation that inscribes an ambivalence at the very origins of colonial authority, indeed, within the originary documents of British colonial history itself.[37]

Colonial signification thus appears to render the Western sign ambivalent, and if Bhabha's account ended here it would indeed imply that the Western sign enjoys a pre- and non-ambivalent status. But Bhabha disputes the temporality that sees colonialism's pure enunciation as something that is corrupted by its ensuing (hybridizing) interpretation. Indeed, Bhabha repeatedly insists – in 'Sly Civility' and in his subsequent writing – that colonial discourse and its hybridization are inseparable and simultaneous: colonial articulations arrive only through the vexed disavowal of the colonized, so they are from the outset hybridized. Just as Bhabha reminds us that truth and falsity, on a more schematic plane, dialectically inform each other, so he situates colonial instruction as being both within and determined by the (hybridized) colonial context. Indeed, 'Signs Taken for Wonders' states precisely that this is the case: 'To see the cultural not as the *source* of conflict – *different* cultures – but as the *effect* of discriminatory practices – the production of cultural *differentiation* as signs of authority – changes its value and its rules of recognition'.[38] To speak of colonizer and colonized, then, is to speak of groups that belong to the same discursive system, but who are inscribed differently within that system;[39] this means that the ambivalence effected by the colonized is an extension of colonialism's hidden schizophrenia, as well as operating as a resistance to its manifest assumptions.

Bhabha's notion of hybridity may not rest on the contradiction that is identified by Young, but other questions are nevertheless triggered by Bhabha's account of ambivalence. His response to the notion of disjunctive repetition that Derrida advances in 'The Double Session', for example, would seem to imply that both the differential distribution of power and its rupture can be found in the West's earliest articulations. This line of reasoning raises the question of whether Western cultural apparatuses are intrinsically colonial, but this question is not one that Bhabha addresses. Implicit in much of *The Location of Culture* is the idea that colonialism should be seen as a specific moment in a general cultural continuum: that is, colonial texts merely re-enact the West's dividing practices under particular historical and political circumstances, and thus represent just one manifestation of a larger cultural anxiety. Colonialism, according to this view, would no longer be seen as a particular cultural moment that alters distributions of power, modifies concepts of cultural identity and difference, or transfigures Western history: instead, colonialism would embody a mode of thought and a form of cultural power that both precedes it and continues after the decline of Europe's high colonial period. The problem here is that the task of theory would no longer be to examine colonial rule and its consequences. Rather, theory should presumably shift its concerns away from a restricted focus on colonialism, and it should instead begin to interrogate the general structure that surrounds and produces colonial authority. If Bhabha does indeed leave this reading of his work open – if theory should place general questions of knowledge and identity over a more situated interrogation of colonial power – then his criticism of Derrida would consequently lose its force, since the disinclination to offer precise readings of colonial inscriptions could no longer be seen as a critical shortcoming.

Hybridity and multiculturalism

Implied in Young's claim that two contradictory arguments are at work in Bhabha's account of cultural hybridity and colonial ambivalence is the idea that this account could be lucid and should make sense – an idea that Young goes on to dismiss in the closing pages of his chapter. *White Mythologies* ends its reading of Bhabha by arguing that the contradictions in his work mimic and deride the contradictions of colonial authority: Bhabha's 'use of disparate and conflicting theories produces just that kind of ambivalence which subjects the reader to the effects of colonial discourse's disconcerting uncertainty'.[40] Inconsistency, Young comes to conclude, is critically provocative because it allows Bhabha's writing to take on a heteroglossic quality, to parade the disjunctive undecidability that is central to colonial discourse, and thus to depart from the principles of reasoned, unequivocal, and transparent exposition that have informed intellectual work in the West.

This conclusion not only mitigates the force of Young's initial criticism of Bhabha. It also blunts his assertion that the notion of hybridity disappears noiselessly from Bhabha's agenda, since the increasing complexity of Bhabha's work would no longer demand a corresponding departure from conceptual ambiguity. Certainly, Bhabha's work after the initial appearance of *White Mythologies* in 1990 corroborates Young's support for the plurivocal quality of Bhabha's thinking, but it also returns to the concept of hybridity in ways that Young neither anticipates in 1990 nor addresses in the 2004 edition of *White Mythologies*. Charting theory's departure at the *fin de siècle* from its earlier apocalyptic and neophilic tendencies, Bhabha's introduction to *The Location of Culture*, for example, argues that questions of culture and cultural identity now turn on ideas of interstitiality. 'What is theoretically innovative, and politically crucial', he insists,

> is the need to think beyond narratives of originary and initial subjectivities and to focus on those moments or processes that are produced in the articulation of cultural differences. These 'in-between' spaces provide the terrain for elaborating strategies of selfhood – singular or communal – that initiate new signs of identity, and innovative sites of collaboration, and contestation, in the act of defining the idea of society itself.[41]

Once again, hybridity – a condition between polarized identities – is here seen as an inalienable alienation that is essential to the West's self-identification, and this internal differentiation demands a divergence from notions of cultural singularity and national particularity. And Bhabha's introduction continues to maintain that hybridity can contribute to the counter-narratives that develop in resistance movements:

> cultures of a postcolonial *contra-modernity* may be contingent to modernity, discontinuous or in contention with it, resistant to its oppressive, assimilationist technologies; but they also deploy the cultural hybridity of their borderline conditions to 'translate', and therefore reinscribe, the social imaginary of both metropolis and modernity.[42]

The Location of Culture therefore continues to submit a theory of hybridity that refuses to draw a line between the colonizer's multiple identifications and the colonized's capacity for anti-colonial struggle.

Bhabha's 1998 essay 'Culture's In Between' extends this work by exploring how the attention to hybridity can help to dispute liberal notions of cultural diversity. Informing liberalism's celebration of diversity is, for Bhabha, a blindness to difference: rather than loosening the bonds that hold European concepts of nationality together, liberalism seeks only to admit excluded groups to a more generalized – but nonetheless European – understanding of national identity.[43] Importantly, liberalism attempts to perform this cultural manoeuvre by reducing history to a 'nondifferential concept of cultural time'.[44] In claiming this, Bhabha returns to his argument that colonial and postcolonial hierarchies have been maintained through the idea that different races and national cultures occupy disparate moments within the same temporality. 'Race, time and the revision of modernity', the closing chapter of *The Location of Culture*, examines this ambivalence in detail. Drawing upon Lacan's theory of the 'time-lag' (which exposes the gap that opens up when the subject renegotiates and represents itself within the symbolic order) and Fanon's vision of history as a zone where blackness is incorporated into white culture (through the construction of the black body as not yet white), Bhabha here claims that national identity defies final closure, that nationality is always a belated and contingent inscription, and that this disjunctive nonpresence can mobilize political intervention. Thus, resistance to colonial structures no longer takes the form of a 'separatist emphasis on simply elaborating an anti-imperialist or black nationalist tradition "in itself"'; instead, Bhabha points to work that attempts 'to interrupt the Western discourses of modernity through these displacing, interrogative subaltern or postslavery narratives and the critical-theoretical perspectives they engender'.[45]

'Culture's In Between' develops this questioning of modernity's temporality by challenging the pluralism that has, in recent years, become a prominent feature of political discourse, and in this respect Bhabha shares other theorists' misgivings about cultural diversity. Slavoj Žižek, for example, identifies two key problems in the liberal multiculturalism that now prevails in Europe. First, he argues, those advocating multiculturalism arrogate to themselves a tolerance that masks their racist and intolerant judgment that other cultures are racist. This displacement of aggressivity – from the civilized European onto the barbarian racist – for Žižek can be seen in the recent disavowal of 'the Balkan Other'. Europe finds its racist past unpalatable but, rather than acknowledging or confronting this traumatic history, Europe now simply declares its respect for other cultures – a respect that it seeks to confirm by righteously condemning the Balkans as a zone of ethnic intolerance. 'The Balkans are *Europe's ghost'*, Žižek writes, because around them there has developed a

> 'reflexive' Politically Correct racism: The multiculturalist perception of the Balkans as a terrain of ethnic horrors and intolerance, of primitive irrational warring passions, to be opposed to the post-nation-state liberal-democratic process of solving conflicts through rational negotiation, compromise and mutual respect.[46]

Europe once again attempts to determine its human (and humanitarian) virtues by establishing others' brutality and inhumanity, and this is one critical shortcoming that lies hidden in the notion of an inclusive and respectful transculturalism. The second problem, for Žižek, concerns the way in which questions of ethnicity and globalization have taken centre stage in both popular political discourse and recent cultural theory. This preoccupation has resulted in a corresponding inattention to the issue of class subordination: many of those who, in an earlier critical idiom, might have fallen into the category of 'worker' are now treated by cultural theory exclusively as part of an immigrant body. This critical shift means that 'the *class* problematic of workers' exploitation is transformed into the *multiculturalist* problematic of the "intolerance of Otherness"'.[47] Since it is concerned to protect the rights of immigrants only insofar as they form an ethnic minority, what liberal multiculturalism fails to offer is a sense of how migrant labour is the expression of capitalism's recent transnational desires. To counter liberal multiculturalism's benevolent appeal for inter-ethnic respect, Žižek proposes a radical intolerance:

> confronted with ethnic hatred and violence, one should thoroughly reject the standard multiculturalist idea that, against ethnic intolerance, one should learn to respect and live with the Otherness of the Other, to develop a tolerance for different lifestyles, and so on – the way to fight ethnic *hatred* effectively is not through its immediate counterpart, ethnic tolerance; on the contrary, what we need is *even more hatred*, but proper political hatred: hatred directed at the common *political* enemy.[48]

Bhabha is similarly unconvinced that liberal theories of ethnic diversity recognize minority groups in the way that they assume, and for him too multiculturalism can only acquire its progressive character through the disavowal of cultures that are seen to be barbaric and brutal. But for Bhabha cultural theory also needs to confront how multiculturalist thinking strangely renders minor groups both visible and invisible. Liberal notions of diversity not only subject different cultural groups to a uniform understanding identity (and thus render the specificity of minority groups invisible), they also – contradictorily – turn the minority subject into a hyper-visible alien. As Henry Giroux explains, 'conservative and liberal discourses that conflate multiculturalism with the imperatives of a "common culture" generally suppress any attempts to call into question the norm of whiteness as an ethnic category that secures its dominance by appearing to be invisible'.[49] Other cultures' differences vanish when humanity's universality is asserted, then, but at the same time liberalism finds itself constantly declaring that minority groups belong to this universal norm. This dual treatment of difference allows majoritarian culture to remain beyond critical reflection, since the nation is treated as an invisible given that emerges from the shadows and assumes its identity only when it responds to those seen as foreigners.

Exemplifying this process of humanitarian subjection for Bhabha is the colonial temporality that persists in multiculturalist thinking: even though it acknowledges the uneven distribution of power between cultures, liberal notions of diversity also rely on a sense of universal contemporaneity.

> It is not that liberalism does not recognize racial or sexual discrimination – it has been in the forefront of those struggles. But there is a recurrent problem with its notion of equality: liberalism contains a nondifferential concept of cultural time. At the point at which liberal discourse attempts to normalize cultural difference, to turn the presumption of equal cultural respect into the recognition of *equal cultural worth*, it does not recognize the disjunctive, 'borderline' temporalities of partial, minority cultures. The sharing of equality is genuinely intended, but only so long as we start from historically congruent space.[50]

Bhabha's insistence that nationality constantly slides away from determinable identification – that it can, at best, be described as an impure interstitiality – troubles this normative benevolence. Bhabha's critical agenda here includes exposing the unspoken and invisible status of the 'we' that informs liberal notions of European culture. But he goes further by questioning liberalism's assumption that nationality is the local expression of an indivisible and innate human character. In doing so, he develops the notion of hybridity that is explored in *The Location of Culture*: rather than just offering this concept as a foil to colonialism's discriminating essentialisms or as a rejoinder to the Manichean thinking that persists in postcolonial studies, 'Culture's In Between' underlines the mismatch between poststructuralism's regard for culture's differentiated constitution – an originary hybridization that precludes determination of a national ontology[51] – and pluralist celebrations of a consensual diversity. 'Borderline negotiations of cultural difference', he maintains, 'often violate liberalism's deep commitment to representing cultural diversity as plural choice'.[52] What liberalism's normative benevolence cannot conceive is that the incorporation of minority groups and populations into an otherwise unaltered tradition would not result in their sudden emancipation. Against such thinking, Bhabha maintains that cultural difference can only be perceived if there is a corresponding departure from the system of recognition that treats minorities as those who need to exhibit their contemporaneity with a universal present. Again operating as both a constitutive uncertainty and the ground for interventionist strategies, hybridity remains at the forefront of Bhabha's concerns because it allows cultural theory to disclose and act upon the discriminating – colonial – temporality that operates in liberal theories of multicultural diversity.

'Though unrepresentable in itself...'[53]

Bhabha's recent writings emphasize the continuing importance of hybridity, but they also restate and underline his commitment to the idea that theories of cultural change require a concept of agency. Indeed, a recent essay by John Kraniauskas reminds us that if hybridity can be seen as the source for resistant activity, then this concept necessarily triggers questions about cultural praxis. In Bhabha's work, he writes,

What emerges is an attempt to think an alternative temporality to established grand narratives, not from the point of view of their crisis as established by conventional postmodernist critique but their putting into question, their interruption from the point of view of a counter-modernity or, more specifically, a *post-colonial agency*.[54]

The idea that a different form of agency operates in postcolonial translations of hegemonic discourse is one to which Bhabha frequently returns. Indeed, the subject's capacity for subversive action is so important to him that it needs to be seen – along with hybridity, colonial ambivalence, postcolonial mimicry, and disjunctive temporalities – as one of the many conceptual centres from which his reading of cultural power and minority insurgence unfolds.

According to Bhabha, agency is to be located not in the willed actions of a purposive individual: *The Location of Culture* argues that the subject is not a deliberative and intending individual which knows itself, moves freely in the world, and is the source and guarantor of meaning. But Bhabha also disputes the kind of elementary determinism that regards the subject's ontology as one cohesively shaped and entirely constrained by social structures or biological characteristics; rather, just as nations lack the self-originating autonomy that is often attributed to them, so the subject's identity is, he maintains, formed by differentiating and disjunctive processes. 'The subject', he writes in 'On Cultural Choice', 'is a strategy of authorization and differentiation that produces an anteriority before the beginning, and a futurity beyond the end, where the present is the time of decision and choice, at once deliberative and disjunctive, at once survival and sovereignty'.[55] This notion of agency hangs on the contingency and undecidability that stems from the subject's multiple constitution, and when developing this notion he turns to the dramatic rethinking of the self that is staged by a range of thinkers, including Althusser, Arendt, Bakhtin, Barthes, Benjamin, Derrida, and Fanon.

Of particular importance to Bhabha's theory of agency is Lacan's work on the place of language in the formation of the subject. For Lacan, structuralist readings of the signifier/signified relationship rethink language as an unmotivated system of rules, and urge us to cast off the illusion that the signifier is burdened by an irredeemable debt to the signified. But although structuralism provokes a turning away from the assumption that language possesses a referential quality, Lacan argues that it fails to consider how this rethinking might impact upon the speaking subject's sovereignty, and that this approach mistakenly finds linear order in language's metaphoricity. Thus, Lacan makes the now rudimentary assertion that the subject's emergence in language results in the death, as much as the birth, of the self as it is commonly conceived: 'the subject, too, if he can appear to be the slave of language is all the more so of a discourse in the universal moment in which his place is already inscribed at birth, if only by virtue of his proper name'.[56]

To this assertion Lacan adds the further claim that language's deracination reveals it to be an unreliable and unstable apparatus, rather than an ordered communicative system. The process of differentiation that is so central to Saussure's account of the formation of meaning becomes radicalized in Lacan's model: here, the spaces that open up between signifiers – the gaps and fissures that are forged by differentiation – make language fail at the very moment that communication becomes possible. These interruptions for Lacan represent unconscious desires that continuously boil over and spill into rational discourse, and it is against these ruptures that the symbolic order constantly rages. Finding itself alienated in such a system – a system which continuously interpellates, resignifies, and over-determines the subject's sovereignty – the subject's response is not to see itself as an artifice, but to misrecognize itself as an autochthonous unity, attempting to re-centre itself with nostalgic phantasies of a recoverable wholeness. Since this recentring is always split, however, the subject can never find a coherent narrative with which to shape and fix itself; rather, it is 'the self's radical ex-centricity to itself with which man is confronted'.[57] What language offers, Lacan argues, is the opportunity to replace '*one word for another*',[58] to choose between competing narratives, and, ultimately, to depart from the imperative to use language as an unambiguously expressive discourse; signification discloses 'the possibility I have, precisely in so far as I have this language in common with other subjects, that is to say, in so far as it exists as a language, to use it in order to signify *something quite other* than what it says'.[59] In other words, the agency that Lacan promotes is a one in which the speaking 'I' renounces its claim to individuated and intentional utterance, where the self becomes a subject without subjectivity by following the wandering course of the errant signifier.

It is this subjectless subject that informs Bhabha's petition for a transfigured notion of agency: just as Lacan argues that meaning emerges precariously from processes of differentiation, so Bhabha states that cultural identity is displaced at the moment of its arrival. Rather than simply assuming that this displacement renders the subject inactive (since it is perpetually out of joint with itself), Bhabha submits that this dislocation allows the subject (however provisionally) to negotiate its relocation:

The individuation of the agent occurs in a moment of displacement. It is a pulsional incident, the split-second movement when the process of the subject's designation – its fixity – opens up beside it, uncannily *abseits*, a supplementary space of contingency. In this 'return' of the subject, thrown back across the distance of the signi-fied, outside the sentence, the agent emerges as a form of retro-activity, *Nachträglichkeit*. It is not agency as itself (transcendent, transparent) or in itself (unitary, organic, autonomous). As a result of its own splitting in the time-lag of signification, the moment of the subject's individuation emerges as an effect of the intersubjec-tive – as the return of the subject as agent.[60]

The capacity to act undoubtedly does exist for Bhabha, but he insists that the ideas of agent and action need to be fundamentally rethought. And he extends this notion of displaced identity to his understanding of counter-colonial and postcolonial resistance: resistance movements have been able to effect cultural transformations, but these move-ments' capacity to act needs to be seen neither as the expression of an authentic ethnicity, nor as an act of ventriloquism that unwittingly voices colonial authority by proxy. For Derrida, as Chapter 2 shows, the entry of the minority into a dominant language transfigures the system of dominance, and Bhabha similarly argues that resistance movements unlock the possibility for cultural intervention by expos-ing colonialism's disjunctive differentiations.

Crucially, just as Lacan's excentric 'I' departs from sense, so Bhabha's agent is one who is irreducible to predicative signification ('The *who* of agency bears no mimetic immediacy or adequacy of representation'[61]) and moves beyond theory:

This 'beyond theory' is itself a liminal form of signification that creates a space for the contingent, indeterminate articulation of social 'experience' that is particularly important for envisaging emergent cultural identities. But it is a representation of 'experience' without the transparent reality of empiricism and outside the inten-tional mastery of the 'author'. Nevertheless, it is a representation of social experience as the contingency of history – the indeterminacy that makes subversion and revision possible – that is profoundly concerned with questions of cultural 'authorization'.[62]

'Beyond theory' here does not signify theory's exteriority. Theory, he argues, already inhabits the 'beyond' of analysis or hypothesis because it does not just explain, reveal, or reflect on an independent and observable reality that lies outside of thought. Rather, theory moves beyond theory as it is often conceived – theory as an explanatory system or pure thematization – because it is always a form of practice, one shaping the reality it represents. Approaching theory in this way, as 'not quite experience, not yet concept; part dream, part analysis; neither signifier nor signified', as an 'intermediate space between theory and practice',[63] for Bhabha allows the subjectless subject to consider culture's contingent and discordant hybridity, but in a discourse that itself provokes the collapse of predicative signification. To illustrate this inescapably elusive concept, Bhabha turns to Barthes' idea (formulated while 'Half-asleep on his banquette in a bar'[64] in Tangiers) of a language that can signify otherwise. Barthes writes:

> [T]hrough me passed words, syntagms, bits of formulae and no sentence formed, as though that were the law of such a language. This speech at once very cultural and very savage, was above all lexical, sporadic; it set up in me, through its apparent flow, a definitive discontinuity: this non-sentence was in no way something that could not have acceded to the sentence, that might have been before the sentence; it was: what is... *outside the sentence.*[65]

Some readers of *The Pleasure of the Text* might find Morocco romanticized in this account,[66] but for Bhabha Barthes is not another tourist who yet again proclaims the mysteries of the East or indulges himself in a mythification of the Orient. Rather than being the site of an exotic pre-history or the locus for an intuitive encounter with primitive inscrutability, the Tangiers of Barthes' account reveals a crisis in 'the semiotic project' of 'enumerating all the languages within earshot'[67] and induces him to seek a departure from a European coding of theory. This loosening of pedagogy and monolingualism – this waking reverie that drifts from sense, this space in-between – is the aperture in the apparatus that provides the subject with an agency without subjectivity. 'It opens up a narrative strategy for the emergence and negotiation of those agencies of the marginal, minority, subaltern, or diasporic that incite us to move through – and beyond – theory', Bhabha writes.[68]

The West?

Redefining agency in this way, Bhabha attempts to steer a course through the concepts that tend to dominate debates about political action and anti-colonial resistance. Often, these debates inexorably replay the same arguments, with the participants perpetually frozen into two irreconcilable camps. Marshalled on one side, according to recurring characterizations of theory, are those who believe that subordinated populations possess the faculty to comprehend culture's complexity, and have the will to engage in effective – oppositional – action. Ranged on the other side of this tableau are the celebrants of simulacra, those who flaunt identity's radical indeterminacy and, as a consequence, leave subaltern groups without a secure footing from which to launch counter-cultural insurgence. As this book has argued, reasonably straightforward divisions between a naive counter-culturalism and an irresponsible poststructuralism turn out, upon closer inspection, to be neither reasonable nor straightforward. Certainly, Derrida, Deleuze and Guattari, Kristeva, and Spivak are not easily accommodated within such a dichotomy, and Bhabha's work plainly shows that any division between postcolonial theory (as a politically sensitive and committed mode of inquiry) and poststructuralist theory (as a decontextualized ludicism that declares the world to be a pure fiction) is an unhelpful and unsustainable one. Indeed, in Bhabha's work, poststructuralism and postcolonial theory inform each other as much as they expose each other's potential shortcomings, and its response to Derrida typifies this equivocating bricolage. By rethinking agency in the way that he does, Bhabha rejects the adversarial distinction between grounded and ungrounded subjectivity, and he argues for a form of intervention that neither begins in voluntarism nor ends in the infinite dispersion of the subject's capacity for resistance. Rather, his focus lies with the shifting and transitional processes of differentiation that shape and reshape identities. Sidestepping the 'wasting argument' between essentialists and anti-essentialists, Bhabha insists that there is

> a far more significant contemporary question about *where* the 'subject' of difference lies: Is the moment of differentiation internal to the history of a culture and integral to its communal existence? Or, are cultural differences to be read as borderline, liminal 'effects', signs of identification produced in those translational movements in which minorities negotiate their rights and representations?[69]

Bhabha's attempts to alter the terms of this debate do not, however, always convince his critics. Moore-Gilbert's *Postcolonial Theory: Contexts, Practices, Politics* draws attention to a series of political limitations that, for it, hamper Bhabha's notion of agency. Thus, Moore-Gilbert questions whether 'psychological guerrilla warfare' is as successful in effecting social and cultural transformations as Bhabha believes it to be, and he extends the now familiar charge of textualism in Derrida's work to Bhabha's emphasis on 'the semiotic as the prime site of post-colonial resistance'.[70] This emphasis means that theory can construe postcoloniality only as a response to the dominant, only as an act of writing back, but such a view for Moore-Gilbert 'depends upon the continuing authority of the dominant for its operation and consequently risks reconstituting that dominant'.[71] For Moore-Gilbert these problems derive in part from Bhabha's failure satisfactorily to navigate a route through two theoretical models that remain at the forefront of postcolonial theory, namely Fanon's later work on resistance as an expression of the individual's sovereignty and Said's suggestion that subaltern groups wholly derive their identity (and, hence, their intentionality) from Western discursive systems.

These problems also arise, according to *Postcolonial Theory*, from Bhabha's reliance on Lacanian thought. Interestingly, however, when Moore-Gilbert questions Bhabha's debt to Lacan, he does so by focusing not on 'the agency of the letter' – the unruly signifier that ruptures meaning and leaves the subject without the capacity for deliberative action – but on Lacan's theory of mimicry. According to this intellectual genealogy, Bhabha's debt to Lacan is a problematic one: when Lacan explains his understanding of psychic mimicry he does so by describing equivalent acts in insects (where one insect simulates another in order to protect itself), and this diversion means that Lacan evades the question of whether the subject's mimicry can be conscious or controlled; in contrast, Bhabha's focus on anti-colonial resistance demands a coherent account of whether insurgent mimesis is a willed act, or is purely the outcome of unconscious processes. Thus, Moore-Gilbert states, 'Bhabha fails to clarify the degree to which the various kinds of resistance which he describes are in fact "transitive" or "intransitive", active or passive'.[72] One response to this objection might point out that it diverts critical attention away from Bhabha's claim that processes of differentiation are central to – and thus interrupt – identification: for Bhabha to state whether modes of resistance are transitive or intransitive would mean falling back on either one of the Fanonian or Saidean models that he is so keen to revise. Bhabha's post-Lacanian transformation of the individual into the subjectless subject means that the forms of resistance he describes emerge from the subaltern's multiple and mobile constitution. 'Agency requires a grounding but it does not require a totalization of those grounds', he maintains, 'it requires movement and maneuver but it does not require temporality of continuity or accumulation; it requires direction and contingent closure, but not teleology and holism'.[73] Irreducible to either disempowerment or activism, this nomadic heteronomy instead signifies a series of interventions that see cultural identity as the site for critical negotiation.

For Moore-Gilbert, Bhabha's reluctance to confront this unresolved lacuna in Lacan's work points to a larger inattention to the question of whether psychoanalytic concepts and methods can appropriately contribute to colonial and postcolonial theory. Work on the psycho-analysis-postcolonialism intersection flourished during the 1980s and 1990s, and Moore-Gilbert adds his own voice to those who express reservations about construing colonialism and postcoloniality as prim-arily psychic states, declaring that in Bhabha's work 'There is no conception of psychoanalysis as a specifically *Western* narrative of knowledge which may have been complicit in the production of mod-ernity and, more particularly, modernity's Others'.[74] Moore-Gilbert identifies a significant issue here: problems do indeed exist in psycho-analytic work on race and cultural identity, and Bhabha certainly seems reluctant to consider whether psychoanalysis has a geocultural specificity, or to ask whether it is a recent manifestation of an older Orientalism.[75] However, two responses might be made to these allega-tions. First, as Elizabeth Roudinesco documents in the closing chapter of *Jacques Lacan: Outline of a Life, History of a System of Thought*, psycho-analysis has, during the period of Bhabha's writing, expanded beyond the West: while psychoanalysis has had little institutional support in those regions that are at the forefront of postcolonial studies (Africa, India, the Caribbean), interest in it has nevertheless grown in Latin America and Eastern Europe, and the appearance of number of profes-sional bodies and associations signals this development.[76]

Second, recent work by Derrida and Said has disputed the idea that psychoanalysis is a specifically Western system of thought. In *Archive Fever*, Derrida responds to Yosef Hayim Yerushalmi's *Freud's Moses* by exploring the idea that psychoanalysis is a distinctively Jewish science.[77] Although, as Derrida himself observes, this idea problematically replays the notion that Judaism possesses a singular and exclusive character, it does suggest that psychoanalysis might be a different kind of science, one that even – perhaps – contests principles and procedures that are at the heart of Western scientific inquiry. Said too finds Yerushalmi's book to be provocative, and in *Freud and the Non-European* he considers how Moses – an Egyptian – renders national identity uncertain in Freud's writing.

While recognizing that Freud's interest in non-European cultures extends little further than an 'ethnographic curiosity',[78] Said also finds Moses functioning in a way that is similar to Spivak's native informant. Thus, Moses founds Judaism, but is not – indeed, cannot be – straightforwardly Jewish: in *Moses and Monotheism* there are, Said maintains, deliberate and 'provocative reminders that Judaism's founder was a non-Jew, and that Judaism begins in the realm of Egyptian, non-Jewish monotheism'.[79] For both Derrida and Said, then, psychoanalysis may well operate as a European science, but buried within this insularity is a challenge to the idea that Europe is culturally self-contained, or that nationality can exist in itself. If this is the case – if for Derrida and Said the provenance of psychoanalytic theory cannot be reduced to a cultural singularity – then the accusation that Bhabha thinks colonialism, postcoloniality, and cultural difference in purely Western terms requires further scrutiny. Indeed, if national and cultural ambiguities reside at the heart of Freudian thought, then it would seem to provide Bhabha with an entirely fitting theoretical framework for understanding colonialism and postcoloniality.

  Bhabha's critics seek to identify a series of problems in his work, from claiming that a stylistic and methodological disorder – hyperlexia, mystification, interpretive distortion, critical opportunism – floods his writing, to asserting that he is interested primarily in European texts and relies too heavily on Western cultural theory. And these theoretical shortcomings are not only located in Bhabha's work, but are often levelled against Derrida, Deleuze and Guattari, Kristeva, and Spivak, as well as others associated with poststructuralism. Quite apart from suggesting that theorists should write in a neutral critical discourse – that they should tell the truth plainly – these responses also find the centres of colonial rule to be the places in which poststructuralism has emerged and been most enthusiastically embraced: poststructuralist theory, it is often claimed, is firmly planted in French, North American, and British soil, and the application of poststructuralism to conditions outside of the West is regularly treated as another instance of Western authoritarianism, another stage in colonial rule. Derrida, Deleuze and Guattari, Kristeva, Spivak, and Bhabha contest such a treatment of theory's geopolitical provenance. For them, the West does not exist in the way that it imagines: rather than possessing the essential and exceptional character that it attributes to itself, the West is, they maintain, built on an originary hybridity that it would prefer to keep concealed. It is this buried and traumatic history that allows theory to contest the West's attempts to establish both its own internal character and the foreigner's difference.

A new cosmopolitanism

Poststructuralism and postcolonial theory do not arrive at a cohesive explanatory model that conclusively explains the relationship between cultural power and the nation-state, but they do overlap and converge in ways that provoke a dramatic rethinking of colonialism's legacy, of postcolonial resistance, and of globalization's impact on national identity. Discourses of identification and disavowal remain fundamental to both Western and non-Western centrisms: certainly, the European Union's efforts to establish an increasingly integrated community are founded on the idea of a regional character that is not possessed by other continental groups; more generally, the supposition of nation-states' inherent and distinctive identity continues to function as an a priori principle in international law. Similarly, colonial and formerly-colonial nations seek to reclaim some semblance of national unity by inhibiting the acute erosion of national frontiers – an erosion that is, of course, one consequence of colonial expansion – and, in more recent years, Western nations have been attempting to shore up national security, to tighten border controls, and to limit the flow of migrant workers and asylum seekers. One of the most crucial contributions made by the theorists considered here is the argument that these discourses of national identity need to be challenged, but without ignoring the singularities of geographical, cultural, and historical location, or routinely dismissing national identification as a uniform operation of phobic differentiation. For them, national identity – even nationalism – is not necessarily an affliction that needs to be overcome in order to arrive at an even distribution of wealth and power: different groups engage in, respond to, and rewrite Western narratives of national specificity and, as a result, cultural theory needs to develop more complex analyses of the nation-state and its transfiguration. For Derrida, Deleuze and Guattari, Kristeva, Spivak, and Bhabha, such complex analyses begin with a reading of the intricate and intimate relationship between power and resistance, with the idea that national identity is a double-coding that is both necessary and impossible, and with the sense that the nation-state's intrinsic character is denied in the very moment that it is asserted.

As much these theorists trace both the discriminatory and the counter-cultural effects of national identification, they also dispute the widely-held belief that we now inhabit an increasingly democratic global community. Recent commentaries on nationality, postcoloniality, and globalization often suggest that the theorists considered here rejoice in the indeterminate, revel in the dispersal of former identities, and celebrate the loss of old certainties. Their work has, for some, embraced the transitionality and the transnationality of the new global citizen, and it has declared the demise of the nation-state as a mode of social and political association; the borders of the nation-state have, apparently, crumbled and, rising from the dust, is a new borderless community in which we can become whatever we want because we no longer know who we are. This book has argued that Derrida, Deleuze and Guattari, Kristeva, Spivak, and Bhabha are emphatically not, as some of their critics maintain, the advocates of such a globalist or post-national utopianism. Indeed, they vigorously contest the narratives of multiculturalism, transnationalism, and globalization that have recently arrived and declare the world to be one in which ideas, information, and populations now flow freely. Rather than endorse such a vague internationalism, these theorists develop compelling critiques of the new liberal pluralist hegemony's faith in the freedom that trans-national movements, institutions, and networks seemingly enable – a new hegemony that sits nervously alongside and against an ongoing investment in the nation-state. What they contest, in other words, are recurring and rudimentary claims that national identity either remains fully operative or is in terminal decline; what they provide instead is a series of conceptual vocabularies for thinking the singular, complex, vacillating, and uneven processes of identification and differentiation which not only shape the West's earliest articulations, but which also persist in accounts of emerging transnational and transcultural movements.

The inoperative community, the new International, nomadism, non-nationalitarianism, hospitality, the native informant, hybridity, and postcolonial agency are just some of the concepts that form part of these alternative vocabularies. As this book has shown, however, these concepts do not come together to form a new and enduring lexicon that provides us with the resources for finally understanding the state of the nation-state. Certainly, they effect a profound deracination of the contemporary nation-state, and they challenge the recent equation of globalization with multiculturalism, consensual transnationalism, and participatory democracy. In this sense, the cosmopolitanism that emerges in the work of Derrida, Deleuze and Guattari, Kristeva, Spivak, and Bhabha is a new cosmopolitanism because it provokes a rethinking of current transfrontier movements while also refusing to view these movements as a departure from national authenticity. More importantly, though, the concepts developed by these theorists can effect a significant conceptual shift: rather than subjecting the nation-state's transitions to an unvarying analysis, they instead initiate alternative – geographically, historically, and culturally responsive – ways to rethink national identity as cosmopolitan difference. Always between a post-structuralism and a postcolonial theory that do not really exist, these concepts never allow themselves to become monumentalized as a pro-grammatic theory, systematic method, or critical school. Revealing the precarious contingency of thought and signification that must be embraced by cultural critique, these concepts unfold alongside and against each other in a restless sequence of theoretical invention and intervention that allows theory to think national identity in other terms.

Notes

Chapter 1 Cosmopolitan Locations

1 Terry Eagleton , 'In the Gaudy Supermarket' *London Review of Books*, 21: 10 (1999), 6.
2 Eagleton, 'In the Gaudy Supermarket', 6.
3 Eagleton, 'In the Gaudy Supermarket', 6.
4 Benita Parry, 'Problems in Current Theories of Colonial Discourse', *Oxford Literary Review*, 9: 1–2 (1987), 27–58; Aijaz Ahmad, *In Theory: Classes, Nations, Literatures* (London: Verso, 1992); Arif Dirlik, *The Postcolonial Aura: Third World Criticism in the Age of Global Capitalism* (Boulder: Westview Press, 1992); Bart Moore-Gilbert, 'Spivak and Bhabha', in Henry Schwarz & Sangeeta Ray, (eds), *A Companion to Postcolonial Studies* (Oxford: Blackwell, 2000), pp. 451–66.
5 James Clifford, 'Taking Identity Politics Seriously: "The Contradictory Stony Ground…"', in Paul Gilroy, Lawrence Grossberg & Angela McRobbie (eds), *Without Guarantees: In Honour of Stuart Hall* (London: Verso, 2000), p. 99.
6 Friedrich Nietzsche, *Beyond Good and Evil: Prelude to a Philosophy of the Future*, trans. Marion Faber (Oxford: Oxford University Press, 1998), pp. 143–5.
7 Friedrich Nietzsche, *Twilight of the Idols/The Anti-Christ*, trans. R.J. Hollingdale (London: Penguin, 1990), p. 112.
8 Nietzsche, *Beyond Good and Evil*, p. 133.
9 Friedrich Nietzsche, 'Philosophy in the Tragic Age of the Greeks', trans. M.A. Mügge, in Geoffrey Clive (ed.), *The Philosophy of Nietzsche* (New York: Mentor, 1965), p. 154
10 Nietzsche, *Human, All Too Human*, trans. Marion Faber & Stephen Lehmann (London: Penguin, 1994), p. 228.
11 Nietzsche, *Human, All Too Human*, p. 228.
12 Alan D. Schrift, 'Nietzsche's Contest: Nietzsche and the Culture Wars', in Alan D. Schrift (ed.), *Why Nietzsche Still? Reflections on Drama, Culture, and Politics* (Berkeley: University of California Press, 2000), p. 193.
13 Edmund Husserl, 'Philosophy and the Crisis of European Man', in *Phenomenology and the Crisis of Philosophy*, trans. Quentin Lauer (New York: Harper Torchbooks, 1965), p. 155.
14 Husserl, 'Philosophy and the Crisis of European Man', p. 159.
15 Husserl, 'Philosophy and the Crisis of European Man', p. 157.
16 Husserl, 'Philosophy and the Crisis of European Man', p. 155.
17 Husserl, 'Philosophy and the Crisis of European Man', p. 178.
18 Husserl, 'Philosophy and the Crisis of European Man', p. 157.
19 Husserl, 'Philosophy and the Crisis of European Man', p. 156.
20 Martin Heidegger, 'The Origin of the Work of Art', in *Poetry, Language, Thought*, trans. Albert Hofstadter (London: Harper & Row, 1971), p. 39.
21 Heidegger, 'The Origin of the Work of Art', p. 76.
22 Heidegger, 'The Origin of the Work of Art', p. 23.

23   Heidegger, 'The Origin of the Work of Art', p. 62.
24   Heidegger, 'The Origin of the Work of Art', p. 75.
25   Timothy Clark, *Martin Heidegger* (London: Routledge, 2002), p. 133.
26   Heidegger, 'The Origin of the Work of Art', p. 51.
27   Heidegger, 'The Origin of the Work of Art', p. 74.
28   Leslie Paul Thiele, *Timely Meditations: Martin Heidegger and Postmodern Politics* (Princeton: Princeton University Press, 1995), pp. 148–9.
29   Jacques Derrida, *Of Grammatology*, trans. Gayatri Chakravorty Spivak (Baltimore: The Johns Hopkins University Press, 1976), p. 102.
30   Derrida, *Of Grammatology*, p. 121.
31   Robert J.C. Young, 'Race and Language in the Two Saussures', in Peter Osborne and Stella Sandford (eds), *Philosophies of Race and Ethnicity* (London: Continuum, 2002), p. 78.
32   Emmanuel Levinas, *Totality and Infinity: An Essay on Exteriority*, trans. Alphonso Lingis (Pittsburgh: Duquesne University Press, 1969), p. 281.
33   Homi K. Bhabha, 'Editor's Introduction: Minority Maneuvers and Unsettled Negotiations', *Critical Inquiry* 23: 3 (1997), pp. 438–9.
34   Emmanuel Levinas, *Difficult Freedom: Essays on Judaism*, trans. Seán Hand (London: Athlone, 1990), p. 164.
35   For a further discussion of Levinas's treatment of nationality, of the status of Israel in his work, and the relationship between his 'philosophical' and 'confessional' writings, see Philip Leonard, 'A Supreme Heteronomy?: *Arche* and Topology in *Difficult Freedom*' in Seán Hand (ed.), *Facing the Other: Ethics in the Work of Emmanuel Levinas* (Richmond: Curzon, 1996), pp. 121–39.
36   Roger Scruton, *England: An Elegy* (London: Pimlico, 2001), pp. 16–17.
37   Scruton, *England*, p. 76.
38   Scruton, *England*, p. 77.
39   Scruton, *England*, p. 6.
40   Jürgen Habermas, *The Postnational Constellation: Political Essays*, trans. Max Pensky (London: Polity, 2001), p. 64.
41   Habermas, *The Postnational Constellation*, p. 76.
42   Habermas, *The Postnational Constellation*, pp. 81–2.
43   Habermas, *The Postnational Constellation*, p. 74.
44   Habermas, *The Postnational Constellation*, p. 74

Chapter 2   'Before, Across, and Beyond': Derrida, Without National Community

1   Jean-Luc Nancy, *The Inoperative Community*, trans. Peter Connor, Lisa Garbus, Michael Holland, and Simona Sawney (Minneapolis: University of Minnesota Press, 1991), p. 9.
2   Nancy, *The Inoperative Community*, p. 11.
3   Nancy, *The Inoperative Community*, p. xl.
4   Nancy, *The Inoperative Community*, pp. 25–6.
5   Jacques Derrida, 'Différance', in *Margins of Philosophy*, trans. Alan Bass (Hemel Hempstead: Harvester Wheatsheaf, 1982), p. 17.
6   Jacques Derrida, 'The Ends of Man', in *Margins of Philosophy*, p. 114.
7   Derrida, 'The Ends of Man', p. 113.

8   Derrida, 'The Ends of Man', pp. 113–14.
9   Derrida, 'The Ends of Man', p. 114.
10 Derrida, 'The Ends of Man', p. 115.
11 Derrida, 'The Ends of Man', p. 116.
12 Derrida, 'The Ends of Man', pp. 117–19.
13 Derrida, *Of Grammatology*, p. 225.
14 Derrida, *Of Grammatology*, p. 261.
15 Derrida, *Of Grammatology*, pp. 267–8.
16 See also Derrida's comments on 'the ceremony of the *pharmakos*': 'The city's body *proper* thus reconstitutes its unity, closes around the security of its inner courts, gives back to itself the word that links it with itself from the confines of the agora, by violently excluding from its territory the representative of an external threat or aggression. That representative represents the otherness of the evil that comes to affect or infect the inside by unpredictably breaking into it. Yet the representative of the outside is nonetheless *constituted*, regularly granted its place by the community, chosen, kept, fed, etc., in the very heart of the inside. These parasites were as a matter of course domesticated by the living organism that housed them at its expense'. Jacques Derrida, 'Plato's Pharmacy', in *Dissemination*, trans. Barbara Johnson (Chicago: University of Chicago Press, 1981), p. 133.
17 Jacques Derrida, *Specters of Marx: The State of the Debt, the Work of Mourning and the New International*, trans. Peggy Kamuf (London: Routledge, 1994), p. 15.
18 Derrida, *Specters of Marx*, p. 141.
19 Derrida cannot stress this second point enough: on one page alone he asserts that Marx's languages are marked by a 'non-contemporaneity with themselves', an 'irreducible heterogeneity', an 'internal untranslatability' and a 'lack of system'. Derrida, *Specters of Marx*, p. 33. This is a point, moreover, that Derrida has made in earlier publications. Much of Derrida's work is concerned with challenging the notion of textual totality ('the unity of the Book') and in *Positions* this challenge is directly related to Marx's work: 'No more than I have dealt with Saussure's text, or Freud's or any other, as homogeneous volumes... I do not find the texts of Marx, Engels or Lenin homogeneous critiques'. Jacques Derrida, *Positions*, trans. Alan Bass (Chicago: University of Chicago Press, 1982), pp. 63–4.
20 Derrida, *Specters of Marx*, p. 32.
21 Derrida, *Specters of Marx*, p. 31.
22 Derrida, *Specters of Marx*, p. 57.
23 Derrida, *Specters of Marx*, p. 51.
24 Derrida, *Specters of Marx*, p. 70.
25 Derrida, *Specters of Marx*, p. 68.
26 Derrida, *Specters of Marx*, p. 88.
27 Derrida, *Specters of Marx*, p. 142.
28 This decalogue or table of spectres (*Gespensts*) consists of: 1) 'the supreme being, God'; 2) 'Being or essence'; 3) 'the vanity of the world'; 4) 'good and evil beings'; 5) 'Being and its realm'; 6) 'beings, therefore'; 7) 'the Man-God'; 8) 'man'; 9) 'the spirit of the people'; 10) 'Everything'. Derrida, *Specters of Marx*, pp. 143–6.
29 Derrida, *Specters of Marx*, p. 45.

30 Derrida, *Specters of Marx*, p. 10.
31 Derrida, *Specters of Marx*, p. 75.
32 Daniel T. McGee, 'Post-Marxism: The Opiate of the Intellectuals', *Modern Language Quarterly*, 58: 2 (1997), p. 225.
33 Mark Lilla, 'The Politics of Jacques Derrida', *The New York Review of Books*, 45:11 (25/6/1998), p. 40.
34 Lilla, 'The Politics of Jacques Derrida', p. 41
35 Fredric Jameson, 'Marx's Purloined Letter', *New Left Review*, 209 (1995), p. 80.
36 Derrida, *Specters of Marx*, p. 88.
37 Derrida, *Specters of Marx*, pp. 88–90.
38 Derrida, *Specters of Marx*, p. 168.
39 Derrida, *Specters of Marx*, p. 168.
40 Richard Beardsworth *Derrida & the Political* (London: Routledge, 1996), p. xii. Cf. also Elizabeth Grosz's comments on Derrida and the political: 'That his works are seen as apolitical, as lacking a mode of political address, is surely the result of a certain freezing up of politics and an attempt to constrain it to well-known or predetermined forms, the very forms whose naturalness or stability is contested through deconstruction', Elizabeth Grosz, 'The Time of Violence: Deconstruction and Value', *College Literature*, 26: 1 (1999), p. 9.
41 Beardsworth, *Derrida & the Political*, p. 51.
42 Beardsworth, *Derrida & the Political*, p. 51.
43 Beardsworth, *Derrida & the Political*, p. 51.
44 Francis Fukuyama, *The End of History and the Last Man*, (London: Hamish Hamilton, 1992), p. 202.
45 Derrida, *Specters of Marx*, pp. 60–1.
46 Fukuyama, *The End of History and the Last Man*, p. 203. Cited in Derrida, *Specters of Marx*, p. 61.
47 Interestingly, later chapters of *The End of History and the Last Man* consider some of the constitutive tensions that Fukuyama finds operating between liberal democracy and community. Tocqueville and Hegel stress the 'importance of associational life as a focus for the public spiritedness in the modern state', Fukuyama, *The End of History and the Last Man* p. 322. But for Fukuyama it is the modern state that *threatens* community life: liberty and equality – the founding principles of liberal democracy – attenuate community associations by turning morality into contractual self-interest (rather than rooting it in deontological foundations) and by opposing exclusionary practices. 'In a situation in which all moralisms and religious fanaticisms are discouraged in the interest of tolerance', Fukuyama writes, 'in an intellectual climate that weakens the possibility of belief in any *one* doctrine because of an overriding commitment to be open to *all* the world's beliefs and "value systems", it should not be surprising that the strength of community life has declined in America. This decline has occurred not *despite* liberal principles, but *because* of them. This suggests that no fundamental strengthening of community life will be possible unless individuals give back certain of their rights to communities and accept the return of certain historical forms of intolerance. Liberal democracies, in other words, are not self-sufficient: the community life on which they depend must ulti-

mately come from a source different from liberalism itself'. Fukuyama, *The End of History and the Last Man*, p. 326. It is perhaps disappointing, given that Derrida is so concerned with the idea of community, that *Specters of Marx* does not discuss Fukuyama's consideration of this tension.

48 Theresa Brennan, 'Why the Time Is Out of Joint: Marx's Political Economy of the Subject', *South Atlantic Quarterly*, 97: 2 (1998), p. 263.
49 Jameson, 'Marx's Purloined Letter', p. 107.
50 Robert Young, *White Mythologies: Writing History and the West* 2nd edn (London: Routledge, 2004), p. 51.
51 Jacques Derrida, *'Geschlecht* II: Heidegger's Hand', trans. John P. Leavey Jr., in John Sallis (ed.), *Deconstruction and Philosophy: The Texts of Jacques Derrida* (Chicago: University of Chicago Press, 1987), p. 193.
52 Jacques Derrida & Christie V. McDonald, 'Choreographies', trans. Christie V. McDonald, *Diacritics*, 12: 2 (1982), p. 69.
53 Jacques Derrida, *The Other Heading: Reflections on Today's Europe*, trans. Pascale-Anne Brault & Michael B. Nass (Bloomington: Indiana University Press, 1992), p. 20.
54 Jacques Derrida, 'Racism's Last Word', trans. Peggy Kamuf, *Critical Inquiry*, 12: 1 (1985), p. 292.
55 Derrida, 'Racism's Last Word', p. 294.
56 Derrida, 'Racism's Last Word', p. 297.
57 Jacques Derrida, *Politics of Friendship*, trans. George Collins (London: Verso, 1997), p. 4.
58 Derrida, *Politics of Friendship*, p. 22.
59 Derrida, *Politics of Friendship*, p. viii.
60 Derrida, *Politics of Friendship*, p. 91.
61 Derrida, *Specters of Marx*, p. xix.
62 Derrida, *Specters of Marx*, p. 169.
63 Derrida, *Specters of Marx*, p. 38.
64 Derrida, *Specters of Marx*, p. 85.
65 Rey Chow, 'On Chineseness as a Theoretical Problem', in Osborne and Sandford (eds), *Philosophies of Race and Ethnicity*, (London: Continuum, 2002) p. 149.
66 Pheng Cheah, 'Spectral Nationality: The Living On [*sur–vie*] of the Postcolonial Nation in Neocolonial Globalization', *boundary 2*, 26: 3 (1999), p. 251.
67 See Gayatri Chakravorty Spivak, *A Critique of Postcolonial Reason: Toward a History of the Vanishing Present* (Cambridge, Mass.: Harvard University Press, 1999), pp. 17–18, n. 29, and Robert Young, *Postcolonialism: An Historical Introduction* (Oxford: Blackwell, 2001), p. 419ff.
68 Hélène Cixous, 'My Algeriance', trans. Eric Prenowitz, in *Stigmata: Escaping Texts* (London: Routledge, 1998), p. 155.
69 Hélène Cixous, *Portrait of Jacques Derrida as a Young Jewish Saint*, trans. Beverley Bie Brahic (New York: Columbia University Press, 2004), p. 86.
70 'Unlike "globalization" or *Globalisierung*, *mondialisation* marks a reference to this notion of a world that is charged with a great deal of semantic history, notably a Christian history: the world... is neither the universe, nor the earth, nor the terrestrial globe, nor the cosmos'. Jacques Derrida,

'The University Without Condition', in *Without Alibi*, trans. Peggy Kamuf (Stanford: Stanford University Press, 2002), p. 224.

71   Jacques Derrida, *The Monolingualism of the Other; or, The Prosthesis of Origin*, trans. Patrick Mensah (Stanford: Stanford University Press, 1998), p. 64. It (almost) goes without saying that the 'homo' in 'monoculturalist homo-hegemony' is not given a homogenous or homoeostatic treatment throughout Derrida's work. For alternatives, see *Glas* trans. John P. Leavey Jr. & Richard Rand (Lincoln: University of Nebraska Press, 1986) and 'Circumfession', in Geoffrey Bennington & Jacques Derrida, *Jacques Derrida*, trans. Geoffrey Bennington (Chicago: University of Chicago Press, 1993).

72   Herman Rapaport, *Later Derrida: Reading the Recent Work* (London: Routledge, 2003), p. 40.

73   Derrida, *The Monolingualism of the Other*, p. 30.

74   Derrida, *The Monolingualism of the Other*, p. 31.

75   Derrida, *The Monolingualism of the Other*, p. 7.

76   Jacques Derrida, 'Provocation: Forewords', in *Without Alibi*, p. xxviii.

77   Derrida, *The Monolingualism of the Other*, p. 25.

78   Geoffrey Bennington, 'Double Tonguing: Derrida's Monolingualism', *Tympanum* 4 (2000), http://www.usc.edu/dept/comp-lit/tympanum/4/bennington.html. Accessed 22/1/04.

79   *Of Grammatology* provides one example that suggests that he has not experienced a sudden revelation about nationalism's transformative capacity. Anticipating his later reading of national identity's radical impropriety, *Of Grammatology* responds to Lévi-Strauss's ethnocentric anti-ethnocentrism by observing that for those in the nineteenth century 'it is undoubtedly true that the progress of formal legality, the struggle against illiteracy, and the like, could have functioned as a mystifying force and an instrument consolidating the power of a class or state whose formal-universal significance was confiscated by a particular empirical force'. Derrida, *Of Grammatology*, p. 132. *Of Grammatology* is also anxious to point out that if Lévi-Strauss's argument is followed *in extenso*, then 'it must also be concluded that nonexploitation, liberty and the like "go hand in hand"... with illiteracy'. Derrida, *Of Grammatology*, p. 132. To this Derrida says 'I shall not belabor the obvious', though it is perhaps a pity that he finds the consequences of this extrapolation to be entirely self-evident. It is, of course, 'obvious' that there are problems with the idea that non-exploitation and liberty pre-date the violent introduction of European writing systems to non-European cultures. However, as much as pre-colonial speech (treated as illiteracy by ethnography and anthropology) guarantees neither non-exploitation nor liberty, *Of Grammatology* here suggests that the introduction of European writing systems to non-European cultures opens Western significations to transformative repetition and resignification, to resistant rearticulation and disarticulation; European representations, then, are dislocated or 'confiscated by a particular empirical force' at the very moment that they consolidate 'the power of a class or state'.

80   Frantz Fanon, *The Wretched of the Earth*, trans. Constance Farrington (Harmondsworth: Penguin, 1967), p. 187.

81 Neil Lazarus, 'Disavowing decolonization: Fanon, nationalism, and the question of representation in postcolonial theory', in Anthony C. Alessandrini, ed., *Frantz Fanon: Critical Perspectives* (London: Routledge, 1999), p. 170.
82 Derrida, *The Monolingualism of the Other*, p. 69.
83 Derrida, *The Monolingualism of the Other*, p. 66.
84 Jacques Derrida, 'Autoimmunity: Real and Symbolic Suicides – A Dialogue with Jacques Derrida', in Giovanna Borradori, *Philosophy in a Time of Terror: Dialogues with Jürgen Habermas and Jacques Derrida* (Chicago: University of Chicago Press, 2003), p. 103.
85 Derrida, 'Autoimmunity', p. 92.
86 Derrida, 'Autoimmunity', p. 93.
87 Derrida, 'Autoimmunity', p. 95.
88 Derrida, 'Autoimmunity', p. 94.
89 Derrida, 'Autoimmunity', p. 113.
90 Derrida's apparent willingness to speculate on what 'the good' might constitute, as well as the apocalyptic tone that is implicit his remarks on 'bin Laden's' tactics, could leave some of his readers feeling a little baffled. See, for example, Ivan Callus and Stefan Herbrechter, 'The Latecoming of the Posthuman, Or, Why "We" Do the Apocalypse Differently, "Now"', *Reconstruction* 4: 3 (2004), pp. 19–20. Available at http://www.reconstruction.ws, accessed 19/8/04.
91 Derrida's subsequent denunciation of 'bin Laden's' fanaticism is remarkable, however. 'In this unleashing of violence without name', he writes, 'if I had to take one of the two sides and choose in a binary situation, well, I would. Despite my very strong reservations about the American, indeed European, political posture, about the "international antiterrorist" coalition, despite all the de facto betrayals, all the failures to live up to democracy, international law, and the very international institutions that the states of this "coalition" themselves founded and supported up to a certain point, I would take the side of the camp that, in principle, by right of law, leaves a perspective open to perfectibility in the name of the "political", democracy, international law, international institutions, and so on'. Derrida, 'Autoimmunity', pp. 113–14. Responses to this startlingly blunt declaration might ask Derrida why he feels such a compulsion to choose one of two positions, or why he is prepared here to reduce views on the current world order to two opposing positions, rather than unsettle the easy adversarialism that characterizes contemporary political discourse.
92 Derrida, 'Autoimmunity', p. 123.
93 Derrida, 'Autoimmunity', p. 131.
94 Derrida, 'Autoimmunity', p. 133.
95 Simon Critchley, *Ethics–Politics–Subjectivity: Essays on Derrida, Levinas, and Contemporary French Thought* (London: Verso, 1999), p. 280.
96 Derrida, *Politics of Friendship*, p. 42.
97 Derrida, *The Monolingualism of the Other*, p. 105.
98 Derrida, *Specters of Marx*, pp. 65–6.
99 Derrida, *Specters of Marx*, p. 90.
100 Derrida, *Specters of Marx*, p. 82.
101 Derrida, 'Autoimmunity', p. 133.
102 Derrida, 'The University Without Condition', p. 234.

Chapter 3   'New Concepts for Unknown Lands': Deleuze & Guattari's Non-Nationalitarianisms

1 Michael Hardt and Antonio Negri, *Empire* (Cambridge, Mass.: Harvard University Press, 2000), p. 166.

2 Hardt and Negri, *Empire*, p. 357.

3 Hardt and Negri, *Empire*, p. 28.

4 Hardt and Negri, *Empire*, p. 28.

5 Finding sense in Deleuze and Guattari's work is neither possible nor desirable. Their work is based on an idea of 'writing as a flow, not a code' (Gilles Deleuze, 'Letter to a Harsh Critic', in *Negotiations 1972–1990*, trans. Martin Joughin (New York: Columbia University Press, 1995), p. 7); it is a 'philosophy of the phantasm' (Michel Foucault, 'Theatrum Philosophicum', in *Language, Counter-Memory, Practice: Selected Essays and Interviews*, ed. Donald F. Bouchard, trans. Donald F. Bouchard and Sherry Simon (Oxford: Blackwell, 1977), p. 169), with a 'luminously schematic' style (Fredric Jameson, 'Marxism and Dualism in Deleuze', *South Atlantic Quarterly*, 96: 3 (1997), p. 395); and 'Reduction or extrapolation of their content from this process is almost impossible' (Tom Conley, 'From Multiplicities to Folds: On Style and Form in Deleuze', *South Atlantic Quarterly*, 96: 3 (1997), p. 637). Attempting to avoid a reduction of their ideas, this chapter will focus on particular moments in their collaborative works: '1227: Treatise on Nomadology: – The War Machine' and '7000B.C: Apparatus of Capture' in *A Thousand Plateaus: Capitalism and Schizophrenia*, trans. Brian Massumi (London: Athlone, 1988), 'What is a Minor Literature? in *Kafka: Toward a Minor Literature*, trans. Dana Polan (Minneapolis: University of Minnesota Press, 1986), and 'Geophilosophy' in *What is Philosophy?*, trans. Graham Burchell and Hugh Tomlinson (London: Verso, 1994).

6 Gregory J. Seignworth and J. Macgregor Wise, 'Introduction: Deleuze and Guattari in Cultural Studies', *Cultural Studies* 14: 2 (2000), p. 139.

7 Gilles Deleuze and Félix Guattari, *Anti-Oedipus: Capitalism and Schizophrenia*, trans. Robert Hurley, Mark Seem and Helen R. Lane (London: Athlone, 1984), p. 136.

8 Deleuze and Guattari, *Anti-Oedipus*, p. 151.

9 Deleuze and Guattari, *A Thousand Plateaus*, p. 427.

10 Deleuze and Guattari, *A Thousand Plateaus*, p. 427.

11 Deleuze and Guattari, *A Thousand Plateaus*, p. 428.

12 On Deleuze and Guattari and deconstruction, see Ronald Bogue, *Deleuze and Guattari*, (London: Routledge, 1989), pp. 156–9; Bruce Baugh, 'Making the Difference: Deleuze's Difference and Derrida's Différance', *Social Semiotics* 7: 2 (1997), pp. 127–46. Following Deleuze's death in 1995, Derrida declares his feeling that 'Deleuze undoubtedly still remains, despite so many dissimilarities, the one among all those of my "generation" to whom I have always judged myself to be the closest. I never felt the slightest "objection" arising in me, not even potentially, against any of his works, even if I happened to grumble a bit about one or another of the propositions found in *Anti-Oedipus*... or perhaps about the idea that philosophy consists in "creating" concepts', Jacques Derrida, 'I'm Going to Have to Wander All Alone', trans. Leonard Lawlor, *Philosophy Today*, 42: 1 (1998), p. 3.

13 Deleuze and Guattari, *A Thousand Plateaus*, p. 429.
14 Deleuze and Guattari, *A Thousand Plateaus*, p. 508.
15 Deleuze and Guattari, *A Thousand Plateaus*, p. 509.
16 Deleuze and Guattari, *A Thousand Plateaus*, p. 360.
17 Deleuze and Guattari, *A Thousand Plateaus*, p. 436.
18 Deleuze and Guattari, *A Thousand Plateaus*, pp. 436–7.
19 Deleuze and Guattari, *A Thousand Plateaus*, p. 464.
20 Deleuze and Guattari, *A Thousand Plateaus*, p. 468.
21 Deleuze and Guattari, *A Thousand Plateaus*, p. 465.
22 Deleuze and Guattari, *A Thousand Plateaus*, p. 465, emphasis added.
23 Deleuze and Guattari, *A Thousand Plateaus*, p. 453.
24 Deleuze and Guattari, *A Thousand Plateaus*, p. 454.
25 Deleuze and Guattari, *A Thousand Plateaus*, p. 456.
26 Arjun Appadurai, *Modernity at Large: Cultural Dimensions of Globalization* (Minneapolis: University of Minnesota Press, 1996), p. 37.
27 Manuel de Landa, *A Thousand Years of Non-Linear History* (New York: Zone, 1997), p. 262.
28 de Landa, *A Thousand Years*, p. 260.
29 Gyan Prakash, 'Who's Afraid of Postcoloniality?', *Social Text*, 14: 4 (1996), p. 199.
30 Timothy W. Luke, 'New Order or Neo-World Orders: Power, Politics and Ideology in Informationalizing Glocalities', in Mike Featherstone, Scott Lash and Roland Robertson (eds), *Global Modernities* (London: Sage, 1995), p. 99.
31 Deleuze and Guattari, *A Thousand Plateaus*, p. 380.
32 Deleuze and Guattari, *A Thousand Plateaus*, p. 381.
33 For some commentators, Deleuze and Guattari's characterization of nomadic disruption remains unconvincing. Christopher Miller, for example, recognizes that 'nomad thought' is 'one of the most compelling models of postidentitarian thinking available in the marketplace of theoretical ideas today'. Christopher Miller, *Nationalists and Nomads: Essays on Francophone African Literature and Culture* (Chicago: University of Chicago Press, 1998), p. 173. But he also argues that their reliance upon established anthropological sources allows 'a reading of Deleuze and Guattari's nomadology as representational and arborescent instead of free and rhizomorphous. If Deleuze and Guattari's nomad thought is in fact arborescent, if it is rooted in and follows from the practices of, for example, a violently representational, colonial ethnography while at the same time claiming to be anticolonial, antianthropological, and nonrepresentational, then it might have to be considered as one of the "pseudomultiplicities" that the authors abhor', Miller, *Nationalists and Nomads*, pp. 181–2.
34 Deleuze and Guattari, *A Thousand Plateaus*, p. 379.
35 Deleuze and Guattari, *A Thousand Plateaus*, p. 379.
36 Deleuze and Guattari, *A Thousand Plateaus*, p. 379.
37 Deleuze and Guattari, *A Thousand Plateaus*, p. 379.
38 Deleuze and Guattari, *A Thousand Plateaus*, p. 456.
39 Deleuze and Guattari, *Anti-Oedipus*, p. 202.
40 Deleuze and Guattari, *Anti-Oedipus*, p. 240.
41 Deleuze and Guattari, *Anti-Oedipus*, p. 240.
42 Deleuze and Guattari, *Anti-Oedipus*, p. 241.

43   Deleuze and Guattari, *A Thousand Plateaus*, pp. 4–5.
44   Deleuze and Guattari, *A Thousand Plateaus*, p. 5.
45   Deleuze and Guattari, *A Thousand Plateaus*, p. 5.
46   Deleuze and Guattari, *A Thousand Plateaus*, p. 5.
47   Deleuze and Guattari, *A Thousand Plateaus*, p. 5.
48   Deleuze and Guattari, *Kafka*, p. 22.
49   The notion of a 'major literature' is one that Deleuze appears to move away from in his own, later writing. In 'Literature and Life', for example, he states that all writing is in a process of becoming: 'Writing is a question of becoming, always incomplete, always in the midst of being formed', Gilles Deleuze, 'Literature and Life', in *Essays Critical and Clinical*, trans. Daniel W. Smith and Michael A. Greco (London: Verso, 1998), p. 1. He further claims, following Proust, that all writing effects a deterritorialization of linguistic order, a creation of a new vocabulary and a transformation of discursive nationality: literature 'brings about not only a decomposition or destruction of the maternal language, but also the invention of a new language within language… a foreign language cannot be hollowed out in one language without language as a whole being toppled or pushed to a limit'. Other forms of textual production do exist, though for Deleuze these cannot be called 'writing' or 'literature': 'among all those who make books, even among the mad, there are very few who can call themselves writers', Deleuze, 'Literature and Life', pp. 5–6.
50   Deleuze and Guattari, *Kafka*, p. 17.
51   Deleuze and Guattari, *Kafka*, p. 17.
52   Deleuze and Guattari, *Kafka*, p. 16.
53   Deleuze and Guattari, *Kafka*, p. 22.
54   Réda Bensmaia, 'On the Concept of Minor Literature From Kafka to Kateb Yacine', trans. Jennifer Curtiss Gage, in Constantin V. Boundas and Dorothea Olkowski, *Gilles Deleuze and the Theatre of Philosophy* (London: Routledge, 1994), p. 220.
55   Deleuze and Guattari, *Kafka*, p. 19.
56   Deleuze and Guattari, *Kafka*, p. 18.
57   Leela Gandhi, *Postcolonial Theory: A Critical Introduction* (Edinburgh: Edinburgh University Press, 1998), p. 84.
58   Gilles Deleuze and Claire Parnet, 'On the Superiority of Anglo-American Literature', in *Dialogues*, trans. Hugh Tomlinson and Barbara Habberjam (London: Athlone, 1987), p. 43.
59   Eugene W. Holland, 'Marx and Poststructuralist Philosophies of Difference', *South Atlantic Quarterly*, 96: 3 (1997), pp. 530–1.
60   Deleuze and Guattari, *Kafka*, p. 24.
61   Cf Bhabha: 'The conditions of minority discourse – "deterritoriality", political immediacy, collective value – do not answer the question of emergence-as-enunciation; for it is the performative act of enunciation – Deleuze and Guattari's list of metaphors of minority discourse, such as tearing away, vibrating with a new intensity, a ladder, a circuit – that fleshes out minority inscription as a mode of agency'. Homi Bhabha, 'Editor's Introduction: Minority Maneuvers and Unsettled Negotiations', *Critical Inquiry*, 23: 3 (1997), p. 441.
62   Deleuze and Guattari, *A Thousand Plateaus*, p. 469.
63   Deleuze and Guattari, *A Thousand Plateaus*, p. 470.

64 Deleuze and Guattari, *A Thousand Plateaus,* p. 470.
65 Alice A. Jardine, *Gynesis: Configurations of Woman and Modernity* (Ithaca: Cornell UP, 1985), p. 217.
66 Miller, *Nationalists and Nomads,* p. 192.
67 Rosi Braidotti, 'Toward a New Nomadism: Feminist Deleuzian Tracks; or, Metaphysics and Metabolism', in Boundas and Olkowski (eds), *Gilles Deleuze and the Theatre of Philosophy,* p. 169.
68 Braidotti, 'Toward a New Nomadism', p. 182.
69 Deleuze and Guattari, *A Thousand Plateaus,* p. 276, cited in Elizabeth Grosz, '"A Thousand Tiny Sexes": Feminism and Rhizomatics', in Boundas and Olkowski, *Gilles Deleuze and the Theatre of Philosophy,* p. 207.
70 Grosz, 'A Thousand Tiny Sexes', p. 194.
71 Gilles Deleuze and Claire Parnet, 'Many Politics', in *Dialogues,* p. 128.
72 Deleuze and Guattari, *A Thousand Plateaus,* p. 380.
73 Deleuze and Guattari, *What is Philosophy?,* p. 86.
74 Deleuze and Guattari, *What is Philosophy?,* p. 106
75 Deleuze and Guattari, *What is Philosophy?,* p. 108.
76 Deleuze and Guattari, *What is Philosophy?,* p. 93.
77 Friedrich Nietzsche, *The Will to Power,* trans. Walter Kaufmann and R.J. Hollingdale (New York: Vintage, 1967), p. 231.
78 Nietzsche, *The Will to Power,* p. 231.
79 Nietzsche, *The Will to Power,* p. 231.
80 Deleuze and Guattari, *What is Philosophy?,* p. 86.
81 Deleuze and Guattari, *What is Philosophy?,* p. 87.
82 Deleuze and Guattari, *What is Philosophy?,* p. 87.
83 Deleuze and Guattari, *What is Philosophy?,* p. 87.
84 Deleuze and Guattari, *What is Philosophy?,* pp. 87–8.
85 Deleuze and Guattari, *What is Philosophy?,* p. 89.
86 Deleuze and Guattari, *What is Philosophy?,* p. 90.
87 Deleuze and Guattari, *What is Philosophy?,* p. 93.
88 Deleuze and Guattari, *What is Philosophy?,* p. 93.
89 Deleuze and Guattari, *What is Philosophy?,* p. 94. John Ratchman offers an eloquent and detailed account of the concept in *The Deleuze Connections* (Cambridge, Mass.: MIT Press, 2000).
90 Deleuze and Guattari, *What is Philosophy?,* p. 95.
91 Deleuze and Guattari, *What is Philosophy?,* p. 94.
92 Deleuze and Guattari, *What is Philosophy?,* p. 95.
93 Deleuze and Guattari, *What is Philosophy?,* p. 109.
94 Deleuze and Guattari, *What is Philosophy?,* p. 93.
95 Deleuze and Guattari, *What is Philosophy?,* p. 109.
96 Deleuze and Guattari, *What is Philosophy?,* p. 88.
97 Deleuze and Guattari, *What is Philosophy?,* p. 97.
98 In this manner, Deleuze and Guattari bring together two issues – the birth of Europe and the emergence of capitalism – that concern Samir Amin: 'The myth of Greek ancestry performs an essential function in the Eurocentric construct. It is an emotional claim, artificially constructed in order to evade the real question – why did capitalism appear in Europe before it did elsewhere? – by replacing it instead, amidst a panoply of false answers, with the idea that the Greek heritage predisposed Europe to rationality. In this myth, Greece was the mother of rational philosophy,

while the "Orient" never succeeded in going beyond metaphysics'. Samir Amin, *Eurocentrism*, trans. Russell Moore (London: Zed Books, 1989), p. 91.
99   Deleuze and Guattari, *What is Philosophy?*, p. 10.
100 Deleuze and Guattari, *What is Philosophy?*, p. 225, n. 15.
101 Deleuze and Guattari, *What is Philosophy?*, p. 104.
102 Deleuze and Guattari, *What is Philosophy?*, p. 104.
103 Deleuze and Guattari, *What is Philosophy?*, p. 105.
104 Deleuze and Guattari, *What is Philosophy?*, p. 106.
105 Deleuze and Guattari, *What is Philosophy?*, p. 105.
106 Deleuze and Guattari, *What is Philosophy?*, p. 102.
107 Deleuze and Guattari, *What is Philosophy?*, p. 104.
108 Deleuze and Guattari, *What is Philosophy?*, p. 6.
109 Deleuze and Guattari, *What is Philosophy?*, p. 99.
110 Deleuze and Guattari, *What is Philosophy?*, p. 110.
111 What differentiates Deleuze and Guattari's work from that of Hardt and Negri is the recognition of the way in which conceptual invention is shaped by, as well as a critical response to, established systems of thought. Timothy Brennan asks: 'How does one borrow ideas without assuming their contextual resonances as first formulated in a system, regardless of whether such a system is summoned for contemporary use? Because Hardt and Negri ignore this logical difficulty, they have little choice but to revert to a *functional* relationship to the concepts they adduce. As such, their "new constellations" are rendered vulgarly pragmatic'. Timothy Brennan, 'The Empire's New Clothes', *Critical Inquiry*, 29: 2 (2003), p. 359.
112 Jean-Luc Nancy, 'The Deleuzian Fold of Thought', in Paul Patton (ed.), *Deleuze: A Critical Reader* (Oxford: Blackwell, 1996), pp. 110–11.
113 Gilles Deleuze, 'A Portrait of Foucault', in *Negotiations*, p. 103.

Chapter 4   'Atopic and Utopic': Kristeva's Strange Cosmopolitanism

1   Anna Smith, *Julia Kristeva: Readings of Exile and Estrangement* (Basingstoke: Macmillan, 1996), p. 11.
2   Julia Kristeva, 'Women's Time', trans. Alice Jardine and Harry Blake, in Toril Moi (ed.), *The Kristeva Reader* (Oxford: Blackwell, 1986), p. 189.
3   Kristeva, 'Women's Time', p. 190.
4   Kristeva, 'Women's Time', p. 188.
5   Julia Kristeva, *About Chinese Women*, trans. Anita Barrows (London: Marion Boyars, 1977), pp. 11–12.
6   Kristeva, *About Chinese Women*, p. 13.
7   Kristeva, *About Chinese Women*, p. 14.
8   Kristeva, *About Chinese Women*, p. 12.
9   Kristeva also pursues this rethinking in 'Europe Divided: Politics, Ethics, Religion', in *Crisis of the Subject*, trans. Susan Fairfield (New York: Other Press, 2000), pp. 111–62.
10   Julia Kristeva, *Nations Without Nationalism*, trans. Leon S. Roudiez (New York: Columbia University Press, 1993), p. 50.
11   Julia Kristeva, *Strangers to Ourselves*, trans. Leon S. Roudiez (London: Harvester Wheatsheaf, 1991), p. 127.
12   Kristeva, *Strangers to Ourselves*, p. 1.

13   Kristeva, *Strangers to Ourselves*, p. 192.
14   Kristeva, *Strangers to Ourselves*, p. 167.
15   Kristeva, *Nations Without Nationalism*, p. 57.
16   Kristeva, *Strangers to Ourselves*, p. 133.
17   Franz Neumann, 'Editor's Introduction', in Baron de Montesquieu, *The Spirit of the Laws*, trans. Thomas Nugent (New York: Hafner Press, 1949), p. xxiv.
18   Emile Durkheim, *Montesquieu and Rousseau: Forerunners of Sociology* (Michigan: Ann Arbor, 1965), p. 17.
19   Durkheim, *Montesquieu and Rousseau*, p. 21.
20   Louis Althusser, *Politics and History: Montesquieu, Rousseau, Hegel and Marx*, trans. Ben Brewster (London: NLB, 1972), p. 31.
21   Althusser, *Politics and History*, p. 47.
22   Montesquieu, *Spirit of the Laws*, p. 221.
23   Montesquieu, *Spirit of the Laws*, p. 293.
24   Kristeva, *Strangers to Ourselves*, p. 128.
25   Kristeva, *Strangers to Ourselves*, p. 129.
26   Kristeva, *Strangers to Ourselves*, p. 131.
27   Kristeva, *Nations Without Nationalism*, p. 32.
28   *Nations Without Nationalism* vacillates curiously between the idea that French thought can contribute to a reactivation of notions of national belonging, and the idea that it provides a superlative conceptual model that other cultures should embrace. Initially, she argues that 'In the face of a resurgence of the French national spirit, and without being aware of the difficulty of living in France as a foreigner, I nevertheless assert that there exists a French national idea that can make up the *optimal rendition* of the nation in the contemporary world'. Kristeva, *Nations Without Nationalism*, p. 39. Later, however, she remarks 'Far be it from me to suggest a model, much less the optimal national model. I shall merely turn to a line of reasoning that put its stamp on French political thought during the Enlightenment and attempt to draw from it a few lessons for the national problem today'. Kristeva, *Nations Without Nationalism*, p. 53.
29   Kristeva, *Nations Without Nationalism*, p. 57.
30   Kristeva, *Nations Without Nationalism*, p. 32.
31   Kristeva, *Nations Without Nationalism*, p. 35.
32   Kristeva, *Nations Without Nationalism*, p. 50. *Nations Without Nationalism* constantly stresses this developmental approach to the Enlightenment idea of the nation: here maintains the importance 'not to reject the idea of the nation in a gesture of wilful universalism but to modulate its less repressive aspects' (Kristeva, *Nations Without Nationalism*, p. 7), and she speaks of 'the optimal version of integration and of the nation today' (Kristeva, *Nations Without Nationalism*, p. 31), the imperative to 'raise the concept of the nation beyond its regressive, exclusionary, integrative, or racial pitfalls (Kristeva, *Nations Without Nationalism*, p. 59).
33   Pheng Cheah, 'Introduction Part II: The Cosmopolitical – Today', in Pheng Cheah and Bruce Robbins (eds), *Cosmopolitics: Thinking and Feeling Beyond the Nation* (Minneapolis: University of Minnesota Press, 1998), p. 38.
34   Sheldon Pollock, Homi K. Bhabha, Carol A. Breckenridge, and Dipesh Chakrabarty, 'Cosmopolitanisms', *Public Culture* 12: 3 (2000), p. 581.
35   Pollock et al., 'Cosmopolitanisms', p. 582.

36   Homi Bhabha and John Comaroff, 'Speaking of Postcoloniality, in the Continuous Present: A Conversation', in David Theo Goldberg and Ato Quayson (eds), *Relocating Postcolonialism* (Oxford: Blackwell, 2002), p. 24.
37   James Clifford, 'Mixed Feelings', in Cheah and Robbins (eds), *Cosmopolitics*, p. 364.
38   Clifford, 'Mixed Feelings', p. 365.
39   Kristeva, *Strangers to Ourselves*, p. 169.
40   Immanuel Kant, 'Perpetual Peace: A Philosophical Sketch', in Hans Reiss (ed.), *Kant: Political Writings*, trans. H.B. Nisbet (Cambridge: Cambridge University Press, 1991), p. 108.
41   Immanuel Kant, 'Idea for a Universal History with a Cosmopolitan Purpose', in Reiss (ed.) *Kant: Political Writings*, p. 52.
42   Kant, 'Idea for a Universal History', p. 52.
43   Kant, 'Perpetual Peace' p. 105
44   Kant, 'Idea for a Universal History', p. 44.
45   Kant, 'Idea for a Universal History', p. 44.
46   Kant, 'Idea for a Universal History', p. 46.
47   Kant, 'Idea for a Universal History', p. 47.
48   Kristeva, *Strangers to Ourselves*, pp. 171–3.
49   Kristeva, *Strangers to Ourselves*, p. 172.
50   Kant, 'Perpetual Peace', p. 106.
51   Cf. Walter D. Mignolo's claim that Kant's *Anthropology from a Pragmatic Point of View* fosters a wholly Eurocentric characterization of the human person: 'The fact that the "person" is Kant's beginning and reference point is already indicative of the presuppositions implied in the universal neutral imaginary that for him constitutes the person. Kant obviously was not thinking about the Amerindians, the Africans, or the Hindus as paradigmatic examples of his characterization'. Walter D. Mignolo, 'The Many Faces of Cosmo-polis: Border Thinking and Critical Cosmopolitanism', *Public Culture*, 12: 3 (2000), p. 734.
52   Kant, 'Perpetual Peace', p. 105.
53   Allen W. Wood, 'Kant's Project for Perpetual Peace', in Pheng Cheah and Bruce Robbins (eds), *Cosmopolitics*, p. 62.
54   Jacques Derrida, 'On Cosmopolitanism', in *On Cosmopolitanism and Forgiveness*, trans. Mark Dooley and Michael Hughes (London: Routledge, 2001), p. 22.
55   Derrida, 'On Cosmopolitanism', pp. 22–3.
56   Kristeva, *Nations Without Nationalism*, p. 32.
57   Gayatri Chakravorty Spivak, 'French Feminism in an International Frame', in *In Other Worlds: Essays in Cultural Politics* (London: Routledge, 1988), p. 140. Lisa Lowe develops Spivak's critique in '*Des Chinoises*: Orientalism, Psychoanalysis, and Feminine Writing', in Kelly Oliver (ed.), *Ethics, Politics, and Difference in Julia Kristeva's Writing* (London: Routledge, 1993), pp. 150–63.
58   Julia Kristeva, 'My Memory's Hyperbole', cited in Spivak, *A Critique of Postcolonial Reason,* p. 66.
59   Spivak, *A Critique of Postcolonial Reason*, p. 66, n. 83. Elsewhere, Spivak states that she is 'repelled by Kristeva's politics... banal historical narrative... christianizing psychoanalysis'. Gayatri Chakravorty Spivak, 'In a Word: Interview', in *Outside in the Teaching Machine* (London: Routledge,

1993), p. 145. *Nations Without Nationalism* mitigates the inflammatory sense of a rigid division of Judeo-Christian Europe and the US versus the Third World: 'the cohesion of the American nation centered in the Dollar and God keeps troubling those for whom the future of men and women is centered in other values. The fierce struggle for profits, a war as *holy* in Washington as it is in Baghdad but in the name of another god and with incomparable humanitarian precautions (since the *Rights of Man* imposes certain duties): are those truly "national values" the entire world, other "nations", "ethnicities", and "origins" must submit to?'. Kristeva, *Nations Without Nationalism*, 11.

60 Deleuze and Guattari, *What is Philosophy?*, p. 97.
61 Kristeva, *Strangers to Ourselves*, p. 58.
62 Kristeva, *Strangers to Ourselves*, p. 60.
63 Aeschylus, *The Suppliants*, in *Prometheus Bound and Other Plays*, trans. Philip Vellacott (London: Penguin, 1961), p. 85.
64 Aeschylus, *The Suppliants*, p.54
65 Aeschylus, *The Suppliants*, cited in Kristeva, *Strangers to Ourselves*, p. 47.
66 Aeschylus, *The Suppliants*, cited in Kristeva, *Strangers to Ourselves*, p. 48.
67 H.D.F. Kitto, *Greek Tragedy* (London: Methuen, 1961), p. 12.
68 Aeschylus, *The Suppliants*, p. 81.
69 Kristeva, *Strangers to Ourselves*, p. 49.
70 Kristeva, *Strangers to Ourselves*, p. 50.
71 Suzanne Clark, Kathleen Hulley and Julia Kristeva, 'Cultural Strangeness and the Subject in Crisis', in Ross Mitchell Guberman (ed.), *Julia Kristeva: Interviews* (New York: Columbia University Press, 1996), p. 45.
72 Kristeva, *Strangers to Ourselves*, p. 42. This claim is restated in *Nations Without Nationalism*: 'The first foreigners mentioned in Greek mythology are women – the Danaïdes'. Kristeva, *Nations Without Nationalism*, p. 17.
73 Kristeva, *Strangers to Ourselves*, p. 43.
74 Kristeva, *Strangers to Ourselves*, p. 44.
75 Kristeva, *Strangers to Ourselves*, p. 45.
76 Kristeva, *Strangers to Ourselves*, p. 46.
77 Derrida, *Of Grammatology*, p. 145.
78 Kristeva, *Strangers to Ourselves*, p. 3.
79 Kristeva, *Nations Without Nationalism*, p. 3.
80 Kristeva, *Nations Without Nationalism*, p. 16. Bhabha is concerned that Kristeva 'speaks too hastily of the pleasure of exile... without realizing how fully the shadow of the nation falls on the condition of exile'. Homi K. Bhabha, *The Location of Culture* (London: Routledge, 1993), pp. 140–1; At times, however, Kristeva does temper the impression that externality or multiplicity can be attained through a willed act or an unbounded declaration: 'To know that an ostensibly masculine, paternal... identification is necessary to have some voice in the record of politics and history. To achieve this identification in order to escape a smug polymorphism where it is so easy and comfortable for a woman here to remain: and by this identification to gain entry to social experience'. Kristeva, *About Chinese Women*, pp. 37–8.
81 Kristeva, *About Chinese Women*, p. 42.
82 Kristeva, *About Chinese Women*, p. 58. *Nations Without Nationalism* echoes this idea when it briefly considers the relationship between the literary and

the social: 'national literature could, in France, become not the expression of the people's enigmatic intimacy but a charmed space where irony merges with seriousness in order to lay out and break up the changing out-lines of the totally discursive being, which, when all is said and done, constitutes the French nation'. Kristeva, *Nations Without Nationalism*, p. 44.

83   Kristeva, *About Chinese Women*, p. 56.

84   The sense of a distinction between phonetic and graphic writing returns later in the text: 'I wish I'd been able to write the *voices* of the Chinese women: vibrant, velvety, so low as to be almost inaudible in conversation. They begin in the chest or belly, but they can suddenly hiss from the throat and rise sharply to the head, strained in aggression or enthusiasm, excited or threatening...'. Kristeva, *About Chinese Women*, p. 158.

85   Kristeva, *Strangers to Ourselves*, p. 10.

Chapter 5   'In the Shadow of Shadows': Spivak, Misreading, the Native Informant

1   Spivak, *A Critique of Postcolonial Reason*, p. 108.

2   This admiration is qualified elsewhere, however: 'Deleuze and Guattari's fantastic insight, that capital was – let us say "almost" – the abstract as such and capita*lism* codes it – is no longer sufficient. Finance capital is let us say "almost" the abstract as such and world trade codes it'. Gayatri Chakravorty Spivak, 'From Haverstock Hill Flat to U.S. Classroom, What's Left of Theory?', in Judith Butler, John Guillory & Kendall Thomas (eds), *What's Left of Theory? New Work on the Politics of Literary Theory* (London: Routledge, 2000), p. 7.

3   Spivak, *A Critique of Postcolonial Reason*, p. 4ff.

4   Spivak, *A Critique of Postcolonial Reason*, p. 58.

5   Spivak, *A Critique of Postcolonial Reason*, p. 82.

6   Spivak, *A Critique of Postcolonial Reason*, p. 96.

7   Gayatri Chakravorty Spivak, 'Subaltern Studies: Deconstructing Historiography', in *In Other Worlds*, p. 203.

8   Dipesh Chakrabarty, *Provincializing Europe: Postcolonial Thought and Historical Difference* (Princeton: Princeton University Press, 2000), p. 96.

9   Spivak, 'Can the Subaltern Speak?', in Cary Nelson & Lawrence Grossberg (eds), Marxism and the Interpretation of Culture (Basingstoke: Macmillan, 1988) p. 291.

10   Spivak, 'Can the Subaltern Speak?', p. 284.

11   Spivak, 'Can the Subaltern Speak?', p. 297.

12   Spivak, 'Can the Subaltern Speak?', p. 296.

13   Spivak, 'Can the Subaltern Speak?', p. 308.

14   Spivak, *A Critique of Postcolonial Reason*, p. 308. That this remark was inad-visable is demonstrated by some of the readings of 'Can the Subaltern Speak?'. Fernando P. Delgado, for example, asserts that 'What Spivak and like-minded scholars, occupying more centrist and flexible positions, suggest is that marginalization and Otherness lead to a silencing and occlu-sion'. Fernando P. Delgado, 'When the Silenced Speak: The Textualization and Complications of Latina/o Identity', *Western Journal of Communication*, 62: 4 (1998), p. 423.

15   Spivak, *A Critique of Postcolonial Reason*, p. 231.
16   Spivak, *A Critique of Postcolonial Reason*, p. 246.
17   Spivak, 'Can the Subaltern Speak?', p. 104/*A Critique of Postcolonial Reason*, p. 304.
18   Spivak, 'Can the Subaltern Speak?', p. 104/*A Critique of Postcolonial Reason*, p. 304.
19   Spivak, *A Critique of Postcolonial Reason*, p. 309.
20   Spivak, *A Critique of Postcolonial Reason*, p. 309.
21   Spivak, *A Critique of Postcolonial Reason*, p. 248.
22   Spivak, *A Critique of Postcolonial Reason*, p. 271.
23   Spivak, 'Can the Subaltern Speak?', p. 308.
24   Gayatri Chakravorty Spivak, '*Glas*-Piece: A *Compte Rendu*', *Diacritics* 7: 3 (1977), p. 24.
25   Paul de Man, 'Autobiography as De-Facement', in *The Rhetoric of Romanticism* (New York: Columbia University Press, 1984), pp. 67–81.
26   Gayatri Chakravorty Spivak, 'Acting Bits/Identity Talk', *Critical Inquiry*, 18: 4 (1992), p. 795.
27   In this manner, the autobiographical vignettes that are scattered throughout Spivak's work should be seen as alternatives to the confessional and self-regarding tendencies that she excoriates in postcolonial studies. As Robert Young points out, 'Spivak disdains this small-time institutional game, and is always disarmingly up-front about her own provenance'. Robert Young, Review of *Outside in the Teaching Machine*, *Textual Practice* 10: 1 (1996), p. 229. These moments reveal the multiple locations that inform – and thus dislocate – her work, and autobiography here becomes a violent defacement of the articulating self. The Spivak who speaks during these moments, then, can only disappear as an autobiographical – and monocultural – subject. And yet, it might equally be argued that the frequency with which Spivak asserts her hybridity means that it – contradictorily – becomes fixed, stable and readable. Young concurs elsewhere, arguing that 'by announcing her position as investigator so insistently, she runs the inevitable risk of presenting herself as the representative of that very "Third-World Woman"'. Young, *White Mythologies*, p. 171.
28   Gayatri Chakravorty Spivak, 'Deconstruction and Cultural Studies: Arguments for a Deconstructive Cultural Studies', in Nicholas Royle (ed.), *Deconstructions: A User's Guide* (Basingstoke: Palgrave, 2000), p. 30.
29   Derrida, *Politics of Friendship*, p. 31.
30   Derrida, *Politics of Friendship*, p. 31.
31   Derrida, *Politics of Friendship*, p. 33.
32   Jacques Derrida and Alexander Garcia Düttmann, 'Perhaps or Maybe', *PLI: Warwick Journal of Philosophy*, 6 (1997), p. 3.
33   Spivak, 'Deconstruction and Cultural Studies', p. 23.
34   Spivak, 'Deconstruction and Cultural Studies', p. 30.
35   For a detailed account of Spivak's misgivings about the rush to embrace her notion of strategy, especially strategic essentialism, see 'In a Word: Interview', in *Outside in the Teaching Machine*, pp. 1–23.
36   Gayatri Chakravorty Spivak, 'Resident Alien', in David Theo Goldberg and Ato Quayson (eds), *Relocating Postcolonialism* (Oxford: Blackwell, 2002), p. 47.

37 Spivak, '*Glas*-Piece', p. 30.
38 Spivak, '*Glas*-Piece', p. 32.
39 Julian Wolfreys, *Deconstruction•Derrida* (Basingstoke: Macmillan, 1998), p. 47.
40 Gayatri Chakravorty Spivak, 'At the *Planchette* of Deconstruction is/in America', in Anselm Haverkamp (ed.), *Deconstruction is/in America: A New Sense of the Political* (New York: New York University Press, 1995), p. 240. In another essay of the same year Spivak hopes that Derrida 'will not be dismayed if I say that in this sketching of the three-step where communism is a figuration of the impossible in view of which capitalism can be effortlessly perceived as socialism's *différence*, I have brutally reduced his work to formulas'. Gayatri Chakravorty Spivak, 'Supplementing Marxism', in Bernd Magus & Stephen Cullenberg (eds), *Whither Marxism?: Global Crises in International Perspective* (London: Routledge, 1995), p. 111.
41 'Does not the notion of context harbor, behind a certain confusion, very determined philosophical presuppositions?'. Derrida, 'Signature Event Context', in *Margins of Philosophy*, p. 310.
42 Stephen Morton, *Gayatri Chakravorty Spivak* (London: Routledge, 2003), p. 25.
43 Gayatri Chakravorty Spivak, 'Translation as Culture', in Isabel Carrera Suárez et al. (eds), *Translating Cultures* (Oviedo: KRK Ediciones; Hebden Bridge, Dangaroo, 1999), p. 17.
44 Gayatri Chakravorty Spivak, 'The Politics of Translation', in *Outside in the Teaching Machine*, p. 197.
45 Spivak, 'At the *Planchette* of Deconstruction is/in America', p. 241. Spivak restates this criticism in an interview with Peter Osborne: 'There are important new directions of resistance where Marxism has been reconstellated in various ways since the experiment of international communism showed itself to have certain kinds of problem. Derrida's readerly involvement with *that* practice has not been very close'. Gayatri Chakravorty Spivak, 'Setting to Work (Transnational Cultural Studies)', in Peter Osborne (ed.), *A Critical Sense: Interviews with Intellectuals* (London: Routledge, 1996), p. 175.
46 Spivak, 'At the *Planchette* of Deconstruction is/in America', p. 242.
47 Gayatri Chakravorty Spivak, 'Limits and Openings of Marx in Derrida', in *Outside in the Teaching Machine*, p. 99.
48 Jacques Derrida, 'White Mythology: Metaphor in the Text of Philosophy', in *Margins of Philosophy*, p. 217, n. 13
49 Gayatri Chakravorty Spivak, 'Speculation on reading Marx: after reading Derrida', in Derek Attridge, Geoffrey Bennington & Robert Young, (eds), *Post-Structuralism and the Question of History* (Cambridge: Cambridge University Press, 1987), p. 53.
50 Spivak, 'Limits and Openings', p. 100.
51 Spivak, 'Limits and Openings', p. 100.
52 Spivak, 'Limits and Openings', p. 100.
53 Spivak, 'Limits and Openings', p. 101
54 Spivak, 'Limits and Openings', p. 105.
55 Spivak, 'Limits and Openings', p. 106.
56 Jacques Derrida, *The Other Heading*, cited by Spivak in 'Limits and Openings', p. 112.
57 Derrida, *Specters of Marx*, p. 13.

58 Spivak, 'Limits and Openings', p. 112.
59 Spivak, 'Limits and Openings', p. 113.
60 Spivak, 'Limits and Openings', pp. 112–13
61 Spivak, 'Limits and Openings', p. 118.
62 Gayatri Chakravorty Spivak, 'Ghostwriting', *Diacritics*, 25: 2 (1995), p. 65.
63 Spivak, 'Ghostwriting', p. 65.
64 Spivak, 'Ghostwriting', p. 67.
65 Derrida, *Specters of Marx*, p. 82.
66 Derrida identifies ten such 'plagues' that are passed over in celebrations of the new world order: 1) unemployment; 2) 'the massive exclusion of homeless citizens from any participation in the democratic life of States'; 3) economic war between nations and its consequences for the implementation of international law; 4) 'the inability to master the contradictions in the concept, norms, and reality of the free market'; 5) 'the aggravation of the foreign debt'; 6) the centrality of the arms industry in Western democracies; 7) 'the spread... of nuclear weapons, maintained by the very countries that say they want to protect themselves from it'; 8) inter-ethnic wars; 9) the 'worldwide power of those super-efficient and properly capitalist phantom-states that are the mafia and the drug cartels on every continent'; 10) 'the present state of international law and its institutions'. Derrida, *Specters of Marx*, pp. 81–4.
67 Spivak, 'Ghostwriting', p. 68. An early footnote in *A Critique of Postcolonial Reason* similarly makes this claim: 'Thus industrial (and specifically postindustrial) capitalism is now in an interruptive *différance* with commercial capital; World Trade with finance capital markets. To notice this *différance* is to learn from Derrida; yet Derrida's own resolute ignoring of the difference between the two is caught within it'. Spivak, *A Critique of Postcolonial Reason*, p. 3, n. 4. Cf. Peggy Kamuf's observation that Derrida's list of the ten plagues of the new world order is 'an ironic reversal of the ten plagues called down on Egypt before it granted self-determination to the people of Israel. Here, on the contrary, the plagues plague precisely the determination to enforce any national, ethnic, or territorial frontiers against the incursion of forces from without, indeed, against all the new forms of enslavement invented by economic liberalism and its offshoots or parasites'. Peggy Kamuf, 'Violence, Identity, Self-Determination, and the Question of Justice: on *Specters of Marx*', in Hent de Vries & Samuel Weber, (eds), *Violence, Identity and Self-Determination* (Stanford: Stanford University Press, 1997), p. 273.
68 Spivak, 'Ghostwriting', p. 71. Spivak restates this claim in 'A Note on the New International': 'In *Politics of Friendship*, Derrida makes a plea for slow reading, even at a time of political urgency, arguing carefully that it must remain always inadequate. As so often, I echo him on another register, and make a plea for the patient work of learning to learn from below – a species of "reading" perhaps – how to mend the torn fabric of subaltern ethics with the thread of the subject whose trace is in the madness of a universal declaration of human rights – necessarily bending curvature into *droiture* – straightness, rights, uprightness. If this interests you, I have not altogether misread Derrida'. Gayatri Chakravorty Spivak, 'A Note on the New International', *Parallax*, 7: 3 (2001), p. 15.

69 Gayatri Chakravorty Spivak, 'Foreword', in *Outside in the Teaching Machine*, p. x.
70 Spivak, 'Limits and Openings', p. 97.
71 Spivak, 'Limits and Openings', p. 112.
72 Spivak, 'Limits and Openings', p. 115.
73 Bart Moore-Gilbert, *Postcolonial Theory: Contexts, Practices, Politics* (London: Verso, 1997), p. 78.
74 Spivak, 'Ghostwriting', p. 72.
75 Spivak, 'Ghostwriting', p. 72.
76 Spivak, 'Ghostwriting', p. 70.
77 Spivak, 'Ghostwriting', p. 65.
78 Spivak, '*Glas*-Piece', p. 24.
79 Jacques Derrida, 'Signature Event Context', p. 328.
80 Gayatri Chakravorty Spivak, 'Responsibility', *boundary 2*, 21: 3 (1994), p. 62.
81 Jacques Derrida, 'Marx & Sons', trans. G.M. Goshgarian, in Michael Sprinker (ed.), *Ghostly Demarcations: A Symposium on Jacques Derrida's Specters of Marx* (London: Verso, 1999), p. 215.
82 Derrida, 'Marx & Sons', p. 222.
83 Derrida, 'Marx & Sons', p. 222.
84 Derrida, 'Marx & Sons', p. 223.
85 Spivak, 'Ghostwriting', p. 79.
86 Derrida, 'Marx & Sons', p. 223.
87 Herman Rapaport, *The Theory Mess: Deconstruction in Eclipse* (New York: Columbia University Press, 2001), p. 63.
88 Spivak, 'Ghostwriting', p. 71.
89 Writing about différance ('the other... different and deferred in the economy of the same') 'Limits and Openings' even suggests that the ability to see is somehow tied to subject-position: 'Given my context, I can see the trace of this relationship between postcoloniality (strictly speaking) and migrancy (or the other way around). Derrida, given his, between "Europe" and migrancy (or the other way around)'. Spivak, 'Limits and Openings', p. 114.
90 Young, *White Mythologies*, p. 216.
91 Spivak, 'Foreword', in *Outside in the Teaching Machine*, p. x.
92 Spivak, 'Neocolonialism and the Secret Agent of Knowledge', *Oxford Literary Review*, 13: 1–2 (1991), p. 242.

Chapter 6 'To Move Through – and Beyond – Theory': Bhabha, Hybridity, and Agency

1 Jacques Derrida, 'The Double Session', in *Dissemination*, p. 189.
2 Bhabha, *The Location of Culture*, p. 82.
3 Bhabha, *The Location of Culture*, p. 10.
4 Bhabha, *The Location of Culture*, pp. 128–32.
5 Bhabha, *The Location of Culture*, p. 59.
6 Bhabha, *The Location of Culture*, p. 108.
7 Bhabha, *The Location of Culture*, p. 109.

8   Homi K. Bhabha, 'Day by Day... With Frantz Fanon', in Alan Read (ed.), *The Fact of Blackness: Frantz Fanon and Visual Representation* (London: ICA/Seattle: Bay Press, 1996), p. 191.
9   Bhabha, 'Day by Day', pp. 190–91.
10 Bhabha, 'Day by Day', p. 191.
11 Indeed, when Bhabha later reworks sections from 'Day by Day... With Franz Fanon', he reminds Derrida that it is not just transnational dislocations that inform the emerging global order, but that 'racism, community, blood and borders haunt the new international and have gained remarkable ideological and affective power'. Homi K. Bhabha, 'On the Irremovable Strangeness of Being Different', *PMLA*, 113: 1 (1998), p. 34.
12 Bhabha, 'Day by Day', p. 191.
13 Bhabha, 'Day by Day', p. 191.
14 Moore-Gilbert, *Postcolonial Theory*, p. 118.
15 Bhabha, *The Location of Culture*, p. 71.
16 Bhabha's privileging of *Black Skin, White Masks* over *The Wretched of the Earth* or *Studies in a Dying Colonialism* is now well documented. For Neil Lazarus, reading Fanon in this way is tendentious because 'Bhabha concedes the existence of a revolutionary-redemptive ethic in Fanon... but he insists that the real value of Fanon's work lies elsewhere, in a psychoanalytic interrogation of the problematics of colonial desire'. Lazarus, 'Disavowing decolonization', p. 164. According to Patrick Williams, 'Bhabha proceeds to what many might regard as just such an act of possession, marginalising Fanon the theorist of nationalism (*The Wretched of the Earth*) in favour of Fanon the theorist of narcissism (*Black Skin, White Masks*), when in fact one of the more important aspects of Fanon's own re-routing is from the analysis of the politics of psychological states to that of the politics of emergent nation states'. Patrick Williams, 'Frantz Fanon: The Routes of Writing', in Sam Haigh (ed.), *An Introduction to Caribbean Francophone Writing: Guadeloupe and Martinique* (Oxford: Berg, 1999), p. 52. Henry Louis Gates' 'Critical Fanonism' surveys some of the different positions that are adopted by Fanon's readers. Henry Louis Gates Jr., 'Critical Fanonism', *Critical Inquiry*, 17: 3 (1991), pp. 457–70.
17 Frantz Fanon, *Black Skin, White Masks*, trans. Charles Lam Markmann (London: Pluto, 1986), p. 111.
18 Fanon, *Black Skin, White Masks*, p. 231.
19 Bhabha, *The Location of Culture*, p. 40.
20 Bhabha, 'Day by Day... With Frantz Fanon', p. 190. Such a reading of Fanon permeates Bhabha's work. In respect of *Black Skin, White Mask*, 'A Question of Survival: Nations and Psychic States', for example, claims that 'From that marked void or caesura that splits any naively liberatory or sovereign sentence of freedom there emerges a political vision of equality. It is a vision articulated at the "edge" of *not* that will not allow any national or cultural "unisonance" in the imagined community of the future'. Homi K. Bhabha, 'A Question of Survival: Nations and Psychic States', in James Donald (ed.), *Psychoanalysis and Cultural Theory* (Basingstoke: Macmillan, 1991), p. 102.

21   Bhabha is not, however, entirely convinced that Deleuze and Guattari's – or, for that matter, Lacan's – work accounts for the forms of invention that are produced by cultural anxiety: the 'scenario of the anxious subject is crucial to its emergence and constitutive of its emergence as *an agency* that translates external cause into fantasmatic identifications. It is almost mimicked in Deleuze and Guattari's constitution of the minority subject, give or take a little. If you give in just a little to the Lacanian *objet petit a* and take away slightly more from Deleuze and Guattari's Nietzschean *becoming*, you will see how the double reflexivity of the middle voice works in the minority subject – as-circuit, emerging as an anxious, yet inventive, questioning about what takes the place of the subject beyond the two designations of author and character, hero and victim'. Bhabha, 'Minority Maneuvers and Unsettled Negotiations', p. 444.

22   Bhabha, *The Location of Culture*, p. 110.

23   Bhabha, *The Location of Culture*, pp. 110–11. Cf also Bhabha's comments in 'The White Stuff': 'The subversive move is to reveal within the very integuments of "whiteness" the agonistic elements that make it the unsettled, disturbed form of authority that it is – the incommensurable "differences" that it must surmount; the histories of trauma and terror that it must perpetrate and from which it must protect itself; the amnesia it imposes on itself; the violence it inflicts in the process of becoming a transparent and transcendent force of authority'. Homi K. Bhabha, 'The White Stuff', *Artforum*, 36: 9 (1998), p. 21.

24   Bhabha, *The Location of Culture*, p. 112.

25   Bhabha, *The Location of Culture*, p. 225.

26   Bhabha, *The Location of Culture*, p. 116. In this manner, Bhabha's theory of hybridity differs from that of Néstor García Canclini, for whom hybridity is the characteristic of a modernity typified by interzones like Tijuana: 'today all cultures are border cultures... cultures lose the exclusive relation with their territory, but they gain in communication and knowledge'. Néstor García Canclini, *Hybrid Cultures: Strategies for Entering and Leaving Modernity*, trans. Christopher L. Chiappari and Silvia L. Lopez (Minneapolis: University of Minnesota Press, 1995), p. 261.

27   Nikos Papestergiadis, 'Restless Hybrids', *Third Text*, 32 (1995), p. 11.

28   Bhabha, *The Location of Culture*, p. 5

29   Since the appearance of *The Location of Culture*, Bhabha's attention has been inclined towards visual representations of cultural and national identity as much as it has been concerned with literary texts. Vivan Sundaram's painting *People Come and Go*, for example, 'with its citations, imitations, and enigmatic, unreadable canvas that hits the sightline at a peripheral, even anamorphic angle, raises for us the issue of identity and cultural authenticity'. Homi K. Bhabha, 'Halfway House', *Artforum*, 35: 9 (1997), p. 125. In Anish Kapoor's work there is 'the intimation of a movement that obliterates perceptual space and supplements it with a disruptive, disjunctive time through which the spectator must pass – "reverse, affirm, negate"'. Homi K. Bhabha, 'Anish Kapoor: Making Emptiness', in *Anish Kapoor* (London: Hayward Gallery/Berkeley: University of California Press, 1998), p. 14.

30   Jean Bernabé, Patrick Chamoiseau and Raphaël Confiant, *Éloge de la Créolité/In Praise of Creoleness*, trans. M.B. Taleb-Khyar (Paris: Gallimard, 1993), pp. 87–8.
31   Ania Loomba, *Colonialism/Postcolonialism* (London: Routledge, 1998), p. 178.
32   To say that these issues are absent from his work is, of course, inaccurate. Indeed, *The Location of Culture* even considers the role played by striking miners' wives in 1984–5: 'Their testimonies would not be contained simply or singly within the priorities of the politics of class or the histories of industrial struggle. Many of the women began to question their roles within the family and the community – the two central institutions which articulated the meanings and mores of the *tradition* of the labouring classes around which ideological battle was enjoined'. Bhabha, *The Location of Culture*, p. 27.
33   Bernabé, Chamoiseau & Confiant, *Éloge de la Créolité/In Praise of Creoleness*, pp. 92–3.
34   Young, *Colonial Desire*, p. 5.
35   Young, *White Mythologies*, p. 191.
36   Young, *White Mythologies*, p. 191.
37   Bhabha, *The Location of Culture*, p. 95.
38   Bhabha, *The Location of Culture*, p. 114.
39   Benita Parry offers a different reading, arguing that Bhabha flattens colonizing and resistance groups into a sameness devoid of conflict: 'To speak then of metropolis and colony as inhabiting the same in-between, interstitial ground, occludes that this territory was differentially occupied, and that it was contested space, being the site of coercion and resistance, and not of civil negotiation between evenly placed contenders'. Benita Parry, 'Signs of Our Times: Review of Homi Bhabha's *The Location of Culture*', *Third Text*, 28/29 (1994), p. 19.
40   Young, *White Mythologies*, p. 197.
41   Bhabha, *The Location of Culture*, pp. 1–2.
42   Bhabha, *The Location of Culture*, p. 6.
43   One example of this kind of thinking can be found, Bhabha tells us, in Charles Taylor et al., *Multiculturalism: Examining the Politics of Recognition* (New Jersey: Princeton University Press, 1994).
44   Homi K. Bhabha, 'Culture's In Between', *Artforum*, 32: 1 (1998), p. 168.
45   Bhabha, *The Location of Culture*, p. 241.
46   Slavoj Žižek, *The Fragile Absolute – or, Why is the Christian Legacy Worth Fighting For?* (London: Verso, 2000), p. 5.
47   Slavoj Žižek, *The Fragile Absolute*, p. 10.
48   Slavoj Žižek, *The Fragile Absolute*, p. 11.
49   Henry A. Giroux, 'Post-Colonial Ruptures and Democratic Possibilities: Multiculturalism as Anti-Racist Pedagogy', *Cultural Critique*, 21 (1992), p. 15.
50   Bhabha, 'Culture's In Between', p. 168.
51   It is important to note here that Bhabha warns against turning concepts like 'ambivalence' or 'hybridity' into formulae that appear fully to capture the nature of culture, since these terms point to the unnameable that resides at the heart of discourse, to those alterities that slip away from the

appropriative strictures of European thought: 'Is ambivalence quasi-transcendental?', he asks, 'I don't think so. I think the whole nature of what I call an analytic of ambivalence will not allow you to make statements like "all forms of authority are always already ambivalent", "all forms of subjectivity are always already split", because there is something about the temporality of ambivalence… which does not allow this "always already" move'. Gary Hall and Simon Wortham, 'Rethinking Authority: Interview with Homi K. Bhabha', *Angelaki*, 2: 2 (1995), p. 61.

52 Bhabha, 'Culture's In Between', p. 167.
53 Bhabha, *The Location of Culture*, p. 37.
54 John Kraniauskas, 'Hybridity in a transnational frame: Latin-Americanist and post-colonial perspectives on cultural studies', in Avtar Brah & Annie E. Coombes (eds), *Hybridity and its Discontents: Politics, Science, Culture* (London: Routledge, 2000), p. 240.
55 Homi K. Bhabha, 'On Cultural Choice', in Marjorie Garber et al. (eds), *The Turn to Ethics* (London: Routledge, 2000), p. 188.
56 Jacques Lacan, 'The agency of the letter in the unconscious or reason since Freud', in *Écrits: A Selection*, trans. Alan Sheridan (London: Routledge, 1977), p. 148.
57 Lacan, 'The agency of the letter', p. 171.
58 Lacan, 'The agency of the letter', p. 157.
59 Lacan, 'The agency of the letter', p. 155.
60 Bhabha, *The Location of Culture*, p. 185.
61 Bhabha, *The Location of Culture*, p. 189.
62 Bhabha, *The Location of Culture*, p. 179.
63 Bhabha, *The Location of Culture*, p. 181.
64 Bhabha, *The Location of Culture*, p. 180.
65 Roland Barthes, *The Pleasure of the Text*, cited in Bhabha, *The Location of Culture*, p. 180.
66 Moore-Gilbert, for example, argues that 'much of Barthes work in the 1970s, including *The Pleasure of the Text* as well as the books on Japan and China published either side of it, can be understood as an unwitting reinscription of an older tradition of Orientalist ideas…. While the East may function as a means by which to deconstruct the authority of the West… it is still being reappropriated… as a solution to 'internal' Western cultural problematics'. Moore-Gilbert, *Postcolonial Theory*, p. 128. However, Bhabha himself recognizes this problem in Barthes', and others', work: 'the site of cultural difference can become the mere phantom of a dire disciplinary struggle in which it has no space or power. Montesquieu's Turkish Despot, Barthes's Japan, Kristeva's China, Derrida's Nambikwara Indians, Lyotard's Cashinahua are part of this strategy of containment where the Other is forever the exegetical horizon of difference, never the active agent of articulation'. Bhabha, *The Location of Culture*, p. 31.
67 Bhabha, *The Location of Culture*, p. 180.
68 Bhabha, *The Location of Culture*, p. 181.
69 Bhabha, 'On Cultural Choice', p. 189.
70 Moore-Gilbert, *Postcolonial Theory*, p. 137.
71 Moore-Gilbert, *Postcolonial Theory*, p. 138.

Notes 181

72 Moore-Gilbert, *Postcolonial Theory*, p. 133.
73 Homi K. Bhabha 'In a Spirit of Calm Violence', in Gyan Prakash (ed.), *After Colonialism: Imperial Histories and Postcolonial Displacements* (New Jersey: Princeton UP, 1995), p. 330. Such a claim seems to deny Eagleton's claim that 'Bhabha romanticizes the marginal and the transgressive, and can find almost nothing of value in unity, coherence or consensus'. Terry Eagleton, 'Goodbye to the Enlightenment', *The Guardian* 8/2/94, p. 12.
74 Moore-Gilbert, *Postcolonial Theory*, p. 141.
75 The troubled relationship between psychoanalysis and national identity is the subject of increasing levels of critical activity; some of the most recent studies in this area include Christopher Lane (ed.), *The Psychoanalysis of Race* (New York: Columbia University Press, 1998), Anne Anlin Cheng, *The Melancholy of Race: Psychoanalysis, Assimilation, and Hidden Grief* (Oxford: Oxford UP, 2001), and Celia Britton, *Race and the Unconscious: Freudianism in French Caribbean Thought* (Oxford: Legenda, 2002).
76 Elizabeth Roudinesco, *Jacques Lacan: Outline of a Life, History of a System of Thought*, trans. Barbara Bray (New York: Columbia University Press, 1997), pp. 428–42. Cf. Derrida's claim that 'there is practically no psychoanalysis in Africa, white or black, just as there is no psychoanalysis in Asia or the South Seas. These are among those parts of "the rest of the world" where psychoanalysis has never set foot, or in any case where it has never taken off its European shoes'. Jacques Derrida, 'Geopsychoanalysis: "… and the rest of the world", in Lane (ed.), *Psychoanalysis and Race*, p. 69. In contrast with Roudinesco, Derrida points out that Latin America has been one area that the International Psychoanalytic Association has reduced to the rank of 'the rest of the world'.
77 Jacques Derrida, *Archive Fever: A Freudian Impression*, trans. Eric Prenowitz (Chicago: University of Chicago Press, 1996).
78 Edward W. Said, *Freud and the Non-European* (London: Verso, 2003), p. 15.
79 Said, *Freud and the Non-European*, p. 44.

Bibliography

Aeschylus, *The Suppliants*, in *Prometheus Bound and Other Plays*, trans. Philip Vellacott (London: Penguin, 1961).

Ahmad, Aijaz, *In Theory: Classes, Nations, Literatures* (London: Verso, 1992).

Ahmad, Aijaz, 'The politics of literary postcoloniality', *Race & Class*, 36: 3 (1995), pp. 1–20.

Al-Kassim, Dina, The Face of Foreclosure', *Interventions: International Journal of Postcolonial Studies*, 4: 2 (2002), pp. 168–74.

Althusser, Louis, *Politics and History: Montesquieu, Rousseau, Hegel and Marx*, trans. Ben Brewster (London: NLB, 1972).

Amin, Samir, *Eurocentrism*, trans. Russell Moore (London: Zed Books, 1989).

Anderson, Benedict, *Imagined Communities: Reflections on the Origin and Spread of Nationalism*, 2nd edn. (London: Verso, 1991).

Ansell-Pearson, Keith (ed.), *Deleuze and Philosophy: The Difference Engineer* (London: Routledge, 1997).

Appadurai, Arjun, *Modernity at Large: Cultural Dimensions of Globalization* (Minneapolis: University of Minnesota Press, 1996).

Ashcroft, Bill, *Postcolonial Transformation* (London: Routledge, 2001).

Attridge, Derek (ed.), *Acts of Literature* (London: Routledge, 1992).

Bal, Meike, 'Three-Way Misreading', *Diacritics*, 30: 1 (2000), pp. 2–24.

Bataille, Georges, *The Impossible*, trans. Robert Hurley (San Francisco: City Lights Books, 1991).

Baugh, Bruce, 'Making the Difference: Deleuze's Difference and Derrida's Différance', *Social Semiotics*, 7: 2 (1997), pp. 127–46.

Beardsworth, Richard, *Derrida & the Political* (London: Routledge, 1996).

Bennington, Geoffrey, *Legislations: The Politics of Deconstruction* (London: Verso, 1994).

Bennington, Geoffrey 'Double Tonguing: Derrida's Monolingualism', *Tympanum*, 4 (2000), http://www.usc.edu/dept/comp-lit/tympanum/4/ bennington.html. Accessed 22/1/04.

Bernabé, Jean, Chamoiseau, Patrick, and Confiant, Raphaël, *Éloge de la Créolité/ In Praise of Creoleness*, trans. M.B. Taleb-Khyar (Paris: Gallimard, 1993).

Beverley, John, *Subalternity and Representation: Arguments in Cultural Theory* (Durham: Duke University Press, 1999).

Bhabha, Homi K., 'A Question of Survival: Nations and Psychic States', in James Donald (ed.), *Psychoanalysis and Cultural Theory* (Basingstoke: Macmillan, 1991), pp. 89–103.

Bhabha, Homi K., *The Location of Culture* (London: Routledge, 1993).

Bhabha, Homi K., 'Frontierlines/Borderposts', in Angelika Bammer (ed.), *Displacements: Cultural Identity in Question* (Bloomington: Indiana University Press, 1994), pp. 269–272.

Bhabha, Homi K., 'In a Spirit of Calm Violence', in Gyan Prakash (ed.), *After Colonialism: Imperial Histories and Postcolonial Displacements* (New Jersey: Princeton UP, 1995), pp. 326–43.

Bhabha, Homi K., 'Day by Day... With Frantz Fanon', in Alan Read (ed.), *The Fact of Blackness: Frantz Fanon and Visual Representation* (London: ICA/Seattle: Bay Press, 1996), pp. 186–205.

Bhabha, Homi, 'Editor's Introduction: Minority Maneuvers and Unsettled Negotiations', *Critical Inquiry*, 23: 3 (1997), pp. 431–59.

Bhabha, Homi K., 'Halfway House', *Artforum*, 35: 9 (1997), pp. 11–12, p. 125.

Bhabha, Homi K., 'Anish Kapoor: Making Emptiness', in *Anish Kapoor* (London: Hayward Gallery/Berkeley: University of California Press, 1998), pp. 11–41.

Bhabha, Homi K., 'Foreword: Joking Aside: The Idea of a Self-Critical Community', in Bryan Cheyette and Laura Marcus (eds), *Modernity, Culture, and 'the Jew'* (Cambridge: Polity, 1998), pp. vv–xx.

Bhabha, Homi K., 'On the Irremovable Strangeness of Being Different', *PMLA*, 113: 1 (1998), pp. 34–9.

Bhabha, Homi K,. 'Culture's In Between', *Artforum*, 32: 1 (1998), pp. 167–8, 211–14.

Bhabha, Homi K., 'The White Stuff', *Artforum*, 36: 9 (1998), pp. 21–4.

Bhabha, Homi K., 'On Cultural Choice', in Marjorie Garber et al. (eds), *The Turn to Ethics* (London: Routledge, 2000), pp. 181–200.

Bhabha, Homi K., 'On minorities: cultural rights', *Radical Philosophy*, 100 (2000), pp. 3–6.

Bhabha, Homi, and Comaroff, John, 'Speaking of Postcoloniality, in the Continuous Present: A Conversation', in David Theo Goldberg and Ato Quayson (eds), *Relocating Postcolonialism* (Oxford: Blackwell, 2002), pp. 15–46.

Blanchot, Maurice, *The Step Not Beyond*, trans. Lycette Wilson (New York: State University of New York Press, 1992).

Bogue, Ronald, *Deleuze and Guattari* (London: Routledge, 1989).

Boundas, Constantin V., and Olkowski, Dorothea, *Gilles Deleuze and the Theatre of Philosophy* (London: Routledge, 1994).

Brennan, Theresa, 'Why the Time Is Out of Joint: Marx's Political Economy of the Subject', *South Atlantic Quarterly*, 97: 2 (1998), pp. 263–80.

Brennan, Timothy, 'The Empire's New Clothes', *Critical Inquiry*, 29: 2 (2003), pp. 337–67.

Britton, Celia, *Edouard Glissant and Postcolonial Theory: Strategies of Language and Resistance* (Charlottesville: University Press of Virginia, 1999).

Britton, Celia, *Race and the Unconscious: Freudianism in French Caribbean Thought* (Oxford: Legenda, 2002).

Callus, Ivan and Herbrechter, Stefan, 'The Latecoming of the Posthuman, Or, Why "We" Do the Apocalypse Differently, "Now"', *Reconstruction*, 4: 3 (2004). Accessed 19/8/04.

Chakrabarty, Dipesh, *Provincializing Europe: Postcolonial Thought and Historical Difference* (Princeton: Princeton University Press, 2000).

Chatterjee, Partha, *Nationalist Thought and the Colonial World: A Derivative Discourse* (London: Zed Books, 1986).

Cheah, Pheng, and Robbins, Bruce (eds), *Cosmopolitics: Thinking and Feeling Beyond the Nation* (Minneapolis: University of Minnesota Press, 1998).

Cheah, Pheng, 'Spectral Nationality: The Living On [*sur–vie*] of the Postcolonial Nation in Neocolonial Globalization', *boundary 2*, 26: 3 (1999), pp. 225–52.

Cheng, Anne Anlin, *The Melancholy of Race: Psychoanalysis, Assimilation, and Hidden Grief* (Oxford: Oxford UP, 2001).

Chow, Rey, *Ethics After Idealism: Theory–Culture–Ethnicity–Reading* (Bloomington: Indiana University Press, 1998).

Cixous, Hélène, 'My Algeriance', trans. Eric Prenowitz, in *Stigmata: Escaping Texts* (London: Routledge, 1998), pp. 153–72.

Cixous, Hélène, *Portrait of Jacques Derrida as a Young Jewish Saint*, trans. Beverley Bie Brahic (New York: Columbia University Press, 2004).

Clark, Suzanne, Hulley, Kathleen, and Kristeva, Julia, 'Cultural Strangeness and the Subject in Crisis', in Ross Mitchell Guberman (ed.), *Julia Kristeva: Interviews* (New York: Columbia University Press, 1996), pp. 141–5.

Clark, Timothy, *Martin Heidegger* (London: Routledge, 2002).

Clifford, James, 'Taking Identity Politics Seriously: "The Contradictory Stony Ground..."', in Paul Gilroy, Lawrence Grossberg & Angela McRobbie (eds), *Without Guarantees: In Honour of Stuart Hall* (London: Verso, 2000), pp. 94–112.

Conley, Tom, 'From Multiplicities to Folds: On Style and Form in Deleuze', *South Atlantic Quarterly*, 96: 3 (1997), pp. 629–46.

Critchley, Simon, *The Ethics of Deconstruction: Derrida and Levinas* (Oxford: Blackwell, 1992).

Critchley, Simon, *Ethics–Politics–Subjectivity: Essays on Derrida, Levinas and Contemporary French Thought* (London: Verso, 1999).

de Landa, Manuel, *A Thousand Years of Non-Linear History* (New York: Zone, 1997).

Deleuze, Gilles, *Negotiations 1972–1990*, trans. Martin Joughin (New York: Columbia University Press, 1995).

Deleuze, Gilles, *Essays Critical and Clinical*, trans. Daniel W. Smith and Michael A. Greco (London: Verso, 1998).

Deleuze, Gilles, and Guattari, Félix, *Anti-Oedipus: Capitalism and Schizophrenia*, trans. Robert Hurley, Mark Seem and Helen R. Lane (London: Athlone, 1984).

Deleuze, Gilles, and Guattari, Félix, *Kafka: Toward a Minor Literature*, trans. Dana Polan (Minneapolis: University of Minnesota Press, 1986).

Deleuze, Gilles, and Guattari, Félix, *A Thousand Plateaus: Capitalism and Schizophrenia*, trans. Brian Massumi (London: Athlone, 1988).

Deleuze, Gilles, and Guattari, Félix, *What is Philosophy?*, trans. Graham Burchell and Hugh Tomlinson (London: Verso, 1994).

Deleuze, Gilles, and Parnet, Claire, *Dialogues*, trans. Hugh Tomlinson and Barbara Habberjam (London: Athlone, 1987).

Delgado, Fernando P., 'When the Silenced Speak: The Textualization and Complications of Latina/o Identity', *Western Journal of Communication*, 62: 4 (1998), pp. 420–38.

de Man, Paul, 'Autobiography as De-Facement', in *The Rhetoric of Romanticism* (New York: Columbia University Press, 1984), pp. 67–81.

Derrida, Jacques, *Of Grammatology*, trans. Gayatri Chakravorty Spivak (Baltimore: The Johns Hopkins University Press, 1976).

Derrida, Jacques, *Writing and Difference*, trans. Alan Bass (London: Routledge & Kegan Paul, 1978).

Derrida, Jacques, *Dissemination*, trans. Barbara Johnson (Chicago: University of Chicago Press, 1981).

Derrida, Jacques & McDonald, Christie V., 'Choreographies', trans. Christie V. McDonald, *Diacritics*, 12: 2 (1982), pp. 66–76.

Derrida, Jacques, *Margins of Philosophy*, trans. Alan Bass (Hemel Hempstead: Harvester Wheatsheaf, 1982).

Derrida, Jacques, *Positions*, trans. Alan Bass (Chicago: University of Chicago Press, 1982).

Derrida, Jacques, 'Racism's Last Word', trans. Peggy Kamuf, *Critical Inquiry*, 12: 1 (1985), pp. 290–9.

Derrida, Jacques, 'Deconstruction and the other', in Richard Kearney, (ed.), *Dialogues with Contemporary Continental Thinkers: The Phenomenological Heritage* (Manchester: Manchester University Press, 1986), pp. 105–26.

Derrida, Jacques, *Glas*, trans. John P. Leavey Jr. & Richard Rand (Lincoln: University of Nebraska Press, 1986).

Derrida, Jacques, '*Geschlecht* II: Heidegger's Hand', trans. John P. Leavey Jr., in John Sallis (ed.), *Deconstruction and Philosophy: The Texts of Jacques Derrida* (Chicago: University of Chicago Press, 1987), pp. 161–96.

Derrida, Jacques, 'Like the Sound of the Sea Deep within a Shell: Paul de Man's War', trans. Peggy Kamuf, *Critical Inquiry*, 14: 3 (1988), pp. 590–652.

Derrida, Jacques, *Limited Inc*, trans. Samuel Weber & Jeffrey Mehlmann (Evanston: Northwestern University Press, 1988).

Derrida, Jacques, 'Biodegradables: Seven Diary Fragments', *Critical Inquiry*, 15: 4 (1989), pp. 812–73.

Derrida, Jacques, *Of Spirit: Heidegger and the Question*, trans. Geoffrey Bennington and Rachel Bowlby (Chicago: University of Chicago Press, 1989).

Derrida, Jacques, 'Force of Law: The "Mystical Foundation of Authority"' trans. Mary Quaintance, in Drucilla Cornell, Michel Rosenfeld & David Gray Carlson (eds), *Deconstruction and the Possibility of Justice* (London: Routledge, 1992), pp. 3–67.

Derrida, Jacques, *The Other Heading: Reflections on Today's Europe*, trans. Pascale-Anne Brault & Michael B. Nass (Bloomington: Indiana University Press, 1992).

Derrida, Jacques, 'Circumfession', in Geoffrey Bennington & Jacques Derrida, *Jacques Derrida*, trans. Geoffrey Bennington (Chicago: University of Chicago Press, 1993).

Derrida, Jacques, *Specters of Marx: The State of the Debt, the Work of Mourning and the New International*, trans. Peggy Kamuf (London: Routledge, 1994).

Derrida, Jacques, *Archive Fever: A Freudian Impression*, trans. Eric Prenowitz (Chicago: University of Chicago Press, 1996).

Derrida, Jacques and Garcia Düttmann, Alexander, 'Perhaps or Maybe', *PLI: Warwick Journal of Philosophy*, 6 (1997), pp. 1–18.

Derrida, Jacques, *Politics of Friendship*, trans. George Collins (London: Verso, 1997).

Derrida, Jacques, 'The Villanova Roundtable: A Conversation with Jacques Derrida', in John. D. Caputo, (ed.), *Deconstruction in a Nutshell: A Conversation with Jacques Derrida* (New York: Fordham University Press, 1997), pp. 3–28.

Derrida, Jacques, 'I'm Going to Have to Wander All Alone', trans. Leonard Lawlor, *Philosophy Today*, 42: 1 (1998), pp. 3–5.

Derrida, Jacques, *The Monolingualism of the Other; or, The Prosthesis of Origin*, trans. Patrick Mensah (Stanford: Stanford University Press, 1998).

Derrida, Jacques, 'Marx & Sons', trans. G.M. Goshgarian, in Michael Sprinker (ed.), *Ghostly Demarcations: A Symposium on Jacques Derrida's Specters of Marx* (London: Verso, 1999), pp. 213–69.

Derrida, Jacques, 'On Cosmopolitanism', in *On Cosmopolitanism and Forgiveness*, trans. Mark Dooley and Michael Hughes (London: Routledge, 2001), pp. 3–24.

Derrida, Jacques, *Without Alibi*, trans. Peggy Kamuf (Stanford: Stanford University Press, 2002).

Derrida, Jacques, 'Autoimmunity: Real and Symbolic Suicides – A Dialogue with Jacques Derrida', in Giovanna Borradori, *Philosophy in a Time of Terror: Dialogues with Jürgen Habermas and Jacques Derrida* (Chicago: University of Chicago Press, 2003), pp. 85–136.

Dews, Peter, *Logics of Disintegration: Poststructuralist Thought and the Claims of Critical Theory* (London: Verso, 1987).

Dirlik, Arif, *The Postcolonial Aura: Third World Criticism in the Age of Global Capitalism* (Boulder: Westview Press, 1992).

Dirlik, Arif, 'How the grinch hijacked radicalism: further thoughts on the post-colonial', *Postcolonial Studies*, 2: 2 (1999), pp. 149–63.

Dumm, Thomas L., 'The Problem of "We"; or, The Persistence of Sovereignty', *boundary 2*, 26: 3 (1999), pp. 55–61.

Durkheim, Emile, *Montesquieu and Rousseau: Forerunners of Sociology* (Michigan: Ann Arbor, 1965).

Eagleton, Terry, *Walter Benjamin: Or Towards a Revolutionary Criticism* (London: Verso, 1981).

Eagleton, Terry, *Nationalism, Colonialism and Literature: Nationalism, Irony and Solidarity*, Field Day Pamphlet no. 13 (Derry: Field Day Theatre Company, 1988).

Eagleton, Terry, *Literary Theory: An Introduction* 2nd edn. (Oxford: Blackwell, 1990).

Eagleton, Terry, 'Goodbye to the Enlightenment', *The Guardian* 8/2/94, p. 12.

Eagleton , Terry, 'In the Gaudy Supermarket' *London Review of Books*, 21: 10 (1999), pp. 3–6.

Eagleton, Terry, 'Capitalism, modernism and postmodernism', in David Lodge and Nigel Wood (eds), *Modern Criticism and Theory: A Reader*, 2nd edn. (Harlow: Longman, 2000), pp. 360–86.

Fanon, Frantz, *The Wretched of the Earth*, trans. Constance Farrington (Harmondsworth: Penguin, 1967).

Fanon, Frantz, *Black Skin, White Masks*, trans. Charles Lam Markmann (London: Pluto, 1986).

Finlayson, Alan, and Valentine, Jeremy (eds), *Politics and Poststructuralism: An Introduction* (Edinburgh: University of Edinburgh Press, 2002).

Foucault, Michel, 'Theatrum Philosophicum', in *Language, Counter-Memory, Practice: Selected Essays and Interviews*, Donald F. Bouchard (ed.), trans. Donald F. Bouchard and Sherry Simon (Oxford: Blackwell, 1977), pp. 165–96.

Fukuyama, Francis, *The End of History and the Last Man* (London: Hamish Hamilton, 1992).

Gandhi, Leela, *Postcolonial Theory: A Critical Introduction* (Edinburgh: Edinburgh University Press, 1998).

García Canclini, Néstor, *Hybrid Cultures: Strategies for Entering and Leaving Modernity*, trans. Christopher L. Chiappari and Silvia L. Lopez (Minneapolis: University of Minnesota Press, 1995).

Gates, Henry Louis Jr, 'Critical Fanonism', *Critical Inquiry*, 17: 3 (1991), pp. 457–70.

Giroux, Henry A., 'Post-Colonial Ruptures and Democratic Possibilities: Multi-culturalism as Anti-Racist Pedagogy', *Cultural Critique*, 21 (1992), pp. 5–39.

Goodchild, Philip, *Deleuze and Guattari: An Introduction to the Politics of Desire* (London: Sage, 1996).

Grosz, Elizabeth, 'The Time of Violence: Deconstruction and Value', *College Literature*, 26: 1 (1999), pp. 8–18.

Habermas, Jürgen, *The Philosophical Discourse of Modernity: Twelve Lectures* (Cambridge: Polity, 1987).

Habermas, Jürgen, *The Postnational Constellation: Political Essays*, trans. Max Pensky (London: Polity, 2001).

Hall, Gary, and Wortham, Simon, 'Rethinking Authority: Interview with Homi K. Bhabha', *Angelaki*, 2: 2 (1995), pp. 59–63.

Hardt, Michael and Negri, Antonio, *Empire* (Cambridge, Mass.: Harvard University Press, 2000).

Heidegger, Martin, *Introduction to Metaphysics*, trans. Ralph Manheim (London: Oxford University Press, 1959).

Heidegger, Martin, 'The Origin of the Work of Art', *Poetry, Language, Thought*, trans. Albert Hofstadter (London: Harper & Row, 1971), pp. 15–87.

Heidegger, Martin, 'The Self-Assertion of the German University: Address Delivered on the Solemn Assumption of the Rectorate of the University of Frieburg', trans. Karsten Harries, *Review of Metaphysics*, 38: 3 (1985), pp. 470–80.

Hillis Miller, J./Asensi, Miguel, *Black Holes/J. Hillis Miller; or, Boustrophedonic Reading* (Stanford: Stanford University Press, 1999).

Holland, Eugene W., 'Marx and Poststructuralist Philosophies of Difference', *South Atlantic Quarterly*, 96: 3 (1997), pp. 525–41.

Husserl, Edmund, 'Philosophy and the Crisis of European Man', in *Phenomenology and the Crisis of Philosophy*, trans. Quentin Lauer (New York: Harper Torchbooks, 1965), pp. 149–92.

Jameson, Fredric, *The Political Unconscious: Narrative as a Socially Symbolic Act* (London: Methuen, 1981).

Jameson, Fredric, 'Marx's Purloined Letter', *New Left Review*, 209 (1995), pp. 75–109.

Jameson, Fredric, 'Marxism and Dualism in Deleuze', *South Atlantic Quarterly*, 96: 3 (1997), pp. 393–416.

JanMohamed, Abdul R., and Lloyd, David, *The Nature and Context of Minority Discourse* (Oxford: Oxford University Press, 1990).

Jardine, Alice A,. *Gynesis: Configurations of Woman and Modernity* (Ithaca: Cornell UP, 1985).

Kamuf, Peggy, (ed.), *A Derrida Reader: Between the Blinds* (Hemel Hempstead: Harvester Wheatsheaf, 1991).

Kamuf, Peggy, 'Violence, Identity, Self-Determination, and the Question of Justice: on *Specters of Marx*', in Hent de Vries & Samuel Weber (eds), *Violence, Identity and Self-Determination* (Stanford: Stanford University Press, 1997), pp. 271–83.

Kitto, H.D.F., *Greek Tragedy* (London: Methuen, 1961).

Kraniauskas, John, 'Hybridity in a transnational frame: Latin-Americanist and post-colonial perspectives on cultural studies', in Avtar Brah & Annie E. Coombes (eds), *Hybridity and its Discontents: Politics, Science, Culture* (London: Routledge, 2000), pp. 235–71.

Kristeva, Julia, *About Chinese Women*, trans. Anita Barrows (London: Marion Boyars, 1977).

Kristeva, Julia, 'Women's Time', trans. Alice Jardine and Harry Blake, in Toril Moi (ed.), *The Kristeva Reader* (Oxford: Blackwell, 1986), pp. 187–213.

Kristeva, Julia, *Strangers to Ourselves*, trans. Leon S. Roudiez (London: Harvester Wheatsheaf, 1991).

Kristeva, Julia, *Nations Without Nationalism*, trans. Leon S. Roudiez (New York: Columbia University Press, 1993).

Kristeva, Julia, 'Europe Divided: Politics, Ethics, Religion', in *Crisis of the Subject*, trans. Susan Fairfield (New York: Other Press, 2000), pp. 111–62.

Lacan, Jacques, 'The agency of the letter in the unconscious or reason since Freud', in *Écrits: A Selection*, trans. Alan Sheridan (London: Routledge, 1977), pp. 146–78.

Lacoue-Labarthe, Philippe, *Heidegger, Art and Politics: The Fiction of the Political*, trans. Chris Turner (Oxford: Blackwell, 1990).

Lane, Christopher (ed.), *The Psychoanalysis of Race* (New York: Columbia University Press, 1998).

Lazarus, Neil, 'Disavowing decolonization: Fanon, nationalism, and the question of representation in postcolonial theory', in Anthony C. Alessandrini, (ed.), *Frantz Fanon: Critical Perspectives* (London: Routledge, 1999), pp. 161–94.

Leonard, Philip, 'A Supreme Heteronomy?: *Arche* and Topology in *Difficult Freedom*' in Seán Hand (ed.), *Facing the Other: Ethics in the Work of Emmanuel Levinas* (Richmond: Curzon, 1996), pp. 121–39.

Levinas, Emmanuel, *Totality and Infinity: An Essay on Exteriority*, trans. Alphonso Lingis (Pittsburgh: Duquesne University Press, 1969).

Levinas, Emmanuel, *Otherwise than Being or Beyond Essence* trans. Alphonso Lingis (The Hague: Martinus Nijhoff, 1981).

Levinas, Emmanuel, *Difficult Freedom: Essays on Judaism*, trans. Seán Hand (London: Athlone, 1990).

Lilla, Mark, 'The Politics of Jacques Derrida', *The New York Review of Books*, 45: 11 (25/6/1998), pp. 36–41.

Loomba, Ania, *Colonialism/Postcolonialism* (London: Routledge, 1998).

Lowe, Lisa, '*Des Chinoises*: Orientalism, Psychoanalysis, and Feminine Writing', in Kelly Oliver (ed.), *Ethics, Politics, and Difference in Julia Kristeva's Writing* (London: Routledge, 1993), pp. 150–63.

Luke, Timothy W., 'New Order or Neo-World Orders: Power, Politics and Ideology in Informationalizing Glocalities', in Mike Featherstone, Scott Lash and Roland Robertson (eds), *Global Modernities* (London: Sage, 1995), pp. 91–107.

Lyotard, Jean-François, *Heidegger and "the Jews"*, trans. Andreas Michel and Mark Roberts (Minneapolis: University of Minnesota Press, 1990).

McGee, Daniel T., 'Post-Marxism: The Opiate of the Intellectuals', *Modern Language Quarterly*, 58: 2 (1997), pp. 201–25.

McQuillan, Martin, *Paul de Man* (London: Routledge, 2001).

Marks, John, *Deleuze: Vitalism and Multiplicity* (London: Pluto, 1998).

May, Todd, *Reconsidering Difference: Nancy, Derrida, Levinas, and Deleuze* (Pennsylvania: Pennsylvania University Press, 1997).

Mignolo, Walter D., 'The Many Faces of Cosmo-polis: Border Thinking and Critical Cosmopolitanism', *Public Culture*, 12: 3 (2000), pp. 721–48.

Miller, Christopher, *Nationalists and Nomads: Essays on Francophone African Literature and Culture* (Chicago: University of Chicago Press, 1998).

Montesquieu, Baron de, *The Spirit of the Laws*, trans. Thomas Nugent (New York: Hafner Press, 1949).

Moore-Gilbert, Bart, *Postcolonial Theory: Contexts, Practices, Politics* (London: Verso, 1997).

Moore-Gilbert, Bart, 'Spivak and Bhabha', in Henry Schwarz & Sangeeta Ray, (eds), *A Companion to Postcolonial Studies* (Oxford: Blackwell, 2000), pp. 451–66.

Moreiras, Alberto, 'Hybridity and Double Consciousness', *Cultural Studies*, 13: 3 (1999), pp. 373–407.

Morton, Stephen, *Gayatri Chakravorty Spivak* (London: Routledge, 2003).

Mullarkey, John, 'Deleuze and Materialism: One or Several Matters?', *South Atlantic Quarterly*, 96: 3 (1997), pp. 439–63.

Nancy, Jean-Luc, *The Inoperative Community*, trans. Peter Connor, Lisa Garbus, Michael Holland, and Simona Sawney (Minneapolis: University of Minnesota Press, 1991).

Nietzsche, Friedrich, 'Philosophy in the Tragic Age of the Greeks', trans. M.A. Mügge, in Geoffrey Clive (ed.), *The Philosophy of Nietzsche* (New York: Mentor, 1965), pp. 152–83.

Nietzsche, Friedrich, *The Will to Power*, trans. Walter Kaufmann and R.J. Hollingdale (New York: Vintage, 1967).

Nietzsche, Friedrich, *Twilight of the Idols/The Anti-Christ*, trans. R.J. Hollingdale (London: Penguin, 1990).

Nietzsche, Friedrich. *Human, All Too Human*, trans. Marion Faber & Stephen Lehmann (London: Penguin, 1994).

Nietzsche, Friedrich, *Beyond Good and Evil: Prelude to a Philosophy of the Future*, trans. Marion Faber (Oxford: Oxford University Press, 1998).

Norris, Christopher, 'Dialectics and Difference: On the Politics of Deconstruction – A Review Essay', *Southern Humanities Review*, 19: 2 (1985), pp. 159–69

Norris, Christopher, *Uncritical Theory: Postmodernism, Intellectuals and the Gulf War* (London: Lawrence and Wishart, 1992).

Osborne, Peter, and Sandford, Stella (eds), *Philosophies of Race and Ethnicity* (London: Continuum, 2002).

Papestergiadis, Nikos, 'Restless Hybrids', *Third Text*, 32 (1995), pp. 9–18.

Parry, Benita, 'Problems in Current Theories of Colonial Discourse', *Oxford Literary Review*, 9: 1–2 (1987), pp. 27–58.

Parry, Benita, 'Signs of Our Times: Review of Homi Bhabha's *The Location of Culture*', *Third Text*, 28/29 (1994), pp. 5–24.

Patton, Paul, (ed.), *Deleuze: A Critical Reader* (Oxford: Blackwell, 1996).

Patton, Paul, *Deleuze & the Political* (London: Routledge, 2000).

Pollock, Sheldon, Bhabha, Homi K., Breckenridge, Carol A., and Chakrabarty, Dipesh, 'Cosmopolitanisms', *Public Culture*, 12: 3 (2000), pp. 577–89.

Prakash, Gyan (ed.), *After Colonialism: Imperial Histories and Postcolonial Displacements* (New Jersey: Princeton University Press, 1995).

Prakash, Gyan, 'Who's Afraid of Postcoloniality?', *Social Text*, 14: 4 (1996), pp. 187–203.

Rapaport, Herman, *The Theory Mess: Deconstruction in Eclipse* (New York: Columbia University Press, 2001).

Rapaport, Herman, *Later Derrida: Reading the Recent Work* (London: Routledge, 2003).

Ratchman, John, *The Deleuze Connections* (Cambridge, Mass.: MIT Press, 2000).

Réda Bensmaia, 'On the Concept of Minor Literature From Kafka to Kateb Yacine', trans. Jennifer Curtiss Gage, in Constantin V. Boundas and Dorothea

Olkowski, *Gilles Deleuze and the Theatre of Philosophy* (London: Routledge, 1994), pp. 213–228.

Reiss, Hans (ed.), *Kant: Political Writings*, trans. H.B. Nisbet (Cambridge: Cambridge University Press, 1991).

Roudinesco, Elizabeth, *Jacques Lacan: Outline of a Life, History of a System of Thought*, trans. Barbara Bray (New York: Columbia University Press, 1997).

Ryan, Michael, *Marxism and Deconstruction* (Baltimore: Johns Hopkins University Press, 1982).

Said, Edward W., 'Criticism Between Culture and System,' in *The World, the Text and the Critic* (London: Vintage, 1991), pp. 178–225.

Said, Edward W., 'Invention, Memory and Place', *Critical Inquiry*, 26: 2 (Winter, 2000), pp. 175–92.

Said, Edward W., *Freud and the Non-European* (London: Verso, 2003).

Schrift, Alan D., 'Nietzsche's Contest: Nietzsche and the Culture Wars', in Alan D. Schrift (ed.), *Why Nietzsche Still? Reflections on Drama, Culture, and Politics* (Berkeley: University of California Press, 2000), pp. 184–201.

Scruton, Roger, *England: An Elegy* (London: Pimlico, 2001).

Seignworth, Gregory J., and Macgregor Wise, J., 'Introduction: Deleuze and Guattari in Cultural Studies', *Cultural Studies*, 14: 2 (2000), pp. 139–46.

Sheppard, Darren, Sparks, Simon, and Thomas, Colin (eds), *On Jean-Luc Nancy: The Sense of Philosophy* (London: Routledge, 1997).

Shetty, Sandya, and Bellamy, Elizabeth Jane, 'Postcolonialism's Archive Fever', *Diacritics*, 30: 1 (2000), pp. 25–48.

Smith, Anna, *Julia Kristeva: Readings of Exile and Estrangement* (Basingstoke: Macmillan, 1996).

Smith, Anne-Marie, *Julia Kristeva: Speaking the Unspeakable* (Pluto, 1998).

Spivak, Gayatri Chakravorty, '*Glas*-Piece: A *Compte Rendu*', *Diacritics*, 7: 3 (1977), pp. 22–43.

Spivak, Gayatri Chakravorty, 'Speculation on reading Marx: after reading Derrida', in Derek Attridge, Geoffrey Bennington & Robert Young, (eds), *Post-Structuralism and the Question of History* (Cambridge: Cambridge University Press, 1987), pp. 30–62.

Spivak, Gayatri Chakravorty, 'Can the Subaltern Speak?', in Cary Nelson & Lawrence Grossberg (eds), *Marxism and the Interpretation of Culture* (Basingstoke: Macmillan, 1988), pp. 271–313.

Spivak, Gayatri Chakravorty, *In Other Worlds: Essays in Cultural Politics* (London: Routledge, 1988).

Spivak, Gayatri Chakravorty, 'Poststructuralism, Marginality, Postcolonialism and Value', in Peter Collier & Helga Geyer-Ryan (eds), *Literary Theory Today* (Cambridge, Polity, 1990), pp. 219–44.

Spivak, Gayatri Chakravorty, *The Postcolonial Critic: Interviews, Strategies, Dialogues* (New York: Routledge, 1990).

Spivak, Gayatri Chakravorty, 'Neolocolonialism and the Secret Agent of Knowledge', *Oxford Literary Review*, 13: 1–2 (1991), pp. 220–51.

Spivak, Gayatri Chakravorty, 'Acting Bits/Identity Talk', *Critical Inquiry*, 18: 4 (1992), pp. 770–803.

Spivak, Gayatri Chakravorty, *Outside in the Teaching Machine* (London: Routledge, 1993).

Spivak, Gayatri Chakravorty, 'Responsibility', *boundary 2*, 21:3 (1994), 19–64.

Spivak, Gayatri Chakravorty, 'At the *Planchette* of Deconstruction is/in America', in Anselm Haverkamp (ed.), *Deconstruction is/in America: A New Sense of the Political* (New York: New York University Press, 1995), pp. 237–49.

Spivak, Gayatri Chakravorty, 'Ghostwriting', *Diacritics*, 25: 2 (1995), pp. 65–84.

Spivak, Gayatri Chakravorty, 'Supplementing Marxism', in Bernd Magus & Stephen Cullenberg (eds), *Whither Marxism?: Global Crises in International Perspective* (London: Routledge, 1995), pp. 109–19.

Spivak, Gayatri Chakravorty, 'Setting to Work (Transnational Cultural Studies)', in Peter Osborne (ed.), *A Critical Sense: Interviews with Intellectuals* (London: Routledge, 1996), pp. 163–77.

Spivak, Gayatri Chakravorty, 'Attention: Postcolonialism!', *Journal of Caribbean Studies*, 12: 2–3 (1998), pp. 159–70.

Spivak, Gayatri Chakravorty, *A Critique of Postcolonial Reason: Toward a History of the Vanishing Present* (Cambridge, Mass.: Harvard University Press, 1999).

Spivak, Gayatri Chakravorty, 'Translation as Culture', in Isabel Carrera Suárez et al. (eds), *Translating Cultures* (Oviedo: KRK Ediciones; Hebden Bridge: Dangaroo, 1999), pp. 17–30.

Spivak, Gayatri Chakravorty, 'Deconstruction and Cultural Studies: Arguments for a Deconstructive Cultural Studies', in Nicholas Royle (ed.), *Deconstructions: A User's Guide* (Basingstoke: Palgrave, 2000), pp. 14–43.

Spivak, Gayatri Chakravorty, 'From Haverstock Hill Flat to U.S. Classroom, What's Left of Theory?', in Judith Butler, John Guillory and Kendall Thomas (eds), *What's Left of Theory? New Work on the Politics of Literary Theory* (London: Routledge, 2000), pp. 1–39.

Spivak, Gayatri Chakravorty, 'The New Subaltern: A Silent Interview', in Vinayak Chaturvedi (ed.), *Mapping Subaltern Studies and the Postcolonial* (London: Verso, 2000), pp. 324–40.

Spivak, Gayatri Chakravorty, 'Thinking Cultural Questions in "Pure" Literary Terms', in Paul Gilroy et al. (eds), *Without Guarantees: In Honour of Stuart Hall* (London: Verso, 2000), pp. 335–57.

Spivak, Gayatri Chakravorty, 'A Note on the New International', *Parallax*, 7: 3 (2001), pp. 12–16.

Spivak, Gayatri Chakravorty, 'Resident Alien', in David Theo Goldberg and Ato Quayson (eds), *Relocating Postcolonialism* (Oxford: Blackwell, 2002), pp. 47–65.

Taylor, Charles, et al., *Multiculturalism: Examining the Politics of Recognition* (New Jersey: Princeton University Press, 1994).

Thiele, Leslie Paul, *Timely Meditations: Martin Heidegger and Postmodern Politics* (Princeton: Princeton University Press, 1995).

Williams, James, *Lyotard & the Political* (London: Routledge, 2000).

Williams, Patrick, 'Difficult Subjects: Black British Women's Poetry', in David Murray (ed.), *Literary Theory and Poetry: Extending the Canon* (London: Batsford, 1989), pp. 108–26.

Williams, Patrick, *Ngugi wa Thiong'o* (Manchester: Manchester University Press, 1999).

Williams, Patrick, 'Frantz Fanon: The Routes of Writing', in Sam Haigh (ed.), *An Introduction to Caribbean Francophone Writing: Guadeloupe and Martinique* (Oxford: Berg, 1999), pp. 51–68.

Williams, Raymond, *Resources of Hope: Culture, Democracy, Socialism* (ed.) Robin Gable (London: Verso, 1989).

Wolfreys, Julian, *Deconstruction•Derrida* (Basingstoke: Macmillan, 1998).

Yale French Studies, 82 (1993), 'Post/Colonial Conditions: Exiles, Migrations and Nomadisms'.

Young, Robert J.C., *Colonial Desire: Hybridity in Theory, Culture and Race* (London: Routledge, 1995).

Young, Robert, Review of *Outside in the Teaching Machine*, *Textual Practice*, 10: 1 (1996), pp. 228–38.

Young, Robert, *Postcolonialism: An Historical Introduction* (Oxford: Blackwell, 2001).

Young, Robert J.C., 'Race and Language in the Two Saussures', in Peter Osborne and Stella Sandford (eds), *Philosophies of Race and Ethnicity* (London: Continuum, 2002), pp. 63–78.

Young, Robert, *White Mythologies: Writing History and the West*, 2nd edn. (London: Routledge, 2004).

Žižek, Slavoj, *The Fragile Absolute – or, Why is the Christian Legacy Worth Fighting For?* (London: Verso, 2000).

Index

Aeschylus, 79–102
agency, 113, 145–54, 166 n.61,
  178 n.21
Ahmad, Aijaz, 1, 123–4, 132
Algeria, 37–8, 42
alienation, 38–9, 96, 141
Althusser, Louis, 80–2, 146
ambivalence, 15, 27–8, 62, 64, 84,
  87–8, 92, 98, 128–30, 133–42,
  146, 179 n.51
anthropology, 23–5, 31, 91, 98, 99,
  111, 162 n.79, 165 n.33
apartheid, 34
Appadurai, Arjun, 57
Asia, 103, 115, 136–7, 181 n.76
Asiatic Mode of Production, the,
  103–5
autobiography, 37, 110, 173 n.27

Bakhtin, Mikhail, 38, 146
Balkans, the, 143
Barthes, Roland, 146, 149, 180 n.66
Bataille, Georges, 47
Beckett, Samuel, 63
Benjamin, Walter, 33, 146
Bernabé, Jean, 136–7
Bhabha, Homi, 1–2, 11, 12, 13, 17,
  19, **127–54**
  on cosmopolitanism, 85
  'Culture's In Between', 142, 145
  'Day by Day... With Frantz Fanon',
    131, 133–4, 177 n.11
  and Deleuze and Guattari, 134,
    178 n.21
  and Derrida, 127–32, 140, 146, 148,
    151, 177 n.11
  on disavowal, 128, 134–5, 139
  on globalization, 131–2, 177 n.11
  on hybridity, 132–49, 178 n.26,
    179 n.51
  and Kristeva, 171 n.80
  on minority groups, 131–2, 144–6,
    148–9, 166 n.61

on multiculturalism, 85
on nationalism, 142, 177 n.16
'On Cultural Choice', 146
on race, 128, 133, 136–7, 142–4, 152
on resistance, 126, 134, 138–9,
  141–2, 145, 148, 150–1,
  179 n.39
'Signs Taken for Wonders', 138–9
'Sly Civility', 138–9
and Spivak, 129, 132
The Location of Culture, 12, 127–54
Bhaduri, Bhubaneswari, 106–7
bin Laden, Osama, 44, 163 n.90,
  163 n.91
blackness, 34, 66–7, 128, 133, 142
Blanchot, Maurice, 27, 47

capitalism, 16, 39, 46, 51, 55–7, 68,
  74, 85, 103, 114–21, 172 n.2,
  175 n.67
Caribbean, the, 136–7, 152
Chakrabarty, Dipesh, 85, 105
Chamoiseau, Patrick, 136–7
Cheah, Pheng, 37, 84, 86
China, 69–71, 78–9, 91, 99–100,
  172 n.84, 180 n.66
Christianity, 20, 32, 34, 35, 55, 70,
  92, 161 n.70, 170 n.59
citizenship, 18, 80, 83, 85, 94–5
Cixous, Hélène, 37
class, 1, 4, 33, 36, 47,107, 109,
  115–16, 137, 143
colonialism, 2, 7, 13, 22, 35, 39–41,
  48, 56, 65, 72, 85, 104–9, 112,
  114, 118, 120, 125, 127–53
communism, 27–8, 36, 104, 174 n.40,
  174 n.45
community, 3, 9, 10, 13–16, 17, 20–2,
  25–6, 29, 31–6, 47–50, 51, 55,
  62–4, 78, 84, 85–7, 89, 93, 96,
  97–8, 100–1, 120, 131, 154,
  160 n.47, 177 n.11, 177 n.20,
  179 n.32

striated space, 55, 58, 66, 75
subalternity, 18, 57, 105–12, 119–21,
    125–6, 127, 129, 142, 149–52,
    175 n.68
subjectivity, 15–16, 18, 20–2, 31–2,
    50, 58, 61, 67–8, 76–7, 81, 87, 93,
    96, 100–1, 104–12, 128–30,
    133–7, 141–2, 145–51, 173 n.27,
    175 n.68, 178 n.21, 179 n.51
surplus-value, 116–18, 121, 126–7

technology, 13, 16, 28, 36, 45, 65,
    131, 141
teleiopoeisis, 110–14, 129
terrorism, 38, 41–4, 48, 163 n.91
'Third World', the, 56, 64, 67, 91–2,
    103, 107–9, 114, 129, 170 n.59,
    173 n.27
time, 12, 27, 33, 47, 74, 77–8, 101,
    131, 134, 139, 142, 144–6, 148,
    152, 159 n.19, 178 n.29, 179 n.51
tolerance, 46, 142–3, 160 n.47
translation, 8, 24, 41, 113–14, 131,
    141, 146, 150, 159 n.19
transnationality, 2, 5, 13, 16, 19, 27,
    45, 46, 51, 65, 77, 83–7, 99, 117,
    119, 125–6, 127, 134, 143, 154,
    177 n.11

United Nations, 88
United States, 6, 22, 29, 31, 37, 43–5,
    69, 91–2, 113, 153, 160 n.47,
    163 n.91, 170 n.59

universalism, 6–7, 12, 15, 26, 32, 49,
    51, 54, 58, 62, 65–8, 71, 76–95,
    101, 106, 109, 118, 136–7,
    144–7, 169 n.32, 170 n.51,
    175 n.68
use-value, 117, 119
utopianism, 13, 19, 29, 81, 86, 90,
    93

Valéry, Paul, 117–19
value, 6, 17, 81, 95, 100, 103–4,
    116–21, 125–6

we, 5–8, 13, 15–16, 25, 145
West, the, 2–3, 6–8, 11–13, 16–17,
    22–3, 33–7, 40, 43, 44, 56–7, 61,
    64–5, 67, 68, 71–5, 76, 78–9, 85,
    88, 91–2, 97–102, 114–15, 127–9,
    134, 136–42, 149–54
whiteness, 34, 66–8, 106, 133, 142,
    144
women, 67, 77–9, 91–2, 95, 97–102,
    106–9, 120, 126, 129, 170 n.84
writing, 11–12, 26–8, 48, 54, 57–68,
    100–1, 112–13, 120, 127, 129–30,
    136, 140–1, 151, 162 n.79,
    164 n.5, 166 n.49, 172 n.84

Yerulshami, Josef, Hayim, 152–3
Young, Robert, 12, 33, 37, 122, 125,
    137–41

Žižek, Slavoj, 142–3